The New York Times
헤드라인 영어

The New York Times
헤드라인 영어

1판 1쇄 발행 2016년 1월 5일

지은이 토마스 안·벨라 정
펴낸 곳 영어닷컴
디자인 주식회사 Chaeg
주소 서울시 종로구 삼봉로 95 대성 102-1004(견지동)
전화 (02) 739 5333
팩스 (02) 739 5777
전자우편 youngodot@gmail.com

ISBN 979-11-85345-07-9 13740

이 책의 출판권은 영어닷컴이 가지고 있습니다.
저작권 법의 보호를 받는 저작물이므로 무단 전재와 무단 복제를 금합니다.

The New York Times
헤드라인 영어

토마스 안·벨라 정 지음

영어닷컴

CONTENTS

PREFACE
006　헤드라인이란 무엇인가

INTRODUCTION
008　어떻게 헤드라인 퍼즐을 풀 것인가

Part. 1
018　**INTERNATIONAL**

Part. 2
126　**BUSINESS**

Part. 3
214　**OPINION**

Part. 4
270　**LIFE**

CONTENTS

INTERNATIONAL
BUSINESS
OPINION
LIFE

PREFACE

헤드라인이란 무엇인가 ¶

신문과 잡지, TV 뉴스 프로그램 등 매체가 전하고자 하는 기사 제목을 헤드라인Headline이라 한다. 자세한 내용을 한눈에 파악하도록 하기 위하여 가능한 짧고 단순하게 의미를 압축하여 쉽게 알아 볼 수 있도록 굵고 큰 글씨체로 기사 첫머리에 나타낸다. 이것은 특히 신문 상에서 다양한 형태를 접할 수 있다.

    영자신문의 기사 제목도 기능은 동일하지만 한글과 영어의 차이만큼 내용을 이해하기가 쉽지 않다. 뿐만 아니라 전 세계에서 펼쳐지는 복잡한 사건과 다양한 문화는 물론 폭넓은 경제 영역에서 벌어지는 광범위한 사건을 단 한 줄의 짧은 문장으로 표현하기 때문에 헤드라인 영어문장을 접하면 일단 난감함을 느끼게 된다. 게다가 헤드라인에 사용된 각 단어는 분명 쉬운 어휘인데 아무리 뜻을 맞추어 보려고 애를 써도 쉽게 이해하기 어려운 퍼즐처럼 느껴진다. 내포하는 의미가 깊고 강한 것을 감안하면 전하려는 메시지를 알아내기 위해서 하늘만한 상상력이라도 동원해야 하는 것인가.

    모든 대상은 아는 만큼 이해한다고 말한다. 추상화를 감상하는 이해의 정도는 아동, 청년 그리고 성인에 있어서 각자 인생 경험의 크기와 비례할 것이다. 함축된 헤드라인 메시지를 일부만 이해하고 넘어간다면 결코 효율적인 일이라고 말할 수 없고, 정보의 입수도 불확실하다. 누군가 수수께끼를 만들어 놓았다면 우리도 조금만 노력하면 풀어낼 수 있는 것이다. 일단 답을 얻은 후에는 수수께끼가 별 것 아니라는 것을 알게 된다. 즉, 알면 쉽고 모르면 어렵다는 말이 여기서도 적용되는 것이다.

헤드라인 영어문장은 수수께끼다 ¶

기사 전체를 축약하여 만든 헤드라인 영어문장은 그야말로 알쏭달쏭한 퍼즐이다. 단순하고 짧은 길이와 정 반대로 헤드라인에 등장한 단어는 의미가 보다 깊고 포괄적이다. 바로 이 점이 헤드라인 영어에 도전하는 유익함이다. 왜냐하면 '효율'이라는 가치가 중요하다는 것을 누구나 알고 있듯이 하나를 알아서 열을 습득하는 효과를 헤드라인 영어문장에서 거둘 수 있기 때문이다.

이 책은 퍼즐을 풀어가는 탐구과정이다 ¶

퍼즐을 풀어나가듯 헤드라인 영어문장에서 어떤 것을 생략했는지, 어떻게 의미를 전달하는지 문장 형태$^{Matrix\ Core}$를 파헤치고 핵심 포인트를 분석$^{Decoded\ Core}$하는 방법으로 150개의 핵들을 다루는 과정은 상당히 흥미롭다. 그리고 이러한 탐구 과정을 정독하는 가운데 영어에 관하여 한층 폭을 넓히는 한편 세계적인 이슈와 관련된 중요 시사 정보를 보는 시야도 더불어 확대된다.

헤드라인이 읽어진다 ¶

세계적 언론 전문가들이 만든 International, Business, Opinion, Life 4개 분야의 영역 별 헤드라인 영어문장의 내부를 들여다봄으로써 영미 언어문화에 한 걸음 더 가까이 접근하며 비슷하게 모방하는 과정을 훈련한다면 영문시사를 읽을 수 있고, 마침내 엄청난 파괴력을 지닌 힘으로 이어질 것이다.

INTRODUCTION

어떻게 헤드라인 퍼즐을 풀 것인가 ¶

헤드라인은 자세히 기술된 기사 내용을 몇 개 단어만으로 압축하여 만든 제목이다. 그러므로 각 단어는 일반적인 문장보다 더 깊고 폭넓은 의미를 포함하고 있다. 이런 함축적인 문장을 만들기 위해서 전문 편집인들이 모여 글자 수를 고려하며 가장 적절한 어휘를 신중하게 선정한 후 허용되는 글자 크기를 맞추어 기사의 머리 자리에 놓게 된다. 즉, 무기로 말하자면 고도로 압축된 핵폭탄에 비유할 수 있다.

    이렇게 압축된 문장을 만드는 이유는 전달이다. 다양해진 현대는 그 만큼 발생하는 사건이 너무나 많기 때문에 짧은 순간에 보다 많은 정보를 획득할수록 경쟁력이 강화된다. 이를 가능하게 만드는 기능이 헤드라인인 셈이다.

    경쟁력 강화를 위해서는 국내뿐만 아니라 글로벌 사회의 시간대별 움직임도 주요한 정보가 된다. 소셜미디어에 의한 긴급뉴스를 전파할 때도 같은 맥락에서 헤드라인은 제 기능을 발휘한다.

    여기서 말하는 헤드라인은 특히 영문 기사의 제목이다. 영어를 제2의 모국어로 취급해야 하는 현실은 영문 기사를 이해하기 위해 한글로 번역할 짬을 점점 더 허용하지 않고 있다. 실시간 전달된 단 한 줄의 브레이킹 뉴스를 보는 순간 압축된 의미를 풀어내야 한다.

    최근 〈뉴욕타임스〉 일면에 실린 헤드라인이 전하려는 의미를 생각해 보자.

"The locals may find welcome has worn out."

이 헤드라인 문장을 보면 'may, find, welcome, has, worn out' 등 마치 문장 전체가 동사만으로 구성된 것처럼 보인다.
이 수수께끼를 풀어보자.

> **The locals**는 주어로 현지 사람들을 의미하고,
> **find**는 '느끼다(feel)'의 의미가 있다.

> 한 문장 안에 동사가 2개 올 수는 없으므로,
> **may find** 뒤에 that이 생략되어 있다고 생각해볼 수 있다.

> **welcome has worn out**에서 welcome은 '환영'이라는
> 명사임을 알 수 있고 worn out(wear out)의 의미는
> '닳다, 다하다, 점점 없어지다(fade away)'라는 의미가 된다.

즉, 위의 헤드라인을 일반 문장으로 표현하면 다음과 같다.

> **"The local people may find that their welcome has faded away."**

의미는 "현지 사람들은 자신들의 환영의 마음이 점점 약해지고 있음을 느낄지도 모른다"이며, 이것은 아프가니스탄 국민들이 미군에 대한 환영하는 마음이 감소했음을 시사하는 내용의 기사로부터 인용한 것이다.

앞의 예문에서 느낄 수 있듯이 헤드라인은 강하고 깊은 의미를 한 줄의 짧은 문장으로 전하는 것이다. 이 짧은 문장의 이해야말로 영어를 다양하게 알게 하고 수준을 더욱 높이는 지름길이 된다.

이곳에서는 헤드라인에 관한 일반적 이해를 간략하게 설명하고 내포된 의미의 퍼즐을 풀어나가는 방법을 안내한다.

본문은 Headline(헤드라인), Lead Sentence(리드 문장), Matrix Core(문장 형태), Decoded Core(핵심 포인트 해설), Plain Expression(일반 표현), Bilingual Reading(영한 읽기), Word&Phrase(단어 및 구문)로 구성된다. 각각의 내용을 먼저 검토해보자.

Headline ¶

미국 주요 일간지 〈The New York Times〉의 최신 기사를 중심으로 〈The Wall Street Journal〉, 〈The Huffington Post〉, 영국의 〈Financial Times〉 등 최신 기사의 헤드라인 영어문장을 소개한다. 이 책에서 소개하는 헤드라인 영어문장들이 바로 퍼즐이다.

Matrix Core ¶

공식과 같은 독특한 구성 형태를 언급하여 퍼즐의 첫 힌트를 제시한다.
⇒ 헤드라인의 문형을 파악하며 영어에 대한 두려움이 줄어든다.

Decoded Core ¶

헤드라인 영어문장을 이해하기 위한 핵심 포인트를 제시하고 퍼즐의 암호를 풀 수 있는 해설을 제공한다. 이 역할은 핵폭탄 해체 과정에 해당하는 이 책의 가장 중요한 부분이다.

일반 표현

포괄적으로 압축된 헤드라인 영어문장을 쉬운 일반 문장으로 치환하여 의미를 보다 쉽고 정확하게 이해할 수 있도록 돕는다. 여기에서 수수께끼의 답을 얻는다.

Lead Sentence

리드 문장은 기사 첫 단락에 위치하는 사건에 대한 요약문이다. 따라서 헤드라인 문장이 잘 이해되지 않을 때 리드를 읽어서 확실한 의미를 파악할 수 있다.
경우에 따라서는 리드 문장에서 헤드라인의 뜻을 이해하는 경우도 있지만, Matrix Core나 Decoded Core의 기능은 문장의 세밀한 부분까지 정확한 영어 자체를 습득하는 데 중요한 가치가 있다.

Bilingual Reading

영어 구문 별로 한글 의미를 나란히 삽입하여 동시에 읽어갈 수 있도록 표기하였다. 이 의미는 이중 언어 능력자들이 동시에 두 언어의 의미를 파악하는 비결이기도 하다. 바이링구얼 리딩을 통하여 영·한 내용을 동시에 빠르고 정확하게 이해하는 연습이 가능하다. 더불어 영어 구문에 해당하는 적합한 한글 표현도 함께 익힐 수 있다.

Word&Phrase

제시된 영문에 나오는 단어와 주요 구문을 풀이한다.
헤드라인의 영어 단어는 사전의 범위를 훨씬 넘어서서 살아 움직이기 때문에 적합한 의미가 필요하다. 영자신문이나 잡지 및 고급 단계의 수준을 희망하는 경우에는 이 부분에서 제시한 단어와 구문으로 많은 도움을 받을 수 있다.

이 책에서 보여주는 헤드라인 영어의 몇 단계 퍼즐 풀이 과정을 지나면 이해가 점차 또렷해짐을 경험하게 된다. 이제부터는 실제 예문으로 해설 단계를 살펴보자.

헤드라인 영어의 일반적 이해

❶ 헤드라인 영어는 일반적 의미보다 더욱 함축적이다.
⇒ U.S. jobs data narrow rate-rise odds.

❷ 헤드라인 영어는 주로 기본단어와 단순구조를 사용한다.
⇒ U.S. jobs data(주어부) narrow(동사) rate-rise odds(보어).

❸ 헤드라인 영어는 최대 축약 문장이므로 생략을 파악하자.
⇒ U.S. jobs data shows less probability of raising interest rate.

❹ 헤드라인 영어는 아는 만큼 이해의 정도가 다르다.
⇒ jobs 일자리 / narrow 줄다(reduce) / odds 가능성(probability)

❺ 헤드라인 영어의 가장 중요한 역할은 전달 기능이다.
⇒ U.S. jobs data shows less probability of raising interest Rate.
(미국 취업률 통계 자료 발표 후 금리 인상 가능성이 감소했다.)

헤드라인 영어의 퍼즐 풀이 단계의 예시

❶ My tax overhaul to unleash 4% growth

Matrix Core	**Decoded Core**	**Word & Phrase**
헤드라인 영어문장은 조동사를 생략하고 단순시제를 쓴다.	overhaul ⇒ overhauled 충분히 검토되어야 한다	overhaul 검토하다 unleash 놓아주다, 내놓다, 풀다

일반 표현
My tax should be overhauled to unleash 4% hike.

Meaning
4% 인상된 세금을 내려면 나의 납세 내역이 충분히 검토되어야 한다.

❷ China slowdown concern

Matrix Core	**Decoded Core**	**Word & Phrase**
헤드라인 영어문장은 be 동사 생략이 가능하다.	slowdown ⇒ is facing slowdown	slowdown 둔화, 후퇴, 침체

일반 표현
China is facing slowdown concern.

Meaning
중국은 경기 성장 둔화의 위기에 봉착해 있다.

❸ The Chief executive falls on his sword as emission deception engulfs VW ¶

Matrix Core
헤드라인 영어문장은 완료형을 현재로 나타낸다.

Decoded Core
on his sword
⇒ take responsibility
'책임을 지다'의 의미로 상당히 세련된 구문인 'on his sword'를 사용했다.

Word & Phrase
fall on : to be the responsibility of someone
~의 책임이다
cause of deception 책임
engulf 휩쓸리다

일반 표현
The chief has taken responsibility for the emission scandal on VW.

Meaning
배기가스 스캔들로 인해 난관에 빠진 폭스바겐의 사장은 이 사태를 자신의 책임으로 받아들였다.

❹ Peak wage system agreed ¶

Matrix Core
헤드라인 영어문장은 현재완료 수동형을 과거분사로 나타낸다.

Decoded Core
agreed
⇒ has been agreed

Word & Phrase
peak wage system
최고 임금제

일반 표현
Peak wage system has been agreed.

Meaning
최고 임금제는 합의가 이루어졌다.

❺ Successor to be chosen soon ¶

Matrix Core
헤드라인 영어문장은 미래를 to로 나타낸다.

Decoded Core
Successor to be
⇒ Successor will be

Word & Phrase
successor 후임자, 계승자

일반 표현	Meaning
Successor will be chosen soon.	후임자가 곧 선출될 예정이다.

❻ Fed adds to uncertainty ¶

Matrix Core	Decoded Core	Word & Phrase
헤드라인 영어문장은 몇 개의 단어로 나타낸다.	Fed adds ⇒ Fed is increasing	Fed(Federal Reserve System) 연방준비이사회 uncertainty 불안

일반 표현	Meaning
Federal Reserve Board is increasing its uncertainty.	연방준비이사회는 불안을 증폭시키고 있다.

❼ Party's list narrowed to three candidates ¶

Matrix Core	Decoded Core	Word & Phrase
헤드라인 영어문장은 정관사 the를 생략한다. 헤드라인 영어문장은 현재완료 수동형을 과거분사로 나타낸다.	Party's list ⇒ The party's list narrowed ⇒ has been narrowed	candidate 후보자

일반 표현	Meaning
The party's list has been narrowed to three candidates.	그 당의 후보자는 세 명으로 좁혀졌다.

❽ The factory pay cut row ¶

Matrix Core	Decoded Core	Word & Phrase
헤드라인 영어문장은 앞의 명사가 뒤의 명사를 수식한다.	row ⇒ disagreement cut ⇒ reduction	factory pay 공장 임금

일반 표현

Lowering factory pay rows.

Meaning

공장의 임금 삭감이 소란을 빚다.

❾ The scandal wiped 30% off company's value ¶

Matrix Core

헤드라인 영어문장은 첫 리드 문장에서 압축의 의미가 풀린다.

배경을 이해하기 위해 리드 문장을 읽으면 도움이 된다.

Decoded Core

wiped
⇒ has been wiped

Word & Phrase

wipe 제거하다, 없애다
: remove
wipe off 청산하다, 닦아 없애다
: clean off
step down : resign from
사표를 내다, 물러나다
bow to : accept to do
받아들이다

일반 표현

The Scandal lowered the company's value by 30%.

이번 사건은 회사의 주식 가격을 30% 폭락시켰다.

Lead Sentence

Martin WinterKorn stepped down as CEO of Volkswagen, bowing to mounting(increasing) pressure over an emissions-fixing (deception scandal) that wiped (removed) more than 30% off the company's share price.

Bilingual Reading

Martin WinterKorn 마틴 윈터콘은 **stepped down** 물러났다 **as CEO of Volkswagen,** 폭스바겐의 CEO자리에서 **bowing to mounting pressure** 커져가는 압력에 굴복하면서 **over an emissions-fixing** 배기가스 조작 사건으로 **that wiped more than 30% off** 30% 이상이나 없애버린 **the company's share price.** 회사의 주식 가격을

마틴 윈터콘은 회사의 주가를 30% 이상이나 하락시킨 배기가스 조작 사건으로 커져가는 압력에 굴복하면서 폭스바겐의 CEO직에서 물러났다.

How to study ¶

❶ 헤드라인 및 리드 문장

❷ Matrix Core 및 Decoded Core
헤드라인을 이해하기 위한 핵심 사항을 살펴본다.

❸ 일반 표현
헤드라인을 보다 쉬운 일반 문장으로 변환하여 이해한다.

❹ 헤드라인 번역문의 의미

❺ Word&Phrase 주요 단어와 구문

❻ Lead Sentence 뉴스 기사의 요약 문장

❼ Bilingual Reading
영한 이중언어 동시 표현으로 리드 문장의 내용을 파악한다.

❽ 리드 문장의 의미

Part. 1
INTERNATIONAL

The New York Times 헤드라인 영어

Part 1 INTERNATIONAL

INTERNATIONAL
BUSINESS
OPINION
LIFE

Deepening economic ties belie China-Japan tension

Seventy years after World War Two, relations between Asia's two biggest economies are in poor shape-as Beijing's huge military parade shows. But trade, investment and tourism tell a different story. Japan's economic success increasingly depends on China's, and vice versa.

Headline

Deepening economic ties belie China-Japan tension

중국과 일본 간의 경제적 유대관계 강화는 양국의 긴장 상태와는 다르게 보인다.

일반 표현

Intensifying economic relationship is in contradiction with China-Japan tension.

Matrix Core

헤드라인 영어문장은 진행형을 현재분사로 나타낸다. ¶

헤드라인 영어문장은 관계대명사를 be동사와 더불어 생략한다. ¶

Decoded Core

deepening ⇒ (what is) deepening 계속 깊어진다는 것
deepening economic ties 경제적 협력이 강화된다는 것은 ¶

belie ⇒ 모순되다, 다르다, 반대로 나타나다
be in contradiction with 실제와 다르게 보이다 ¶

China-Japan tension ⇒ 중국과 일본 간의 긴장 상태, 중일 갈등 ¶

[01]

Word&Phrase

vice versa 반대의 경우도 마찬가지다

Lead Sentence

Seventy years after World War Two, relations between Asia's two biggest economies are in poor shape-as Beijing's huge military parade shows. But trade, investment and tourism tell a different story. Japan's economic success increasingly depends on China's, and vice versa.

2차 세계대전이 끝난 지 70년 만에 아시아의 두 최대 경제대국 간의 관계는 베이징의 거대한 군사 퍼레이드가 보여주다시피 좋지 못한 상황에 놓여 있다. 하지만 무역, 투자, 관광은 이야기가 다르다. 일본의 경제적 성공은 점점 더 중국에 의존하고 있고, 중국 또한 마찬가지다.

Bilingual Reading

Seventy years after World War Two, 2차 세계대전이 끝난 지 70년 만에 **relations between Asia's two biggest economies** 아시아의 두 최대 경제대국 간의 관계는 **are in poor shape** 좋지 못한 상황에 놓여 있다 **-as Beijing's huge military parade shows.** 즉, 베이징의 거대한 군사 퍼레이드가 보여주다시피 **But trade, investment and tourism** 하지만 무역, 투자, 관광은 **tell a different story.** 이야기가 다르다 **Japan's economic success** 일본의 경제적 성공은 **increasingly depends on China's,** 점점 더 중국에 의존하고 있고 **and vice versa.** 중국도 마찬가지다

Part.1 INTERNATIONAL

White House split on opening talks with Putin

President Obama's administration is debating whether Mr. Obama and President Vladimir V. Putin should try to work out their differences, but fear playing into Mr. Putin's hands.

Headline

White House split on opening talks with Putin

미국 백악관은 푸틴과의 협상 개최를 놓고 의견이 분산되고 있다.

일반 표현

White House has been split on opening talks with Putin.

Matrix Core

헤드라인 영어문장은 현재완료 수동형을 과거분사로 나타낸다. ¶

Decoded Core

split ⇒ (has been) split ¶

White House has been split ⇒ 백악관은 의견이 나누어졌다 ¶

on opening talks ⇒ 협상 개최에 관해 ¶

split ⇒ 분열되다, 사이가 틀어지다 ‡ divide ¶

[02]

Word&Phrase

administration 정부, 행정, 관리
debate 논의, 토론
work out 해결하다, 만들어 내다
play into one's hands 다른 사람의 생각대로 되다, 유리하게 행동하다

Lead Sentence

President Obama's administration is debating whether Mr. Obama and President Vladimir V. Putin should try to work out their differences, but fear playing into Mr. Putin's hands.

오바마 행정부는 오바마 대통령과 블라디미르 푸틴 대통령이 양자의 의견 차이를 해소하기 위해 노력을 해야 하는지를 두고 논쟁을 벌이고 있지만, 푸틴의 손 안에서 놀게 될 것을 우려하고 있다.

Bilingual Reading

President Obama's administration 오바마 대통령의 행정부는 **is debating** 논쟁을 벌이고 있다 **whether Mr. Obama and President Vladimir V. Putin** 오바마와 블라디미르 푸틴 대통령이 **should try** 노력을 해야 하는지를 두고 **to work out their differences,** 그들의 의견 차이를 해소하기 위해 **but fear playing into Mr. Putin's hands.** 그러나 푸틴의 손 안에서 놀게 될 것을 우려하고 있다

Part.1 INTERNATIONAL

23

China to begin cap-and-trade program to limit emissions

China will announce a landmark commitment on Friday to limit and put a price on greenhouse gas emissions, a substantial step by the world's largest polluter.

Headline

China to begin cap-and-trade program to limit emissions

중국은 배기가스를 제한하기 위해 배출권 거래제 프로그램을 시행할 예정이다.

일반 표현

China will begin Cap-Trade program to restrict emission. China plans to take the step of cap and trade program to restrict pollution of emission.

Matrix Core

헤드라인 영어문장은 미래를 to로 나타낸다. ¶

Decoded Core

China to begin ⇒ China will begin ¶

cap-and-trade ⇒ 배출권 거래제 : 환경 보호를 위해 실시하는 일종의 인센티브 제도로 허용 배출 탄소의 상한선을 설정하고 이를 준수할 경우 경제적 이익으로 되돌려주는 계약거래 프로그램이다. ¶

limit emission ⇒ 배기가스 제한 ¶

[03]

Word&Phrase

landmark 두드러진 특징, 표지
commitment policy 공약
substantial 실질적인, 상당한
polluter 오염자, 오염원, 공해 기업

Lead Sentence

China will announce a landmark commitment on Friday to limit and put a price on greenhouse gas emissions, a substantial step by the world's largest polluter.

중국은 세계 최대 오염원으로서 실질적 조치인 온실가스를 제한하고 비용을 부과하기 위한 획기적인 정책을 목요일에 공식적으로 발표할 예정이다.

Bilingual Reading

China 중국은 **will announce** 발표할 예정이다 **a landmark commitment** 획기적인 정책을 **on Friday** 목요일에 **to limit and put a price** 제한하고 비용을 부과하기 위한 **on greenhouse gas emissions,** 온실가스를 **a substantial step** 실질적 조치인 **by the world's largest polluter.** 세계 최대 오염원으로서

Coping with migrant wave tests Germany's reputation for efficiency

The government has been preparing for months as the humanitarian crises on Europe's periphery grew, but as the crisis wears on, states and municipalities are starting to groan under the burden.

Headline

Coping with migrant wave tests Germany's reputation for efficiency

이민자 유입에 관한 대처 방법은 독일의 문제 처리 능력의 명성을 시험하게 될 것이다.

일반 표현

Addressing migrant influx will test German's efficient ability.

Matrix Core

헤드라인 영어문장은 진행형을 현재분사로 나타낸다. ¶

Decoded Core

cope with ⇒ 잘 처리하다, 다루다, 대비하다, 대처하다 ∦ satisfy, fulfill, meet the need ¶

coping with migrant wave ⇒ (what is) coping with migrant wave ¶

Germany's reputation for efficiency ⇒ 독일의 문제 대처 능력의 명성 ∦ ability of Germany's performance ¶

efficiency ⇒ 능력, 효율 ¶

reputation ⇒ 명성, 평판 ¶

[04]

Word&Phrase

humanitarian crises 인도적 난국
periphery 주변의
start to groan under burden 부담 아래 신음하기 시작하다

Lead Sentence

The government has been preparing for months as the humanitarian crises on Europe's periphery grew, but as the crisis wears on, states and municipalities are starting to groan under the burden.

유럽 주변국들의 인도적 요구가 커져감에 따라 독일 정부는 대처 방안을 수 개월 동안 준비를 해왔다. 그러나 위기가 계속되자, 정부와 지방 자치체들은 부담으로 신음하기 시작했다.

Bilingual Reading

The government 정부는 **has been preparing** 준비를 해왔다 **for months** 몇 달 동안 **as the humanitarian crises** 인도적 요구가 **on Europe's periphery grew,** 유럽의 주변 국가들에 커져감에 따라 **but as the crisis wears on,** 그러나 위기가 계속되자 **states and municipalities** 정부와 지방 자치체는 **are starting to groan** 신음하기 시작했다 **under the burden.** 부담으로

Hugo Dixon: Greece may not need debt haircut

No single measure, such as debt to GDP, adequately captures how unsustainable Athens' balance sheet is. Most other yardsticks show Greece needs debt relief. But cutting the face value of its borrowings is probably not required.

Headline

Hugo Dixon: Greece may not need debt haircut

그리스는 부채 삭감이 필요 없을지도 모른다.

일반 표현

Greece may not require structuring to pay off its debt.

Matrix Core

헤드라인 영어문장은 조동사로 가능성을 나타낸다. ¶

Decoded Core

debt haircut ⇒ 부채 삭감, 부채를 갚기 위한 구조조정 ¶

Hugo Dixon: ⇒ Hugo Dixon said, Hugo Dixon은 영국과 유럽의 온라인 뉴스 ‹Breakingviews›의 칼럼니스트이다. ¶

[05]

Word&Phrase

adequately 적절히, 충분히, 알맞게
balance sheet 대차대조표, 재무제표, 경상수지
yardstick 척도, 기준, 자
face value of debt 채무액면가

unsustainable 지탱할 수 없는, 유지할 수 없는
: not able to upheld or defended

Lead Sentence

No single measure, such as debt to GDP, adequately captures how unsustainable Athens' balance sheet is. Most other yardsticks show Greece needs debt relief. But cutting the face value of its borrowings is probably not required.

GDP 대비 부채와 같이 한 가지 척도만으로는 그리스의 경상수지가 어느 정도로 불균형한지 적절히 설명하기 어렵다. 대부분의 다른 판단 기준은 그리스가 채무 지원책이 필요하다고 이야기하고 있다. 그러나 부채 총액을 깎아주는 정도까지는 필요하지 않을지도 모른다.

Bilingual Reading

No 하지 못한다 **single measure, such as debt to GDP,** GDP 대비 부채와 같은 한 가지의 척도는 **adequately captures** 적절한 설명을 **how unsustainable Athens' balance sheet is.** 그리스의 경상수지가 어느 정도로 불균형한지 **Most other yardsticks** 대부분의 다른 판단 기준은 **show** 보여준다 **Greece needs debt relief.** 그리스가 채무 지원책이 필요하다고 **But** 하지만 **cutting the face value of its borrowings** 부채 액면가 삭감까지는 **is probably not required.** 필요하지 않을지도 모른다.

Part.1 INTERNATIONAL

China's yuan devaluation push looks far from done

The central bank weakened the official exchange rate by another 1.6 pct against the U.S. dollar. It's a clear sign the new "market-oriented" yuan is heading down. Until China uses its foreign exchange hoard to prop up the currency, investors will assume there's further to go.

Headline

China's yuan devaluation push looks far from done

위안화 평가절하 추진은 당분간 지속될 것이다.

일반 표현

The measure of China's yuan devaluation can't be helped.

Matrix Core

헤드라인 영어문장은 앞의 명사가 뒤의 명사를 수식한다.

Decoded Core

China's yuan devaluation push 명사로 이어진 구절 ⇒ 중국의 위안화 평가절하 추진 ¶

push ⇒ 추진, 힘으로 밀다, 추진하다, move with force 명사로 사용 ¶

far from done ⇒ 도움이 되기에는 거리가 멀다, 전혀 도움이 되지 않는다 ¶

do ⇒ ~에 도움이 되다 ¶

[06]

Word&Phrase

devaluation 평가절하, 가치 저하
market-oriented 시장 주도의, 시장 중심적
prop up 떠받치다
foreign exchange hoard 외환 비축량, 축적, 저장

There is further to go 아직 갈 길이 남았다, 끝나지 않았다

Lead Sentence

The central bank weakened the official exchange rate by another 1.6 pct against the U.S. dollar. It's a clear sign the new "market-oriented" yuan is heading down. Until China uses its foreign exchange hoard to prop up the currency, investors will assume there's further to go.

중국 중앙은행은 달러 대비 공식 위안화 환율을 또다시 1.6% 낮추었다. 이것은 새로운 '시장 중심'의 위안화 가치 하락의 명백한 신호다. 중국이 외환 비축량을 사용해서 위안화를 떠받칠 때까지 투자가들은 위안화가 더욱 떨어질 것으로 생각할 것이다.

Bilingual Reading

The central bank 중국 중앙은행은 **weakened** 낮추었다 **the official exchange rate** 공식 위안화 환율을 **by another 1.6 pct** 또다시 1.6%까지 **against the U.S. dollar.** 달러 대비 **It's a clear sign** 이것은 명백한 신호다 **the new "market-oriented" yuan** 새로운 시장주도 위안화 가치가 **is heading down.** 떨어지고 있다는 **Until** 때까지 **China uses its foreign exchange hoard** 중국이 외환 비축량을 사용해서 **to prop up the currency,** 위안화를 떠바칠 **investors** 투자가들은 **will assume there's further to go.** 위안화가 더욱 떨어질 것으로 생각할 것이다.

Senate blocks Government funding bill tied to abortion

With less than a week before the government runs out of money, the Senate failed Thursday to advance a bill that would have kept federal offices open, but defunded Planned Parenthood.

Headline

Senate blocks Government funding bill tied to abortion

상원은 낙태와 관련된 정부 자금지원 법안을 부결시켰다.

일반 표현

Senate has blocked Government funding bill related to abortion.

Matrix Core

헤드라인 영어문장은 완료형을 현재로 나타낸다. ¶

Decoded Core

Senate blocks ⇒ Senate has blocked ¶

block ⇒ 저지하다, 막다, obstruct 방해하다, thwart 좌절시키다 ¶

bill tied to abortion ⇒ 낙태에 관련된 법안, bill which is related to abortion ¶

tied 관련된 ¶

abortion ⇒ 낙태, 유산 ¶

[07]

Word&Phrase

with 때문에
defund 자금 혜택을 중단하다
: withdraw the financial help
run out 다 써버리다, ~가 동나다
advance 진행, 나아가다

Federal offices 연방정부 기관
Planned Parenthood 가족계획

Lead Sentence

With less than a week before the government runs out of money, the Senate failed Thursday to advance a bill that would have kept federal offices open, but defunded Planned Parenthood.

일주일 이내로 연방정부 예산이 완전 소진됨에 따라 상원은 연방정부 부처사무실을 열어둘 수 있는 법안 통과 및 진행을 목요일에 중단하고, 가족계획 자금 지급도 중단했다.

Bilingual Reading

With less than a week before 일주일 이내 **the government** 연방정부 **runs out of money,** 예산이 완전 소진됨으로 **the Senate** 상원은 **failed Thursday** 목요일에 중단했고 **to advance a bill** 법안통과 진행을 **that would have kept federal offices open,** 연방정부 부처사무실을 열어둘 수 있는 **but defunded Planned Parenthood.** 가족계획 자금 지급도 중단했다.

Part.1 INTERNATIONAL

33

Friendship between Putin and Xi becomes strained as economies falter

Slowdowns in Russia and China have put energy deals between the countries in question, affecting the once-vaunted relationship between the two leaders.

Headline

Friendship between Putin and Xi becomes strained as economies falter

푸틴 대통령과 시진핑 주석 간의 우정이 경제적 활력을 잃은 후 긴장국면에 처해졌다.

일반 표현

Friendship between Putin and Xi has faced tension after losing economic momentum.

Matrix Core

헤드라인 영어문장은 완료형을 현재로 나타낸다. ¶

Decoded Core

becomes ⇒ (has been) become ¶

becomes strained ⇒ has become strained on, 긴장관계에 빠지다 ¶

falter ⇒ 힘을 잃어버리다, 비틀거리다 : start to lose strength or momentum ¶

[08]

Word&Phrase

slowdown in Russia and China 러시아와 중국의 경기 둔화
once-vaunted 한때 자랑했던
put something in question ~을 의심스럽게 만들다
energy deal 에너지 협정

Lead Sentence

Slowdowns in Russia and China have put energy deals between the countries in question, affecting the once-vaunted relationship between the two leaders.

러시아와 중국의 경기 둔화는 두 나라의 에너지 협정을 의문스럽게 만들며 한때 우호적이던 두 정상 간 관계에 타격을 주었다.

Bilingual Reading

Slowdowns in Russia and China 러시아와 중국의 경기 둔화는 **have put** 던졌고 **energy deals between the countries** 두 나라의 에너지 협정에 **in question,** 의문으로 **affecting** 타격을 주었다 **the once-vaunted relationship** 한때 자랑했던 관계에 **between the two leaders.** 두 정상 사이의

Part.1 INTERNATIONAL

Flat wages add to allure of the 'anti-politician' in reliably Red States

The economy in general and stagnant wages in particular have some Republican voters looking for a leader who is not entrenched in American politics.

Headline

Flat wages add to allure of the 'anti-politician' in reliably Red States

임금 동결로 인해 미국 내 공화당이 우세한 주에서 기존 정치인에 대한 불신이 늘어나고 있다.

일반 표현

Flat wages has increased the sentiment of anti-politician in reliably red states.

Matrix Core

헤드라인 영어문장은 완료형을 현재로 나타낸다. ¶

Decoded Core

add ⇒ has added, 증가시키다, increase의 의미 ¶

anti-politician ⇒ 기존 정치인들에 대한 기피 ¶

allure ⇒ 유혹하다 attract, entice
여기서 allure는 동사가 아니고 명사로 사용했다. ¶

flat wage ⇒ 낮은 임금 ¶

[09]

Word&Phrase

in particular 특히
have (some Republic voters) looking for 일부 공화당 유권자들로 하여금 어떤 사람을 찾게 하다
entrench 굳건하게 자리를 잡다 ¦ establish solidly
stagnant 흐르지 않는, 고여 있는, 발달이 없는

Lead Sentence

The economy in general and stagnant wages in particular have some Republican voters looking for a leader who is not entrenched in American politics.

전반적인 경기 침체와 특히 정체된 임금 문제가 공화당 지지 유권자들로 하여금 미국 정치에 타성화되지 않은 지도자를 찾게 한다.

Bilingual Reading

The economy in general 전반적인 경기와 **and stagnant wages in particular** 특히 정체된 임금 문제가 **have some Republican voters** 공화당 지지 유권자들로 하여금 **looking for a leader** 지도자를 찾게 한다 **who is not entrenched in American politics.** 미국 정치에 타성화되지 않은

Police program aims to pinpoint those most likely to commit crimes

At the request of his probation officer, Tyrone C. Brown came to a community auditorium here in June and sat alongside about 30 other mostly young black men with criminal records—men who were being watched closely by the police, just as he was.

Headline

Police program aims to pinpoint those most likely to commit crimes

프로그램의 목적은 범죄를 저지를 가능성이 있는 사람들을 사전에 예측하는 것이다.

일반 표현

The Police program is to call those who are likely to pull crimes.

Matrix Core

헤드라인 영어문장은 관계대명사를 생략한다. ¶

Decoded Core

those likely to commit crimes ⇒
those (who are) likely to commit crimes ¶

commit ⇒ 저지르다, perform an act, 주로 부정적 의미로 사용 ¶

pinpoint ⇒ 정확히 찾아내다, 정확히 짚어내다 ⁞ to find out ¶

[10]

Word&Phrase

probation 가석방, 보호 관찰, 집행유예
community auditorium 지역 회관
criminal records 범죄 경력
perpetrate a crime 범죄를 저지르다

pull a bank robbery 은행 절도를 저지르다, perpetrate의 동의어로 pull이 있다
predict 예측하다 : foretell, call, forebode, anticipate, promise

Lead Sentence

At the request of his probation officer, Tyrone C. Brown came to a community auditorium here in June and sat alongside about 30 other mostly young black men with criminal records—men who were being watched closely by the police, just as he was.

타이론 브라운은 보호 감찰관의 요청으로 6월 이곳 지역 회관에 와서 대부분 젊고 흑인인 30명의 전과자들과 함께 앉았다. 이들은 모두 그가 이전에 그랬던 것처럼 경찰들이 요주의 인물로 감시하는 사람들이다.

Bilingual Reading

At the request of his probation officer, 보호 감찰관의 요청으로 **Tyrone C. Brown** 타이론 브라운 **came to a community auditorium here** 이곳 지역 회관에 와서 **in June** 6월에 **and sat alongside about 30 other mostly young black men** 대부분 젊고 흑인인 30명의 남자들과 함께 앉았다 **with criminal records** 범죄 기록이 있는—**men** 그들은 **who were being watched closely** 면밀히 관찰되고 있는 사람들이다 **by the police,** 경찰관에 의해서 **just as he was.** 그(타이론)와 마찬가지로

Part. 1 INTERNATIONAL

39

A sacred mission in lunch for the homeless

Pope Francis is compelling the cameras to show a picture some might rather ignore: In Washington, he met the homeless.

Headline

A sacred mission in lunch for the homeless

노숙자와 점심을 같이 하는 성스러운 사명감

일반 표현

It was his sacred mission that he shares lunch with the homeless.

Matrix Core

헤드라인 영어문장은 몇 개의 단어나 기본구조로 나타낸다. ¶

Decoded Core

문장 패턴 ⇒ It is a sacred mission that 구문이 좋다. ¶

sacred mission ⇒ 성스러운 사명감 ¶

[11]

Word&Phrase

Pope 교황
compel 강요하다 : force
rather ignore 다소 무시하다
homeless 집 없는, 노숙자

Lead Sentence

Pope Francis is compelling the cameras to show a picture some might rather ignore: In Washington, he met the homeless.

프란치스코 교황은 카메라에게 사람들이 흔히 무시해 버릴 수 있는 장면을 비추어 달라고 요청하고 있다. 즉 워싱턴에서 그가 노숙자들을 만난 장면이다.

Bilingual Reading

Pope Francis 프란치스코 교황은 **is compelling the cameras** 카메라에게 요청하고 있다 **to show a picture** 장면을 비추어 달라고 **some might rather ignore:** 흔히 무시해 버릴 수 있는 **In Washington,** 워싱턴에서 **he met the homeless.** 그는 노숙자들을 만났다

Vote to take in migrants tests limits of unity in Europe

Overruling four former Soviet bloc countries, European Union ministers approved a plan for individual nations in the bloc to accept a share of 120,000 refugees.

Headline

Vote to take in migrants tests limits of unity in Europe

이주 노동자를 받아들이는 투표는 유럽 내 연합 정도를 시험했다.

일반 표현

A vote to accept migrants tested limits of unity in Europe.

Matrix Core

헤드라인 영어문장은 완료형을 현재로 나타낸다. ¶

Decoded Core

tests ⇒ (has) tested ¶

vote to take in migrant ⇒ 이주 노동자를 받아들이는 문제에 관한 투표 ⋮ vote to accept in migrant ¶

migrant ⇒ 이주 노동자 ⋮ a person who moves to find work ¶

limits of unity in Europe ⇒ 유럽 내 연합 정도 ¶

[12]

Word&Phrase

overrule 뒤엎다, 각하하다, ~을 지배하다 : to set aside
Soviet bloc countries 바르샤바 조약에 가맹한 동구와 중앙유럽의 공산주의 국가들
approve 승인, 찬성
a share 공유, 몫, 분담
refugee 난민, 망명자, 이탈자

Lead Sentence

Overruling four former Soviet bloc countries, European Union ministers approved a plan for individual nations in the bloc to accept a share of 120,000 refugees.

전 소련연방 4개국을 제외한 유럽연합 장관들은 120,000명의 난민을 일정 분량씩 연합 내 각 국가가 받아들이는 계획안을 승인했다.

Bilingual Reading

Overruling four former Soviet bloc countries, 전 소련연방 4개국을 제외한 **European Union ministers** 유럽연합 장관들은 **approved a plan** 계획안을 승인했다 **for individual nations in the bloc** 연합 내 각 국가가 **to accept a share** 일정 분량씩 받아들이는 **of 120,000 refugees.** 120,000명의 난민을

Part.1 INTERNATIONAL

43

Russia has levers to cope with oil squeeze

A low oil price will dent growth and public revenues, and Russia needs rebalancing. Yet President Vladimir Putin can hold the line by drawing on reserves and even inflating regional deficits, while the rouble's fall helps competitiveness. That could enable a fragile equilibrium.

Headline

Russia has levers to cope with oil squeeze

러시아는 낮은 유가 상황을 견딜 수 있는 안전장치를 가지고 있다.

일반 표현

Russia is able to manage low oil price.

Matrix Core

헤드라인 영어문장은 기본구조로 나타낸다. ¶

Decoded Core

lever ⇒ 지렛대, 문제 등을 해결할 수 있는 방법 ¶

cope with ⇒ 문제 등을 해결하다, 처리하다 ⁑ deal, manage, act, move ¶

squeeze ⇒ 압박, 궁지, 곤란, 짜내다, 압착하다, 긴축하다 ¶

[13]

Word&Phrase

dent 움푹 들어가게 하다, 손실을 가져오다
make a dent in economy 경제에 큰 소실을 가져오게 하다
fragile 취약한, 깨지기 쉬운 부진한, 불안정한

Lead Sentence

A low oil price will dent growth and public revenues, and Russia needs rebalancing. Yet President Vladimir Putin can hold the line by drawing on reserves and even inflating regional deficits, while the rouble's fall helps competitiveness. That could enable a fragile equilibrium.

낮은 유가는 경제 성장과 국고 세입에 손실을 가져올 것이고, 러시아는 경제 재균형이 필요하다. 하지만 푸틴 대통령은 외환보유고를 이용하고 러시아 지역 적자에 인플레이션을 야기하여 균형을 잡을 수 있으며, 한편으로는 루블화 가격 하락이 경쟁력을 높일 수도 있다. 하지만 그것은 취약한 균형이 될 것이다.

Bilingual Reading

A low oil price 낮은 석유 가격은 **will dent** 손실을 가져올 것이다 **growth and public revenues,** 러시아의 경제 성장과 국고 세입에 **and Russia needs rebalancing.** 그리고 러시아는 경제 재균형 (수입과 지출)이 필요하다 **Yet President Vladimir Putin** 하지만 블라디미르 푸틴 대통령은 **can hold the line** 균형을 잡을 수 있다 **by drawing on reserves** 외환보유고를 이용하고 **and even inflating regional deficits,** 러시아 지역 적자에 인플레이션을 야기해 **while the rouble's fall** 한편 루블화 가격 하락이 **helps competitiveness.** 경쟁력을 도울 수 있다 **That could enable a fragile equilibrium.** 하지만 그것은 취약한 균형이 될 수 있다

45

Global companies joining climate change efforts

Major companies including Johnson & Johnson, Starbucks and Walmart are setting long-term targets for powering operations entirely with renewable energy.

Headline

Global companies joining climate change efforts

국제 기업들이 배기가스를 줄이는 기후변화 억제 노력에 동참하고 있다.

일반 표현

Global companies are joining climate change efforts.

Matrix Core

헤드라인 영어문장은 대체로 **be 동사를** 생략한다. ¶

Decoded Core

Global companies joining ⇒
Global companies (are) joining ¶

join ⇒ 가입하다, 참여하다 : to put or bring together, to connect ¶

climate change efforts ⇒ (배기가스를 줄임으로써) 기후의 이상 현상을 예방하려는 노력 ¶

Word&Phrase

be setting 정하다
long-tern target 장기적 목표
power operation 공장을 가동시키다
entirely with renewable energy 온전히 재생에너지만으로

Lead Sentence

Major companies including Johnson&Johnson, Starbucks and Walmart are setting long-term targets for powering operations entirely with renewable energy.

존슨&존슨, 스타벅스, 월마트 등 주요 기업들은 온전히 재생에너지만으로 공장을 가동시키겠다는 장기 목표를 세웠다.

Bilingual Reading

Major companies 주요 회사들은 **including** 포함하는 **Johnson & Johnson,** 존슨&존슨 **Starbucks and Walmart** 스타벅스 그리고 월마트를 **are setting long-term targets** 장기 목표를 세웠다 **for powering operations entirely** 공장을 완전히 가동시키는 **with renewable energy.** 재생에너지로

Why oil investors are so behind the curve

> Investors used to assume that the cost of pulling oil out of the ground was relatively static–or changed slowly. Reality is slipperier. Rethinking the way the "cost curve" works may help explain recent gyrations in oil and other commodity markets.

Headline

Why oil investors are so behind the curve

석유 투자가들은 왜 현실을 제대로 파악하지 못하는가?

일반 표현

Why is it that oil investors fail to see the reality right?

Matrix Core

헤드라인 영어문장은 의문부호를 생략한다. ¶

Decoded Core

Why oil investors are so ⇒ Why are oil investors so? 의문부호를 생략하기 위한 도치 ¶

behind the curve ⇒ 변동을 따라가지 못하다 ¶

don't keep up with reality ⇒ 현실을 따라 잡지 못하다 ¶

[15]

Word&Phrase

the cost of pulling oil out of the ground
땅에서 석유를 시추하는 비용
static 정지된, 변함없는, 움직이지 않는 ː not in physical motion
cost curve 비용곡선
slippery 미끄러운, 불안정한 ː causing things to slip or slide
gyration 선회, 회전, 소용돌이 모양 ː turn
commodity 원자재

Lead Sentence

Investors used to assume that the cost of pulling oil out of the ground was relatively static-or changed slowly. Reality is slipperier. Rethinking the way the "cost curve" works may help explain recent gyrations in oil and other commodity markets.

투자가들은 석유 시추 비용이 비교적 변동이 없거나 변하더라도 천천히 변한다고 생각해왔다. 그러나 현실은 보다 불안정하다. '비용곡선'이 움직이는 추이를 다시 생각해보면 최근에 보이는 석유와 원자재 시장의 선회 현상을 이해할 수 있을 것이다.

Bilingual Reading

Investors 투자가들은 **used to assume** 생각해왔다 **that the cost of pulling oil out of the ground** 석유시추 비용은 **was relatively static** 비교적 변동이 없거나 **-or changed slowly.** 아니면 천천히 변한다고 **Reality is slipperier.** 현실은 더욱 불안정하다 **Rethinking** 다시 생각해 보면 **the way the "cost curve" works** "비용곡선"이 움직이는 방식을 **may help explain** 이해할 수 있을 것이다 **recent gyrations** 최근의 선회를 **in oil and other commodity markets.** 석유와 원자재 시장에서

49

Cyberthreat posed by China and Iran confounds White House

President Obama has vowed to deter computer attacks on the United States, but he is struggling to muster the leverage to do so ahead of a state visit from China's leader.

Headline

Cyberthreat posed by China and Iran confounds White House

중국과 이란이 야기하는 사이버위협이 백악관을 당혹스럽게 하고 있다.

일반 표현

China and Iran have posed cyberthreat to the U.S., baffling the White house.

Matrix Core

헤드라인 영어문장은 관계대명사절을 생략한다. ¶

Decoded Core

Cyberthreat posed ⇒ Cyberthreat (which has been) posed ¶

confound ⇒ 당혹스럽고 놀라게 하다 : to surprise and confuse, baffle ¶

pose ⇒ 제기하다, 야기하다 ¶

pose a threat or danger ⇒ 위협 또는 위험을 야기하다 ¶

[16]

Word&Phrase

vow 밝히다, 약속하다 : serious promise
deter 단념시키다, 방해하다, 저지하다
muster 소집하다, 모으다, 집합
leverage 영향력, 효력

Lead Sentence

President Obama has vowed to deter computer attacks on the United States, but he is struggling to muster the leverage to do so ahead of a state visit from China's leader.

오바마 대통령은 미국에 대한 사이버 공격을 저지시키겠다고 약속했다. 하지만 그는 중국 주석의 국빈 방문 전에 이를 실효적으로 이행하는 데 어려움을 겪고 있다.

Bilingual Reading

President Obama 오바마 대통령은 **has vowed** 약속했다 **to deter computer attacks on the United States,** 미국에 대한 사이버 공격을 저지하겠다고 **but he** 하지만 그는 **is struggling** 어려움을 겪다 **to muster the leverage** 영향력을 행사하려고 **to do so** 그렇게 하기 위한 **ahead of a state visit** 국빈 방문 전에 **from China's leader.** 중국 주석의

India beats timely retreat from fiscal tyranny

The finance minister has retracted a flawed plan to tax foreign fund managers' past earnings. Jittery global markets may have hastened the truce. Settling similar disputes with Vodafone and Cairn would show the government is belatedly keeping its promise to end "tax terrorism".

Headline

India beats timely retreat from fiscal tyranny

인도는 경제 독재정책을 적절히 철회했다.

일반 표현

India has timely retracted its fiscal authoritative policy.

Matrix Core

헤드라인 영어문장은 완료형을 현재로 나타낸다. ¶

Decoded Core

beat ⇒ (has) beat 도망가다 ¶

beat timely retreat ⇒ 시기적절하게 도망가다 ¶

beat timely retreat from ⇒ ~로부터 적절한 시기에 철수하다, 정책을 버리다 ¶

retract ⇒ 철회하다 ¶

tyranny ⇒ 폭정, 횡포 ¶

[17]

Word&Phrase

flaw 결함, 흠
jittery 초조해 하는, 불안한
hasten 서두르다, 재촉하다
trace 휴전, 종결

belatedly 뒤늦게
tax terrorism 세금 테러

Lead Sentence

The finance minister has retracted a flawed plan to tax foreign fund managers' past earnings. Jittery global markets may have hastened the truce. Settling similar disputes with Vodafone and Cairn would show the government is belatedly keeping its promise to end "tax terrorism".

인도 재무장관은 외국 펀드 매니저들의 지난 수입에 세금을 부과하는 잘못된 정책을 철회했다. 불안정한 세계 금융시장이 정책 중단을 재촉했는지도 모른다. 보다폰(Vodafone)과 케른(Cairn)과의 유사한 논쟁 해결은 인도 정부도 세금 테러를 끝내겠다는 약속을 뒤늦게 지키려고 한다는 것을 보여줄 것이다.

Part.1 INTERNATIONAL

Bilingual Reading

The finance minister 인도 재무장관은 **has retracted a flawed plan** 잘못된 정책을 철회했다 **to tax** 세금을 부과하는 **foreign fund managers'** 외국 펀드매니저들의 **past earnings.** 이전 수입에 **Jittery global markets** 불안정한 세계 금융시장이 **may have hastened the truce.** 중단을 재촉했는지도 모른다 **Settling similar disputes** 유사한 논쟁 해결은 **with Vodafone and Cairn** 보다폰(영국 이동통신업체)과 케른(정유회사)과의 **would show** 보여주게 될 것이다 **the government** 인도 정부가 **is belatedly** 늦었지만 **keeping its promise** 약속을 지키려고 한다는 것을 **to end "tax terrorism".** 세금 테러를 끝내겠다는

53

Journalist's shaming shows increase in China's press control

When a journalist from Caijing, a reputable business and finance publication, was compelled to confess on television before going to trial, it came as a surprise to many.

Headline

Journalist's shaming shows increase in China's press control

기자들이 받은 모욕은 중국의 언론 통제가 강화되고 있음을 보여준다.

일반 표현

Chinese government dishonors journalist working in China, it means the government is increasing its press control.

Matrix Core

헤드라인 영어문장은 대체로 be 동사를 생략한다. ¶

Decoded Core

shows ⇒ is meant to show ¶

journalist's shaming ⇒ shaming journalist 기자들을 모욕하는 것 ¶

press control ⇒ 언론 통제 ¶

[18]

Word&Phrase

reputable 저명한
compel 강요하다, ~하지 않을 수 없다, 압도적인
confess 고백하다
trial 재판

Lead Sentence

When a journalist from Caijing, a reputable business and finance publication, was compelled to confess on television before going to trial, it came as a surprise to many.

중국의 저명한 경제지 «차이징»의 기자는 재판을 받기 전 TV에 나와 자신의 잘못을 고백해야만 했고, 이것은 많은 사람을 놀라게 했다.

Bilingual Reading

When a journalist from Caijing, 차이징 기자 한 사람은 **a reputable business and finance publication,** 저명한 경제지인 **was compelled to confess** 자기의 잘못을 고백해야만 했다 **on television** TV에 나와 **before going to trial,** 재판을 받기 전 **it came as a surprise to many.** 이것은 많은 사람을 놀라게 했다.

Pope's visit to U.S. is his first ever, for several reasons

Unlike predecessors who traveled to the United States before rising to the papacy, Pope Francis has waited until age 78 to visit the country.

Headline

Pope's visit to U.S. is his first ever, for several reasons

여러 가지 이유에서 교황의 미국 방문은 이번이 처음이다.

일반 표현

Pope will visit U.S. for the first time for several reasons.

Matrix Core

헤드라인 영어문장은 뒤에서 읽는 것이 이해에 더 도움이 되기도 한다. ¶

Decoded Core

first ever ⇒ 지금까지 처음으로
for several reasons ⇒ 여러 가지 이유에서

[19]

Word&Phrase

unlike 다르다, 같지 않다, 달리
predecessor 전임자
Papacy 교황 직위

Lead Sentence

Unlike predecessors who traveled to the United States before rising to the papacy, Pope Francis has waited until age 78 to visit the country.

교황의 자리에 오르기 전 미국을 방문한 전임자들과 달리 프란치스코 교황은 미국을 방문하기 위해 그의 나이 78세가 되기까지 기다렸다.

Bilingual Reading

Unlike predecessors 전임자들과 달리 **who traveled to the United States** 미국을 방문한 **before rising to the papacy,** 교황 지위에 오르기 전에 **Pope Francis** 프란치스코 교황은 **has waited** 기다렸다 **until age 78** 그의 나이 78세가 되기까지 **to visit the country.** 미국을 방문하기 위해

Part.1 INTERNATIONAL

Wealthy gulf nations are criticized for tepid response to Syrian refugee crisis

The affluent nations reject the criticism, insisting they have given generously to humanitarian aid programs and provided work for fleeing Syrians.

Headline

Wealthy gulf nations are criticized for tepid response to Syrian refugee crisis

부유한 걸프 국가들은 시리아 난민 사태에 미온적 태도를 취하고 있다고 비난 받고 있다.

일반 표현

They criticized wealthy gulf nations for their lukewarm interest to Syrian refuge crises.

Matrix Core

헤드라인 영어문장은 현재완료 수동형을 현재 수동형으로 나타낸다. ¶

Decoded Core

wealthy gulf nations are criticized for ⇒ wealthy gulf nations have been criticized for 부유한 걸프 국가들은 비난 받고 있다 ¶

tepid ⇒ 미지근한, 열의가 없는 ※ showing little interest ¶

[20]

Word&Phrase

reject 무엇을 받아들이기를 거절하다 : refuge to accept

give generously to humanitarian aid program 인도적 원조 프로그램에 많은 것을 내놓다

Lead Sentence

The affluent nations reject the criticism, insisting they have given generously to humanitarian aid programs and provided work for fleeing Syrians.

걸프 지역의 부유한 국가들은 그 비난에 반박하면서 자신들이 인도적 원조 프로그램에 많은 것을 내놓았고 탈출한 시리아인들에게 일자리를 제공해주었다고 주장하고 있다.

Bilingual Reading

The affluent nations 걸프 지역 부유국들은 **reject the criticism,** 그 비난을 받아들이지 않고 **insisting** 주장하고 있다 **they** 그들이 **have given generously** 많은 것을 내놓았고 **to humanitarian aid programs** 인도적 원조 프로그램에 **and provided work** 일자리를 제공해 주었다고 **for fleeing Syrians.** 탈출한 시리아인들에게

Part.1 INTERNATIONAL

U.S. is said to rethink Afghan exit

With pressure building on the White House to slow or completely halt the withdrawal of American troops from Afghanistan, White House officials said that president Obama appeared increasingly willing to keep a force there large enough to carry on the hunt for Alqaeda and Islamic militants.

Headline

U.S. is said to rethink Afghan exit

미국은 아프가니스탄 철수를 재고하는 것으로 전해진다.

일반 표현

It is said that the U.S. reconsiders its withdrawal from Afghanistan.

Matrix Core

헤드라인 영어문장은 주체가 불확실할 때 It is said that 구문을 쓴다. ¶

헤드라인 영어문장은 현재완료 수동형을 현재 수동형으로 나타낸다. ¶

Decoded Core

rethink ⇒ 다시 생각하다, 재고하다 ⁞ reconsiders ¶

exit ⇒ 철수, 퇴출 ⁞ withdrawal ¶

[21]

Word&Phrase

with ~ from Afghanistan ~라는 이유로 해서(이유를 설명하는 부사구)
halt 중단, 막다, 마비 : stop, suspend
hunt 찾다, 추적

Lead Sentence

With pressure building on the White House to slow or completely halt the withdrawal of American troops from Afghanistan, White House officials said that president Obama appeared increasingly willing to keep a force there large enough to carry on the hunt for Alqaeda and Islamic militants.

백악관을 향해 아프가니스탄 주둔 미군 철수를 늦추든지 또는 완전히 중단시켜야 한다는 압력이 커짐에 따라 오바마 대통령이 알카에다와 이슬람 용병을 추적할 수 있는 충분한 병력을 그곳에 계속 주둔시키려는 의지가 커져가고 있는 것처럼 보인다고 백악관 관리가 말했다.

Bilingual Reading

With pressure building 압력이 커져감으로 **on the White House** 백악관에 대한 **to slow or completely halt** 속도를 줄이든지 또는 완전히 중단시켜야 한다는 **the withdrawal of American troops** 미군 철수의 **from Afghanistan,** 아프가니스탄으로부터 **White House officials said** 백악관 관리가 말했다 **that president Obama** 오바마 대통령은 **appeared increasingly willing** 의지가 커져가고 있는 것처럼 보인다 **to keep** 계속 유지시키려는 **a force there large enough** 충분한 병력을 그곳에 **to carry on the hunt** 완전히 추적할 수 있는 **for Alqaeda and Islamic militants.** 알카에다나 이슬람 민병대를

Part.1 INTERNATIONAL

Hong Kong slowly losing its neon glow

For nearly four decades, a giant neon cow suspended above a steakhouse in 's Western District was a neighborhood landmark. It was where, if you were giving directions, you told someone to get off the bus or to take the next left.

Headline

Hong Kong slowly losing its neon glow

홍콩은 천천히 네온 불빛을 잃어버리고 있다.

일반 표현

Hong Kong is slowly losing its neon light.

Matrix Core

헤드라인 영어문장은 대체로 **be 동사**를 생략한다. ¶

Decoded Core

slowly losing ⇒ (is) slowly losing 차츰 불이 꺼지다 ¶

lose its neon glow ⇒ 네온 불빛을 잃다, 불빛이 꺼지다 ¶

[22]

Word&Phrase

suspend 달다, 정지하다
landmark 표지물, 눈에 띄는 특색
direction 방향, 지시, 길

Lead Sentence

For nearly four decades, a giant neon cow suspended above a steakhouse in 's Western District was a neighborhood landmark. It was where, if you were giving directions, you told someone to get off the bus or to take the next left.

지난 40여 년 간 홍콩 웨스턴 구역의 어느 스테이크하우스에 걸려있던 소 모양의 대형 네온사인은 지역의 랜드마크였다. 누군가 길을 물어보면 바로 그 건물 앞에서 버스를 내리든지 또는 그 건물 다음 역 왼편에서 버스를 타라고 말을 했었다.

Bilingual Reading

For nearly four decades, 거의 40년 동안 **a giant neon cow** 소 형태의 대형 네온사인 간판 **suspended** 걸려 있던 **above a steakhouse** 한 스테이크하우스 위에 **in Hong Kong's Western District** 홍콩의 웨스턴 구역에 **was a neighborhood landmark.** 이 지역의 랜드마크였다 **It was where,** 여기는 그런 곳이었다 **if you were giving directions,** 길을 가르쳐 줄 일이 있다면 **you** 당신은 **told** 말했던 **someone** 길을 묻는 사람에게 **to get off the bus** 그 건물 앞에서 버스를 내리든지 **or to take the next left.** 또는 그 건물 다음 역 왼편에서 버스를 타라고

Part.1 INTERNATIONAL

Britain urges Saudis to free grandfather facing lethal lash

For more than a year, asthmatic 74 years-old grandfather and former oil executive has sat in a prison, Saudi Arabia, accused of violating the country's strict alcohol after the authorities found bottles of homemade wine in his car.

Headline

Britain urges Saudis to free grandfather facing lethal lash

영국은 사우디아라비아 정부에 치명적인 태형에 처해 있는 노인을 석방시키라고 촉구했다.

일반 표현

Britain encourages Saudis to release grandfather facing lashes.

Matrix Core

헤드라인 영어문장은 진행형을 현재분사로 나타낸다. ¶

Decoded Core

grandfather facing lethal lash ⇒ grandfather (who is) facing lethal lash ¶

urge ⇒ 하도록 설득하다 ⁞ encourage, persuade ¶

lethal ⇒ 치명적인 ¶

lash ⇒ 비난, 공격, 채찍, 아픔 ¶

[23]

Word&Phrase

free 석방시키다
asthmatic 천식의 : release
violate 위반하다
the country's strict alcohol 그 나라의 엄격한 금주법
authorities 당국

Lead Sentence

For more than a year, asthmatic 74 years-old grandfather and former oil executive has sat in a prison, Saudi Arabia, accused of violating the country's strict alcohol after the authorities found bottles of homemade wine in his car.

천식을 앓고 있는 전직 석유회사 사장인 74세의 노인이 1년 이상이나 교도소에 수감되어 있다. 사우디아라비아 당국이 그의 차에서 집에서 빚은 술을 발견하고 자국의 엄격한 금주법 위반 혐의로 기소한 것이다.

Bilingual Reading

For more than a year, 1년 이상 **asthmatic** 천식을 앓고 있는 **74 years-old grandfather** 74세의 노인 **and former oil executive** 전직 석유회사 사장 **has sat in a prison,** 교도소에 수감되어 있다 **Saudi Arabia,** 사우디아라비아는 **accused** 기소했다 **of violating the country's strict alcohol** 그 나라의 엄격한 금주법 위반으로 **after the authorities** 당국이 **found bottles of homemade wine** 집에서 만든 술을 발견한 후 **in his car.** 그의 차에서

Leaderless youth fan Palestinian flames

Armed groups drive rise in violence in Israel, but now social media is the spark.

Headline

Leaderless youth fan Palestinian flames

지도자 없는 젊은이들이 팔레스타인의 적개심을 더욱 자극시키고 있다.

일반 표현

Youth with no leader makes Palestinian more hostile.

Matrix Core

헤드라인 영어문장은 몇 개의 단어나 기본구조로 나타낸다. ¶

Decoded Core

fan ⇒ make fiercer의 의미. 더욱 부추기다, 더욱 격렬하게 만들다 ¶

flames ⇒ hostility의 의미 ¶

Palestinian flames ⇒ 이스라엘인에 대한 팔레스타인의 적대감정 ¶

[24]

Word&Phrase

armed group 무장 단체
drive rise 부추기다
social media 소셜미디어 : forms of electronic to
spark 촉발시키다, 야기하다, 유발, 불꽃 : respond with enthusiasm

Lead Sentence

Armed groups drive rise in violence in Israel, but now social media is the spark.

무장단체들이 이스라엘 내의 폭력을 야기했지만, 현재는 소셜미디어가 촉매제 역할을 하고 있다.

Bilingual Reading

Armed groups 무장단체들이 **drive rise in violence** 폭력을 부추기고 있고 **in Israel,** 이스라엘에서 **but now social media** 지금은 소셜미디어가 **is the spark.** 촉매제다

Part.1 INTERNATIONAL

67

New York Attorney General examining whether Turing restricted drug access

Eric T. Schneiderman has begun an inquiry into whether Turing Pharmaceuticals violated antitrust rules by restricting distribution of a drug, Daraprim, as a way to thwart generic competition.

Headline

New York Attorney General examining whether Turing restricted drug access

뉴욕 주 법무장관은 튜링 제약이 약품 유통(공급)을 제한했는지 조사하고 있다.

일반 표현

New York Attorney General is examining whether Turing Pharmaceuticals restricted drug distribution.

Matrix Core

헤드라인 영어문장은 대체로 be 동사를 생략한다. ¶

Decoded Core

examining ⇒ (is) examining ¶

restrict ⇒ 범위, 숫자, 행동 등을 제한하다 ⁝ limit in extent, number, scope or action, confine, tighten ¶

drug access ⇒ 약품 유통 ⁝ drug distribution ¶

Attorney General ⇒ 법무장관 ¶

Turing pharmaceuticals ⇒ 튜링 제약회사. 합성 생화학 약품 제조회사 ¶

[25]

Word&Phrase

inquiry 조사, 문의, 수사
pharmaceutical 제약의, 조제약
antitrust rules 독점 금지법
: antitrust legislation

thwart 좌절시키다, 방해하다, 가로지르다, 불리하다, 고집 센
generic competition 일반약품 판매경쟁
Daraprim(Pyrimethamine) 프로토졸 감염을 위해 사용하는 약품

Lead Sentence

Eric T. Schneiderman has begun an inquiry into whether Turing Pharmaceuticals violated antitrust rules by restricting distribution of a drug, Daraprim, as a way to thwart generic competition.

에릭 T. 슈나이더만은 튜링 제약회사가 일반의약품 판매 경쟁에서 이기기 위한 방법으로 '다라프림' 약품의 유통량을 제한함으로써 독점판매 금지법을 위반했는지 수사를 시작했다.

Bilingual Reading

Eric T. Schneiderman 에릭 T. 슈나이더만은 **has begun an inquiry** 수사를 시작했다 **into whether Turing Pharmaceuticals** 튜링 제약회사가 **violated antitrust rules** 독점판매 금지법을 위반했는지 **by restricting distribution of a drug, Daraprim,** '다라프림' 약품의 유통량을 제한함으로써 **as a way to thwart generic competition.** 일반의약품 판매 경쟁에 이기기 위한 방법으로

Outside moves shift Syria conflict to proxy war

Rebel commanders say that since Russian airstrikes began, powerful American-made antitank missiles are being readily delivered for the first time, raising morale but making a diplomatic settlement even more unlikely.

Headline

Outside moves shift Syria conflict to proxy war

외부 세력들이 시리아 분쟁을 대리전쟁으로 전환시켰다.

일반 표현

Foreign forces have changed Syria conflict to proxy war.

Matrix Core

헤드라인 영어문장은 기본구조로 나타낸다. ¶

Decoded Core

shift ⇒ change의 의미 ¶
outside move ⇒ 외부세력 ¶
proxy ⇒ 대리, 대리인 ¶
proxy war ⇒ 대리전쟁 ¶

[26]

Word&Phrase

rebel commander 반군 사령관
antitank 대전차용
antitank missile 대전차용 미사일
readily 자진해서, 기꺼이, 당장, 즉시

morale 사기, 의욕, 기세, 용기
settlement 해결, 합의, 타협, 조정

Lead Sentence

Rebel commanders say that since Russian airstrikes began, powerful American-made antitank missiles are being readily delivered for the first time, raising morale but making a diplomatic settlement even more unlikely.

러시아의 공중 폭격이 시작된 이래로 강력한 미제 대전차용 미사일이 처음으로 지급되고 있고, 이는 사기를 끌어올리고 있다. 하지만 외교적 해결의 가능성을 더욱 희박하게 만들고 있다고 반군 사령관들은 말하고 있다.

Bilingual Reading

Rebel commanders say 반군 사령관들이 말하고 있다 **that since Russian airstrikes began,** 러시아의 공중 폭격이 시작된 이래로 **powerful American-made antitank missiles** 강력한 미제 대전차용 미사일이 **are being readily delivered** 지급되고 있고 **for the first time,** 처음으로 **raising morale** 사기를 끌어올리고 있다 **but making** 하지만 만들고 있다고 **a diplomatic settlement** 외교적 해결을 **even more unlikely** 더욱 가능성이 희박하게

Despite nuclear accord, U.S.-Iran tensions are on the rise

Tensions between the U.S. and Iran, rather than easing as a result of July's nuclear accord, are increasing over a wide spectrum of issues tied to the broader Middle East security landscape and to domestic Iranian politics, current and former U.S. officials say.

Headline

Despite nuclear accord, U.S.-Iran tensions are on the rise

핵 협정에도 불구하고 미국과 이란 사이의 긴장은 더 높아지고 있다.

일반 표현

U.S.-Iran tension is increasingly greater despite nuclear deal.

Matrix Core

헤드라인 영어문장은 기본구조로 나타낸다. ¶

Decoded Core

are on the rise ⇒ increase 의미, 점점 더 늘어나고 있다 ⋮ becoming greater, increasing ¶

accord ⇒ 공식적 합의 ⋮ an official agreement, treaty, deal ¶

nuclear accord ⇒ 핵 협정 ¶

[27]

Word&Phrase

conviction 확신, 자각, 설득력
spectrum 범위, 분포 : a complete range of
different opinions 포괄적 의견 차이
landscape 지역, 지형, 경관

Lead Sentence

Tensions between the U.S. and Iran, rather than easing as a result of July's nuclear accord, are increasing over a wide spectrum of issues tied to the broader Middle East security landscape and to domestic Iranian politics, current and former U.S. officials say.

전현직 미국 관리들에 따르면 7월에 합의된 핵 협정의 결과 미국과 이란 사이에 감돌고 있는 긴장이 완화되기는커녕 더 넓은 중동 안보 배경과 이란 국내 정치와 관련 있는 다양한 분야의 이슈에 걸쳐 더욱 높아지고 있다.

Bilingual Reading

Tensions between the U.S. and Iran, 미국과 이란 사이에 감돌고 있는 긴장은 **rather than easing** 완화되기보다 오히려 **as a result of July's nuclear accord,** 7월에 합의된 핵 협정의 결과로서 **are increasing** 더욱 확대되고 있다고 **over a wide spectrum of issues** 다양한 분야의 이슈에 걸쳐 **tied** 관련 있는 **to the broader Middle East security landscape** 더 넓은 중동 안보 배경과 **and to domestic Iranian politics,** 이란 국내 정치와 **current and former U.S. officials say.** 전현직 미국 관리들이 말하고 있다

Part.1 INTERNATIONAL

73

Migration crisis echoes age-old test of finance

The flow of desperate people to Europe has a financial-world parallel. For companies, high returns attract new entrants who threaten incumbents' comfortable state. The options for EU leaders are similar too: shut out competition, or find new, better ways to create profit.

Headline

Migration crisis echoes age-old test of finance

이민자 위기는 유럽 국가들이 높은 소득을 보장함으로써 외국 근로자들이 몰려드는 상황이다.

일반 표현

Migration crisis comes with high returns and flows of new entrants.

Matrix Core

헤드라인 영어문장은 기본구조로 나타낸다. ¶

Decoded Core

echo ⇒ make remember '기억나게 하다'라는 의미 ¶

age-old ⇒ 예전부터 있어왔던, 오래된 ¶

age-old test of finance ⇒ '높은 소득은 새로운 참가자를 끌어들인다'라는 의미 : high returns attracts bring in new entrant ¶

[28]

Word&Phrase

parallel 평행, 유사, 병렬, 대응, 부합, 일치
entrant 참가자, 신입
incumbent 현직, 재직자
shut out 막다, 따돌리다, 가로막다

Lead Sentence

The flow of desperate people to Europe has a financial-world parallel. For companies, high returns attract new entrants who threaten incumbents' comfortable state. The options for EU leaders are similar too: shut out competition, or find new, better ways to create profit.

절망적인 사람들이 유럽으로 몰려드는 것은 금융세계에서는 공통적으로 겪는 일이다. 회사들의 높은 임금은 새로운 유입자들을 끌어들이고 이것은 편안한 생활을 해오던 국가를 위험에 빠뜨리고 있다. 역시 이에 대한 EU 지도자들의 선택도 비슷하다. 즉, 경쟁을 지양하거나 새롭게 더 나은 이익을 창출하는 방법을 찾는 길이다.

Bilingual Reading

The flow of desperate people to Europe 절망적인 사람들이 유럽으로 몰려드는 것은 **has a financial-world parallel.** 금융세계에서는 공통적으로 겪는 일이다 **For companies,** 회사들의 **high returns** 높은 임금은 **attract new entrants** 새로운 유입자들을 끌어들이고 **who threaten incumbents' comfortable state.** 이들은 편안한 생활을 해오던 국가를 위험하고 있다 **The options for EU leaders** 이에 대한 EU 지도자들의 선택도 **are similar too:** 역시 비슷하다 **shut out competition,** 즉, 경쟁을 지양하거나 **or find new,** 새롭게 찾는 길이다 **better ways to create profit.** 더 나은 이익을 창출하는 방법을

Tax havens are turning the U.S. into an unequal aristocracy

French economist Gabriel Zucman, a protégé of Thomas Piketty, has a new book outlining how to avoid this.

Headline

Tax havens are turning the U.S. into an unequal aristocracy

조세 피난처가 미국을 불공평한 특권사회로 만들고 있다.

일반 표현

Tax havens are changing the U.S. into an unequal aristocracy.

Matrix Core

헤드라인 영어문장은 기본구조로 나타낸다. ¶

Decoded Core

tax haven ⇒ 조세 피난처. 국가적인 차원에서 세금이 낮게 부과되거나 전혀 부과되지 않는 나라를 말한다. ¶

turn someone into ⇒ ~를 ~한 상태로 만들다 : to change and become someone ¶

[29]

Word&Phrase

protégé 제자
unequal aristocracy 불평등한 귀족사회

Lead Sentence

French economist Gabriel Zucman, a protégé of Thomas Piketty, has a new book outlining how to avoid this.

토마스 피케티의 제자인 프랑스 경제학자 가브리엘 주크만은 이런 사태를 피할 수 있는 방법을 피력하는 새로운 책을 내놓았다.

Bilingual Reading

French economist Gabriel Zucman, 프랑스 경제학자 가브리엘 주크만은 **a protégé of Thomas Piketty,** 토마스 피케티의 제자인 **has a new book outlining** 피력하는 새로운 책을 내놓았다 **how to avoid this.** 이런 일을 피할 수 있는 방법을

Part. 1 INTERNATIONAL

Greek election may reopen can of worms

Given that no party is likely to emerge from next month's vote with a majority, it may be hard to form a strong government that can implement the country's new bailout deal. There's even a risk that there will be yet more elections. That could tip Greece back into crisis.

Headline

Greek election may reopen can of worms

그리스의 선거는 그 동안 나타나지 않았던 어려운 문제점을 또다시 전개시킬지도 모른다.

그리스 선거 이후 많은 문제점이 다시 나타날 가능성이 있다.

일반 표현

Greek election likely reveals many spoilers.
Many spoilers are likely revealed after Greek's election.

Matrix Core

헤드라인 영어문장에서 may는 likely의 의미로도 쓴다. ¶

Decoded Core

may reopen ⇒ likely reopen, likely reveal ¶

can of worms ⇒ 벌레가 들어있는 캔 통조림, 기피하고 싶은 존재, 즉 귀찮은 장애물, 바이러스 ≑ spoiler ¶

[30]

Word&Phrase

given that ~을 감안하면, 고려하면, ~로 보아, ~점에서, 때문에
emerge 나타나다. 명백해지다, 떠오르다
majority 과반수, 대부분
implement 시행하다, 실시하다, 방법, 운영
bailout deal 긴급 금융지원
tip 기울게 하다

Lead Sentence

Given that no party is likely to emerge from next month's vote with a majority, it may be hard to form a strong government that can implement the country's new bailout deal. There's even a risk that there will be yet more elections. That could tip Greece back into crisis.

어느 정당도 다음 달에 있을 투표에서 다수당이 될 가능성이 없으므로 이 나라의 새로운 금융 긴급 구조 자금 협상을 실행시킬 강한 정부를 형성하기는 어려울지 모른다. 또 다시 선거를 치러야 할 위험도 있고, 그리스를 다시 위기로 이끌 수도 있다.

Bilingual Reading

Given that 때문에 **no party** 어떤 정당도 **is likely to emerge** 가능성이 없기 **from next month's vote** 다음 달에 있을 투표에서 **with a majority,** 다수당이 될 **it may be hard** 어려울지 모른다 **to form a strong government** 강한 정부를 형성하기 위해 **that can implement the country's new bailout deal.** 이 나라의 새로운 금융 긴급 구제 자금 협상을 실행시키는 것이 **There's even a risk** 위험도 있다 **that there will be yet more elections.** 또 다시 선거를 치러야 할 **That could tip Greece back into crisis.** 그리스를 다시 위기로 기울게 할 수도 있다.

Double-duty CEOs are a worrisome trend

Fiat boss Sergio Marchionne may don another hat to run Ferrari. Like Jack Dorsey and Elon Musk, however, he's only human. Investors in public companies, especially young or challenged ones, require full attention from a leader. That's all but impossible when he's running two.

Headline

Double-duty CEOs are a worrisome trend

최근 겸직 CEO 문제가 염려스러운 현상으로 떠오르고 있다.

일반 표현

Investors tend to worry that a CEO does two jobs.

Matrix Core

헤드라인 영어문장은 몇 개의 단어나 기본구조로 나타낸다. ¶

Decoded Core

double-duty ⇒ to do two jobs at one time
한 번에 두 가지 역할을 하는, 겸직 ¶

worrisome ⇒ 걱정되는, 곤란한 ⁑ causing concern, worrying ¶

worrisome trend ⇒ 염려스러운 추세 ¶

[31]

Word&Phrase

don 입다, 쓰다, 신다 = put on, take on

Lead Sentence

Fiat boss Sergio Marchionne may don another hat to run Ferrari. Like Jack Dorsey and Elon Musk, however, he's only human. Investors in public companies, especially young or challenged ones, require full attention from a leader. That's all but impossible when he's running two.

피아트 사의 사장인 세르지오 마르치오네는 페라리를 운영하는 또 하나의 모자를 쓸지도 모른다. 하지만 그도 잭 도시와 엘론 머스크와 마찬가지로 인간일 뿐이다. 상장사, 특히 신생기업이나 도전적인 기업에 투자한 투자자들의 경우 회사의 리더에게 온전한 집중력을 요구한다. 두 개의 직책을 동시에 겸할 때는 회사에 완전한 관심을 기울이는 것이 거의 불가능하다.

Bilingual Reading

Fiat boss Sergio Marchionne 피아트 사의 사장 세르지오 마르치오네는 **may don another hat** 또 하나의 모자(position)를 쓸지 모른다 **to run Ferrari.** 페라리를 운영하는 **Like Jack Dorsey and Elon Musk,** 그도 잭 도시나 엘론 머스크와 마찬가지로 **however,** 하지만 **he's only human.** 인간일 뿐이다 **Investors in public companies,** 상장회사에 투자하는 투자자들은 **especially young or challenged ones,** 특히 신생기업이거나 도전적인 기업일 때 **require full attention from a leader.** 리더로부터 온전한 집중력을 요구한다 **That's** 그것은 **all but impossible** 거의 불가능한 것이다 **when he's running two.** 그가 두 개의 회사를 운영할 때

Fake Goldman Sachs belies a real China strength

The U.S. investment bank joins a long list of counterfeits that includes Apple stores, police stations and British villages. They're easy to mock, but also veil a broader readiness to bend rules in search of profit. Properly channelled, that ingenuity and pluck could be powerful.

Headline

Fake Goldman Sachs belies a real China strength

중국의 가짜 골드만삭스 회사와 실제 중국의 힘과는 다르다.

일반 표현

Fake Goldman Sachs is in contradiction with a real China strength.

Matrix Core

헤드라인 영어문장은 기본구조로 나타낸다. ¶

Decoded Core

belie ⇒ 일치하지 않는다, ~과 모순되다 ‡ to give a false representation, to misrepresent ¶

fake Goldman Sachs ⇒ 중국에 위치한 골드만삭스 금융대출회사 ‡ 중국의 Goldman Sachs financial leasing company. 이 회사는 마치 미국 'Goldman Sachs'와 관계가 있는 듯이 영업을 해왔으나 실제로는 관계가 없는 것으로 밝혀졌고, 이 사건을 가리켜 'Goldman Sachs counterfeit 위조사건'이라 한다. ¶

Goldman Sachs ⇒ 골드만삭스. 국제금융시장에서 기관투자가들에게 금융서비스를 제공하는 미국계 다국적 투자은행 ¶

[32]

Word&Phrase

counterfeit 가짜의, ~을 위조하다
mock 모의의, 가짜의, 조롱하다, 모방하다, 흉내 내다, 속이다
bend 굴절, 휘다, 왜곡하다

ingenuity 교묘한 고안, 창의력, 정교함
pluck 뽑다, 용기, 빼앗다, 따다, 꺾다, 골라내다

Lead Sentence

The U.S. investment bank joins a long list of counterfeits that includes Apple stores, police stations and British villages. They're easy to mock, but also veil a broader readiness to bend rules in search of profit. Properly channelled, that ingenuity and pluck could be powerful.

미국 투자은행 골드만삭스도 애플스토어, 경찰서 그리고 영국 마을까지 포함되어 있는 가짜 리스트에 그 이름을 올리게 되었다. 이런 이름들은 모방하기가 쉽지만 이익을 추구하는 데 룰을 더욱 폭넓게 왜곡할 준비가 되어 있음을 보여준다. 적절히 이용하면 그러한 재주와 대담함은 큰 힘이 될 수도 있다.

Bilingual Reading

The U.S. investment bank 미국 투자은행 골드만삭스도 **joins a long list of counterfeits** 가짜 리스트에 이름을 올리게 되었다 **that includes** 포함되는 **Apple stores, police stations** 애플스토어, 경찰서 **and British villages.** 그리고 영국 마을까지 **They're easy to mock,** 이런 이름들은 모방하기 쉽지만 **but also veil** 보여준다 **a broader readiness to bend rules** 룰을 더욱 폭넓게 왜곡할 준비가 되어있음을 **in search of profit.** 이익을 추구하는 데 **Properly channelled,** 적절히 이용하면 **that ingenuity and pluck** 그러한 재주와 대담함은 **could be powerful.** 큰 힘이 될 수도 있다.

83

Luxury faces tough quest for next big market

China's slowdown and weaker currency have hit share prices of bauble-peddlers LVMH and Swatch. The hunt is on for luxury's next hotspot. India and Brazil show promise, but a mix of scale, rising incomes and inequality is elusive. Better opportunities may be closer to home.

Headline

Luxury faces tough quest for next big market

사치품 분야는 다음 거대시장을 찾는 데 어려움을 겪고 있다.

일반 표현

Luxury goes about hunting next big market.

Matrix Core

헤드라인 영어문장은 대체로 be 동사를 생략한다. ¶

Decoded Core

face ⇒ (is) facing 부딪치다, 직면하다, 다가오다
go about, approach의 의미 ¶

Luxury faces tough quest ⇒ 사치품도 어려움에 직면하다 ¶

Word&Phrase

slowdown 감속, 감산
bauble 겉만 번지르르한 싸구려 물건, 시시한 것, 속 보이는 것
peddler 판매원, 행상인
hotspot 분쟁지대, 곤란한 상황, 위험한 장소
inequality 불평등, 불균형
elusive 알기 어려운, 피하는, 눈에 띄지 않는, 교묘하게 피하는

Lead Sentence

China's slowdown and weaker currency have hit share prices of bauble-peddlers LVMH and Swatch. The hunt is on for luxury's next hotspot. India and Brazil show promise, but a mix of scale, rising incomes and inequality is elusive. Better opportunities may be closer to home.

중국의 경기 침체와 위안화 약세는 염가의 상품을 취급해온 LVMH와 SWATCH의 주가를 급락하게 만들었다. 이 사냥은 사치품의 다음 지역을 향해서 이동하고 있다. 인도와 브라질 시장은 희망적이지만 규모가 커져가는 소득 불균형이 시장 파악을 어렵게 만들고 있다. 더 나은 기회는 국내에 있을지 모른다.

Bilingual Reading

China's slowdown 중국의 경기 침체와 **and weaker currency** 위안화 약세는 **have hit share prices** 주가를 급락하게 만들었다 **of bauble-peddlers LVMH and Swatch.** LVMH와 SWATCH의 염가의 상품을 취급해온 **The hunt** 이 사냥은 **is on** 이동하고 있다 **for luxury's next hotspot.** 사치품의 다음 지역을 향해서 **India and Brazil** 인도와 브라질 시장은 **show promise,** 희망적이지만 **but a mix of scale,** 소득 불균형이 **rising incomes and inequality** 규모가 커져가는 **is elusive.** 시장 파악을 어렵게 만들고 있다 **Better opportunities may be closer to home.** 더 나은 기회는 국내에 있을지 모른다

Stock rout to blow hole in China's deal pipeline

The selloff has brought an abrupt end to a record-breaking run for share sales in the People's Republic. This will hurt local brokers, which dominate onshore listings, more than foreign banks. A sharp slowdown in Chinese M&A, up 70 pct so far this year, also looks inevitable.

Headline

Stock rout to blow hole in China's deal pipeline

주식시장의 혼란은 주가 정보 서비스에 큰 구멍을 내게 될 것이다.

일반 표현

Stock debacle will blow hole in China's transaction information.

Matrix Core

헤드라인 영어문장은 미래를 to로 나타낸다. ¶

Decoded Core

rout to blow ⇒ rout will blow ¶

stock rout ⇒ 주식 혼란, 최근의 중국 주가 폭락을 의미 ¶

blow hole ⇒ 구멍을 내다, 타격을 주다 ¶

China deal pipeline ⇒ 석유 주식 거래정보 ⁑ transaction information ¶

China deal pipeline ⇒ 중국 석유 거래(송유관) ¶

86

Word&Phrase

debacle 붕괴, 와해
selloff 대량 매각, 하락하다, 팔아치우다, 방출하다
abrupt 갑작스러운, 돌연한, 일관성 없는
onshore 연안의
inevitable 피할 수 없는, 당연한

Lead Sentence

The selloff has brought an abrupt end to a record-breaking run for share sales in the People's Republic. This will hurt local brokers, which dominate onshore listings, more than foreign banks. A sharp slowdown in Chinese M&A, up 70 pct so far this year, also looks inevitable.

주식 방매는 중국 주식 판매 기록에 갑작스런 종식을 가져왔다. 이것은 외국 은행들보다 중국 본토의 증시를 지배하고 있는 국내 주식 중개인들에게 더 큰 충격을 줄 것이다. 중국 M&A 시장의 급격한 침체는 올해 지금까지 70%에 달하고 있으며 피할 수 없는 일이다.

Bilingual Reading

The selloff 주식 방매는 **has brought an abrupt end** 갑작스런 종식을 가져왔다 **to a record-breaking run for share sales in the People's Republic.** 중국 주식 판매 기록에 **This** 이것은 **will hurt local brokers,** 국내 주식 중개인들에게 더 큰 충격을 줄 것이다 **which dominate onshore listings,** 중국 본토의 증시를 지배하고 있는 **more than foreign banks.** 외국 은행들보다 **A sharp slowdown in Chinese M&A,** 중국 M&A 시장의 급격한 침체는 **up 70 pct 70%에 달하고 so far this year,** 올해 지금까지 **also looks inevitable.** 역시 피할 수 없는 일이다

Investors struggle to find true safe havens

Boltholes like U.S. and German bonds or the Swiss franc are benefiting less than might be expected amid equity swings and concern over a slowing China. Investors are rightly wary of once-safe assets that have moved erratically of late. The mystery is where they are going instead.

Headline

Investors struggle to find true safe havens

투자가들은 투자의 안전한 피난처를 찾으려고 몹시 노력하고 있다.

일반 표현

Investors are trying hard to find true safe havens.

Matrix Core

헤드라인 영어문장은 진행되고 있는 상황을 현재로 나타낸다. ¶

Decoded Core

struggle ⇒ 긴장(restraint)이나 속박(constriction)에서 벗어나기 위해 애쓰다 ¶

safe haven ⇒ 피난처, 안전한 장소 ¶

[35]

Word&Phrase

bolthole 숨을 수 있는 장소, 안전한 은신처 : a place where a person can escape and hide
benefit 유익하다
equity 주식, 재산
swing 정세, 사정, 흔들기, 변동
erratically 불안하게

Lead Sentence

Boltholes like U.S. and German bonds or the Swiss franc are benefiting less than might be expected amid equity swings and concern over a slowing China. Investors are rightly wary of once-safe assets that have moved erratically of late. The mystery is where they are going instead.

미국, 독일 채권 또는 스위스 프랑과 같은 투자의 은신처도 주가 변동 또는 중국의 경기 둔화 여파로 기대했던 것보다 별로 이익을 내지 못하고 있다. 당연히 투자자들은 한때 안전하게 생각했으나 최근 불안할 정도로 변화가 심한 이 자산에 대해 경계하고 있다. 그 외에 시장의 흐름을 도저히 설명할 수 없다는 것이다.

Bilingual Reading

Boltholes 투자의 은신처도 **like U.S. and German bonds or the Swiss franc** 미국과 독일 채권 또는 스위스 프랑과 같은 **are benefiting less** 별로 이익이 되지 못하고 있다 **than might be expected** 기대할 수 있었던 것보다 **amid equity swings and concern over a slowing China.** 주식가격 변동 또는 중국의 경기 둔화 가운데 **Investors** 투자가들은 **are rightly wary** 당연히 이 자산에 대해 경계를 하고 있다 **of once-safe assets** 한때 안전하게 생각했던 **that have moved erratically of late.** 최근 불안하게 변화가 심한 **The mystery is where they are going instead.** 그 외에 시장의 흐름을 도저히 설명할 수 없다는 것이다

Impossible trinity gives China a difficult choice

Not even the People's Republic can go on cutting interest rates, keep the yuan stable, and allow capital to flow freely. It must choose two out of three. Huge foreign exchange reserves give Beijing some room to muddle through, but not enough to reverse self-fulfilling outflows.

Headline

Impossible trinity gives China a difficult choice

공존이 불가능한 경제의 3요소가 중국에게 어려운 선택을 강요하고 있다.

일반 표현

The trinity is impossible, which gives China a difficult choice.

Matrix Core

헤드라인 영어문장은 기본구조로 나타낸다. ¶

Decoded Core

trinity ⇒ 3개가 한 세트인 요소, 3인조, 삼위일체 ※ 기독교 성 삼위일체 doctrine은 Father: 하나님, the son: 예수님, the Holy Spirit: 성령의 3가지를 갖춘 단 한 분의 하나님. 중국 경제의 삼위일체는 금리, 위안화, 자본 ¶

Not even the People's Republic can go on cutting interest rate ⇒ not이 문장 앞에 전치되어 부정 문장을 강조한다. (Even the People's Republic cannot go on cutting interest rate.) ¶

[36]

Word&Phrase

foreign exchange reserves 외환 보유고
room 여지 : part, space
muddle 혼란, 갈팡질팡 : to cause confusion, to mix up
reverse 뒤집다, 바꾸다, 되돌리다

self-fulfilling 자기 달성의, 자기 충족, 스스로의 힘으로 목적 달성
outflow 유출

Lead Sentence

Not even the People's Republic can go on cutting interest rates, keep the yuan stable, and allow capital to flow freely. It must choose two out of three. Huge foreign exchange reserves give Beijing some room to muddle through, but not enough to reverse self-fulfilling outflows.

중국조차 금리 저하와 위안화 안정, 자본의 자유로운 흐름을 동시에 유지할 수는 없다. 중국은 3가지 중 2가지를 선택해야 한다. 엄청난 외화보유고가 이 어려움에서 빠져나갈 여유를 주지만, 자연적인 현상으로 빠져나가는 유출을 돌려놓기에는 충분치 못하다.

Bilingual Reading

Not even the People's Republic 중국조차 **can go on** 유지할 수 없다 **cutting interest rates,** 금리를 저하하다 **keep the yuan stable,** 위안화를 안정시키다 **and allow capital to flow freely.** 자본의 자유로운 흐름을 허용하다 **It must choose** 중국은 선택해야 한다 **two out of three.** 셋 중 둘을 **Huge foreign exchange reserves** 엄청난 외화보유고가 **give Beijing some room** 여유를 주지만 **to muddle through,** 이 어려움에서 빠져나갈 수 있는 **but not enough** 충분치 못하다 **to reverse self-fulfilling outflows.** 자연적인 현상으로 빠져나가는 유출을 돌려놓기에는

Tech's real China syndrome victims are yet to fall

Facebook, Apple, Amazon and Microsoft lost nearly $200 bln of value in a week. China's woes sparked the rout, but the problem was investors' giddy faith in growth. Public tech stocks may recover. Fantasy valuations of private firms like Uber, though, will take the bigger hit.

Headline

Tech's real China syndrome victims are yet to fall

기술주의 중국 신드롬은 여전히 줄지 않았다.

일반 표현

Tech's real China syndrome victims have not fallen yet.

Matrix Core

헤드라인 영어문장은 기본구조로 나타낸다. ¶

Decoded Core

yet ⇒ 동사구 안에서 부정의 의미 ¶

are yet to fall ⇒ 떨어지지 않았다 ¶

be yet to ⇒ 상황을 부정으로 설명하기 위한 강조 표현 ¶

He has yet to call ⇒ So far he hasn't called
지금까지 그는 전화를 걸지 않았다 ¶

Tech's real China syndrome ⇒ 기술주의 중국 신드롬 ¶

victims ⇒ Facebook, Apple, Amazon을 의미 ¶

[37]

Word&Phrase

woe 슬픔, 비탄
rout 혼란, 무질서한 군중, 고함
giddy 어지러운, 현기증 나는
Uber 우버, 샌프란시스코에 본부를 둔 미국 국제 운송 네트워크 회사

Lead Sentence

Facebook, Apple, Amazon and Microsoft lost nearly $200 bln of value in a week. China's woes sparked the rout, but the problem was investors' giddy faith in growth. Public tech stocks may recover. Fantasy valuations of private firms like Uber, though, will take the bigger hit.

페이스북, 애플, 아마존 그리고 마이크로소프트는 한 주 동안 2천 억 달러의 손실을 입었다. 중국발 재난이 이런 혼란을 발생시켰다. 그러나 문제점은 투자가들의 중국 성장에 대한 경솔한 믿음 때문이었다. 일반 기술주는 회복될지 모른다. 하지만 우버와 같은 개인회사의 환상적인 가치는 더 큰 손실을 입을 수 있다.

Bilingual Reading

Facebook, Apple, Amazon 페이스북, 애플, 아마존 **and Microsoft** 그리고 마이크로소프트는 **lost nearly $200 bln of value in a week.** 한 주 동안 2천 억 달러의 손실을 입었다 **China's woes sparked the rout,** 중국발 재난이 이런 혼란을 발생시켰다 **but the problem** 그러나 문제점은 **was investors' giddy faith in growth.** 투자가들의 중국 성장에 대한 경솔한 믿음 때문이었다 **Public tech stocks** 일반 기술주는 **may recover.** 회복될지 모른다 **Fantasy valuations of private firms** 개인회사의 환상적인 가치는 **like Uber, though,** 하지만 우버와 같은 **will take the bigger hit.** 더 큰 손실을 입을 수 있다.

China's ailing stocks are now contagious

Mainland shares are tumbling again. Unlike in July, this sell-off is hurting currencies, commodities, and other Asian bourses. Two things have changed. There's now the threat of devaluation. And bungled interventions cast doubt on China's ability to manage markets.

Headline

China's ailing stocks are now contagious

중국의 주식 하락 여파가 주변국가로 번지고 있다.

일반 표현

Ailing Chinese stocks impact global market.

Matrix Core

헤드라인 영어문장은 기본구조로 나타낸다. ¶

Decoded Core

contagious ⇒ 감정, 느낌, 태도 등이 다른 사람에게 퍼지고 영향을 줄 가능성이 있는, 전염성의 ‡ spread ¶

China's ailing stocks ⇒ 중국의 병든 주식, 허약한 주식 ¶

ailing ⇒ 병약한, 앓고 있는 ‡ ail 병들다, 괴롭히다 ¶

[38]

Word&Phrase

tumble 굴러 떨어지다, 무너지다, 하락
sell-off 대량 매각, 팔아 치우다, 방출하다
bourse 증권 거래소, 금융시장
devaluation 평가절하, 가치하락
bungle 실수, 서투른 솜씨, 실패
intervention 개입, 중재, 간섭

Lead Sentence

Mainland shares are tumbling again. Unlike in July, this sell-off is hurting currencies, commodities, and other Asian bourses. Two things have changed. There's now the threat of devaluation. And bungled interventions cast doubt on China's ability to manage markets.

중국 주식들이 다시 폭락하고 있다. 7월과 달리 이번 폭락은 환율, 원자재 시장 상품 그리고 아시아 증시에도 상처를 입히고 있다. 두 가지가 변했다. 위안화 평가절하의 위험도 있다. 서투른 역할 개입이 시장을 관리할 수 있는 중국 정부의 능력에 의심을 던지고 있다.

Bilingual Reading

Mainland shares 중국 주식들은 **are tumbling again.** 다시 폭락하고 있다 **Unlike in July,** 7월과 달리 **this sell-off** 이번 폭락은 **is hurting** 상처를 입히고 있다 **currencies, commodities,** 환율, 원자재, 상품 **and other Asian bourses.** 그리고 아시아 증시에도 **Two things have changed.** 두 가지가 변했다 **There's now the threat of devaluation.** 위안화 평가절하의 위험도 있다 **And bungled interventions** 서투른 역할 개입이 **cast doubt** 의심을 던지고 있다 **on China's ability to manage markets.** 시장을 관리할 수 있는 중국 정부의 능력에

Part.1 INTERNATIONAL

Effluent packs economic and environmental punch

Fracker Pioneer National is about to start using treated sewage in its wells. United Airlines may use animal waste as fuel. Recycling feces is now efficient enough to produce both energy and drinking water. This new spin on natural gas offers benefits for the land and air, too.

Headline

Effluent packs economic and environmental punch

하수도 오물을 처리해서 경제적, 환경적 효과를 얻을 수 있다

일반 표현

Effluent may treat economic and environmental flaw.

Matrix Core

헤드라인 영어문장은 기본구조로 나타낸다. ¶

Decoded Core

pack ⇒ 채우다 ⁑ to treat, to fill completely ¶
effluent ⇒ 폐수, sewage, 오물의 의미, 명사로 사용 ¶
punch ⇒ 구멍, 큰 효과, 찌르기, 영향 ¶

[39]

Word&Phrase

flaw 결점, 흠, 결함
sewage 하수, 오수
feces 배설물, 찌꺼기
spin 회전, 의견, (실을) 잣다, 내다, 빙빙 돌다

Lead Sentence

Fracker Pioneer National is about to start using treated sewage in its wells. United Airlines may use animal waste as fuel. Recycling feces is now efficient enough to produce both energy and drinking water. This new spin on natural gas offers benefits for the land and air, too.

프래커 파이오니어 내셔널은 그 회사의 정화조에서 처리된 오물 사용을 시작하려고 한다. 유나이티드 항공사(UA)는 동물의 오물을 연료로 이용하려 한다. 재생 배설물은 에너지와 음료수를 생산하기에 충분히 적당하다. 천연가스에 대한 새로운 견해는 육지와 공기에도 혜택을 준다.

Bilingual Reading

Fracker Pioneer National 프래커 파이오니어 내셔널은 **is about to start** 시작하려고 한다 **using treated sewage in its wells.** 그 회사의 정화조에서 처리된 오물 사용을 **United Airlines** 유나이티드 항공사(UA)는 **may use animal waste** 동물의 오물을 연료로 이용하려 한다 **as fuel Recycling feces** 왜냐하면 재생 배설물 연료는 **is now efficient enough** 충분히 적당하기 때문이다 **to produce both energy and drinking water.** 에너지와 음료수를 생산하기에 **This new spin on natural gas** 천연가스에 대한 새로운 견해가 **offers benefits for the land and air, too.** 육지와 공기에도 혜택을 준다

Rob Cox: Tianjin deserves to be a Cuyahoga moment

The chemical blasts that rocked China's No. 6 city have exposed a lethal coziness between industry, government and party-and an endemic failure to put human life over economic development. Like the time an Ohio river caught fire in 1969, this feels like a wake-up call.

Headline

Rob Cox: Tianjin deserves to be a Cuyahoga moment

텐진 화학약품 폭발 사건은 미국 오하이오 주 쿠야호가 화재 사건을 연상시켰다.

일반 표현

Tianjin blast recalls Cuyahoga fire.

Matrix Core

헤드라인 영어문장은 기본구조로 나타낸다.

Decoded Core

deserve to be ⇒ 당연히 ~라 할 수 있다 ¶

Tianjin's chemical blast ⇒ 중국 텐진 시의 화학물 폭발 사건 ¶

Cuyahoga moment ⇒ 미국 오하이오 주에 있는 쿠야호가 카운티의 화재순간 ⁞ Cuyahoga Valley National Park ¶

Cuyahoga ⇒ 오하이오 주 쿠야호가밸리 국립공원 ¶

Rob Cox ⇒ 로브 콕스. 온라인 뉴스 《Breakingviews》 설립을 도운 칼럼리스트 ¶

Word&Phrase

blast 폭발하다, 공격하다
lethal 치명적인, 치사성의
coziness 편안함, 안락함
endemic 풍토병, 지방병, 특유한
wake-up call 환기하는 경고, 현실 경고, 경각심을 불러일으키다

Lead Sentence

The chemical blasts that rocked China's No. 6 city have exposed a lethal coziness between industry, government and party–and an endemic failure to put human life over economic development. Like the time an Ohio river caught fire in 1969, this feels like a wake-up call.

중국의 여섯 번째 도시를 강타했던 화학약품 폭발 사건은 중국 산업체, 정부 그리고 당 간에 모든 일에 대해 지나칠 정도로 신경을 쓰지 않고 있다는 사실을 폭로시켰다. 즉 인명보다 경제개발을 우선한다는 고질정인 병폐다. 1969년 미국 오하이오 강에 화재가 났을 때와 같이 이것은 일종의 경고음과 같다는 느낌이 든다.

Bilingual Reading

The chemical blasts 화학약품 폭발 사건은 **that rocked China's No. 6 city** 중국의 여섯 번째 도시를 뒤흔든 **have exposed a lethal coziness** 지나칠 정도로 신경 쓰지 않고 있다는 사실을 폭로시켰다 **between industry, government and party** 중국 산업체, 정부 그리고 당 간에 **–and an endemic failure** 고질정인 병폐다 **to put human life** 즉 사람의 생명보다 **over economic development.** 경제개발을 우선한다 **Like the time** 그때와 같이 **an Ohio river** 미국 오하이오 강에 **caught fire in 1969,** 1969년 화재가 났던 **this feels like a wake-up call.** 이것은 일종의 경고음 같은 느낌이 든다.

Glencore tripped up by faith in rational markets

The commodity trader's earnings have disappointed as copper and coal have tumbled. Anticipating the market is getting harder because both rivals' behaviour and Chinese demand for raw materials are even more unpredictable. Glencore is thus focusing on what it can control: cash.

Headline

Glencore tripped up by faith in rational markets

글렌코어는 합리적인 시장을 믿다가 실패했다.

일반 표현

Glencore was tripped up by faith in rational market.

Matrix Core

헤드라인 영어문장은 대체로 **be 동사를** 생략한다. ¶

Decoded Core

tripped up ⇒ (was) tripped up 넘어지다 ¶

trip ⇒ 걸려 넘어지다, 여행, 방문하다 ¶

faith ⇒ 믿음, 신념 ¶

rational market ⇒ 합리적인 시장 ¶

Glencore ⇒ 글렌코어. 스위스에 본사를 둔 세계 최대 석탄 채광 회사 ¶

[41]

Word&Phrase

tumble 하락, 무너지다, 굴러 떨어지다

Lead Sentence

The commodity trader's earnings have disappointed as copper and coal have tumbled. Anticipating the market is getting harder because both rivals' behaviour and Chinese demand for raw materials are even more unpredictable. Glencore is thus focusing on what it can control: cash.

구리와 석탄 채굴업자의 수입은 동과 석탄 가격이 폭락했을 때 실망스러웠다. 시장의 회복을 기대하기는 점점 더 어려워지고 있다. 이유는 경쟁사들의 태도와 중국의 원자재에 대한 수요가 예측 불가능하기 때문이다. 이런 이유로 글렌코어는 직접 관리할 수 있는 일만 신경 쓰고 있다. 바로 현금이다.

Bilingual Reading

The commodity trader's earnings 구리와 석탄 업자의 수입은 **have disappointed** 실망스러웠다 **as copper and coal have tumbled.** 동과 석탄 가격이 폭락했을 때 **Anticipating the market** 시장 회복을 기대하기는 **is getting harder** 점점 더 어려워지고 있다 **because** 이유는 **both rivals' behaviour** 경쟁사들의 태도와 **and Chinese demand for raw materials** 중국의 원자재에 대한 수요가 **are even more unpredictable.** 예측 불가능하기 때문이다 **Glencore** 글렌코어는 **is thus** 이런 이유로 **focusing on** 신경 쓰고 있다 **what it can control:** 직접 관리할 수 있는 일만 **cash.** 바로 현금이다

New bank M&A powerhouse leaves rivals for dead

Regional U.S. lender BB&T's $1.8 bln swoop for National Penn is its fourth deal in a year. The acquisition makes financial sense and is more proof the Fed supports industry tie-ups. The longer other banks stay on the sidelines, the more it'll look like they fear rejection.

Headline

New bank M&A powerhouse leaves rivals for dead

새로운 은행 합병인수
강자가 경쟁사들을 흡수하다.

일반 표현

New bank M&A powerhouse takes rivals.

Matrix Core

헤드라인 영어문장은 기본구조로 나타낸다. ¶

Decoded Core

leave ⇒ 어떤 상태가 되게 만들다 ⁑ cause, allow to remain ¶

powerhouse ⇒ 강자 ⁑ 유력 집단, 강력한 힘을 가지고 있는 조직이나 사람을 의미 ¶

for dead ⇒ 쓸모 없게, 힘을 못 쓰게 ¶

leave rivals for dead ⇒ 경쟁사들을 힘을 못 쓰게 만들다 ¶

[42]

Word&Phrase

lender 돈을 빌려주는 사람이나 회사
swoop 인수, 급강하하다, 갑자기 덮치다, 급습
National Penn 내셔널 펜 은행, 미국 필라델피아에 있는 투자은행
tie-up 제휴, 협력
sideline 측선, 방관

Lead Sentence

Regional U.S. lender BB&T's $1.8 bln swoop for National Penn is its fourth deal in a year. The acquisition makes financial sense and is more proof the Fed supports industry tie-ups. The longer other banks stay on the sidelines, the more it'll look like they fear rejection.

미국 대출회사 BB&T가 내셔널 펜을 18억 달러를 주고 흡수하면서 1년 사이 네 번째 인수를 마쳤다. 이 인수는 금융적인 면에서 현명한 일이고, 또 미국의 연방준비위원회가 산업체 상호 연합을 지지하고 있다는 더 많은 증거다. 다른 은행들이 버티면 버틸수록 독자적으로 영업하기가 점점 더 어려워질 것으로 보인다.

Bilingual Reading

Regional U.S. lender BB&T's 미국 BB&T의 **$1.8 bln swoop for National Penn** 내셔널 펜 18억 달러 인수는 **is its fourth deal in a year.** 이것이 한 해에 네 번째 거래다 **The acquisition** 이 인수는 **makes financial sense** 금융적인 면에서 현명한 일이고 **and is more proof** 더 많은 증거다 **the Fed** 또 미국의 연방준비위원회가 **supports industry tie-ups.** 산업체 상호 연합을 지지하는 **The longer other banks stay** 다른 은행들이 버틸수록 **on the sidelines,** 독자적으로 **the more** 점점 **it'll look like they fear rejection.** 독자적으로 영업하기가 더 어려워질 것으로 보인다

The cost of China's devaluation: Edward Chancellor

Forget about currency wars and global deflation. The true impact of the yuan's sudden decline will be felt by China's dysfunctional credit system, where domestic borrowers and foreign lenders believed the currency could only appreciate.

Headline

The cost of China's devaluation: Edward Chancellor

중국 당국의 위안화 평가절하 선택에 충격을 받았다.

일반 표현

We experienced a sudden impact when Chinese authorities chose to devalue its currency.

Matrix Core

헤드라인 영어문장은 몇 개의 단어로 나타낸다. ¶

Decoded Core

China's devaluation ⇒ 중국 위안화의 갑작스런 평가절하 ¶

cost ⇒ 대가. 여기에서 사용된 cost는 갑작스런 충격을 의미 ¶

Edward Chancellor ⇒ 온라인 뉴스 ‹Breakingviews› 기자 ¶

[43]

Word&Phrase

dysfunctional 기능을 제대로 하지 못하는, 비정상적인
appreciate 평가하다, 절상하다

Lead Sentence

Forget about currency wars and global deflation. The true impact of the yuan's sudden decline will be felt by China's dysfunctional credit system, where domestic borrowers and foreign lenders believed the currency could only appreciate.

화폐전쟁과 글로벌 인플레이션에 대해서는 잊어버리자. 위안화의 갑작스런 평가절하는 기능을 제대로 하지 못하는 중국의 비정상적인 크레디트 시스템의 전반을 느끼게 만들 것이다. 국내 채무자들과 외국 채권자들은 지금까지 화폐가 시장의 원칙에 의해서만이 평가될 수 있다고 믿어왔다.

Bilingual Reading

Forget 잊어버리자 **about currency wars** 화폐전쟁과 **and global deflation.** 글로벌 인플레이션에 대해서는 **The true impact of the yuan's sudden decline** 위안화의 갑작스런 평가절하는 **will be felt** 느끼게 될 것이다 **by China's dysfunctional credit system,** 중국의 비정상적인 크레디트 시스템을 **where domestic borrowers** 국내 채무자들과 **and foreign lenders** 외국 채권자들이 **believed the currency** 화폐가 **could only appreciate.** 시장의 원칙에 의해서만이 평가될 수 있다고 믿어왔던

China's currency could fall another 5 percent

The central bank says it's not out to weaken the yuan. But to recoup China's competitiveness without slipping into deflation, a slide to at least 6.75 to the dollar would be welcome. That could help the mainland, but would give the rest of the world a new headache.

Headline

China's currency could fall another 5 percent

중국 위안화는 추가로 5% 더 떨어질 가능성이 있다.

일반 표현

China's currency is likely to depreciate another 5 percent.

Matrix Core

헤드라인 영어문장은 기본구조로 나타낸다.

Decoded Core

could ⇒ 앞으로 있을 수 있는 가능성을 의미

another 5 percent ⇒ 또다시 5%

could fall another 5% ⇒ 또다시 5% 평가절하될 수 있다

[44]

Word&Phrase

recoup 다시 강화하다, 메우다, 회복
competitiveness 경쟁력, 장점
slide to at least 6.75 to the dollar 달러당 최소 6.75% 평가절하
without slipping into deflation 디플레이션으로 빠지지 않고
mainland 본토, 대륙, 여기서 중국의 의미

Lead Sentence

The central bank says it's not out to weaken the yuan. But to recoup China's competitiveness without slipping into deflation, a slide to at least 6.75 to the dollar would be welcome. That could help the mainland, but would give the rest of the world a new headache.

중국 중앙은행은 이것이 중국 위안화를 약화시키기 위한 것이 아니라고 말한다. 그러나 디플레이션으로 떨어뜨리지 않고 경쟁력을 끌어올리기 위해서는 달러당 최소 6.75% 정도 절하시키는 것이 나을 것이다. 그러한 조치는 중국에게 도움을 줄 수 있으나 세계 나머지 국가들에겐 새로운 두통거리를 줄 것이다.

Bilingual Reading

The central bank says 중국 중앙은행은 말한다 **it's not out to weaken the yuan.** 이것은 위안화를 약화시키기 위한 것이 아니라고 **But** 그러나 **to recoup China's competitiveness** 경쟁력을 끌어올리기 위해서는 **without slipping into deflation,** 디플레이션으로 떨어뜨리지 않고 **a slide to at least 6.75 to the dollar would be welcome.** 달러당 최소 6.75% 정도 절하시키는 일일 것이다 **That could help the mainland,** 그러한 조치는 중국에게 도움을 줄 수 있으나 **but would give** 줄 것이다 **the rest of the world** 세계 나머지 국가들에겐 **a new headache.** 새로운 두통거리를

Greece deal leaves euro intact but fragile

Athens may get its bailout after Prime Minister Alexis Tsipras gave in to reform demands. Quitting the euro is much less likely. It suggests currency union can bear the near-exit of a peripheral state. Economic rifts between core members, though, remain the big future risk.

Headline

Greece deal leaves euro intact but fragile

그리스 구조금융 협정은 유로에 큰 타격을 주지는 않지만 위험요소를 남길 것이다.

일반 표현

Greece deal has no impact on euro dollar, but causes it to be fragile.

Matrix Core

헤드라인 영어문장은 기본구조로 나타낸다. ¶

Decoded Core

leave ⇒ leave + object + adjective
목적어를 어떤 상태로 만들다 ¶

leave euro intact ⇒ 유로 달러에는 피해를 주지 않는다 ¶

fragile ⇒ 매우 엷은, 얄팍한 ⁝ easily broken, flimsy ¶

[45]

Word&Phrase

bailout 긴급 구조금융
give in to reform demand 개혁 요구에 굴복하다, 받아들이다
much less likely 훨씬 가능성이 적은
near-exit 탈퇴에 가까운

currency union 유로존 국가들, EU 회원국들 가운데 유로화를 통화로 채택하고 있는 나라
remain the big future risk 여전히 미래에 큰 위험부담으로 남다

Lead Sentence

Athens may get its bailout after Prime Minister Alexis Tsipras gave in to reform demands. Quitting the euro is much less likely. It suggests currency union can bear the near-exit of a peripheral state. Economic rifts between core members, though, remain the big future risk.

알렉시스 치프라스 총리가 EU의 개혁 요구를 받아들인 후 그리스는 구제 금융을 받게 될 것이다. EU를 탈퇴할 가능성은 훨씬 낮다. 이것은 유로존 국가들이 앞으로 주변 한 국가가 유로존을 탈퇴하더라도 견뎌낼 수 있다는 것을 말해주고 있다. 하지만 핵심 회원국들 간에 경제적 분쟁은 여전히 앞으로 큰 위험부담으로 남는다.

Bilingual Reading

Athens 그리스는 **may get its bailout** 구제금융을 받게 될 것이다 **after Prime Minister Alexis Tsipras** 총리 알렉시스 치프라스가 **gave in to reform demands.** EU의 개혁 요구를 받아들인 후 **Quitting the euro** EU 탈퇴는 **is much less likely.** 가능성이 훨씬 적다 **It suggests** 이것은 말해주고 있다 **currency union** 유로존 국가들이 **can bear** 견뎌낼 수 있다는 것을 **the near-exit** 유로존을 앞으로 탈퇴하더라도 **of a peripheral state.** 주변 한 국가가 **Economic rifts between core members,** 핵심 회원국들 간에 경제적 분쟁은 **though,** 하지만 **remain the big future risk.** 여전히 앞으로 큰 위험부담으로 남는다

Malaysian crisis could do lasting financial damage

Prime Minister Najib Razak's sacking of his deputy opens the door to a protracted power struggle. The economy can ill-afford it. Fading consumer and investor confidence and a slumping currency could mean a long period of high interest rates, anaemic growth and soured loans.

Headline

Malaysian crisis could do lasting financial damage

말레이시아의 위기는 영구적인 금융피해를 야기할 수 있다.

일반 표현

Malaysian crisis may cause lasting financial problem.

Matrix Core

헤드라인 영어문장은 기본구조로 나타낸다.

Decoded Core

do ⇒ do damage 피해를 주다
do lasting financial damage ⇒ 영구적인 금융 손실을 주다
could ⇒ have potential 가능성을 의미, 즉 할 수도 있다

Word&Phrase

sack 해임하다
open the door to something 무엇을 가능하게 만들다 : make something possible
fade 사라지다, 쇠퇴
ill-afford 용납하지 않는, 받아들일 수 없는
anaemic growth 허약한 성장, 무기력한 성장 : weak growth

Lead Sentence

Prime Minister Najib Razak's sacking of his deputy opens the door to a protracted power struggle. The economy can ill-afford it. Fading consumer and investor confidence and a slumping currency could mean a long period of high interest rates, anaemic growth and soured loans.

말레이시아 나지브 라작 총리가 그의 부총리를 해임한 것은 오랫동안 끌어온 권력 투쟁의 가능성을 보여준다. 이로 인해 국가 경제가 타격을 받을 수 있다. 소비자와 투자가들의 확신 감소와 통화 약화는 앞으로 장기간 동안의 높은 금리, 만성적인 제자리에 머문 성장 그리고 높은 담보 대출을 의미할 수도 있다.

Bilingual Reading

Prime Minister Najib Razak's 말레이시아 나지브 라작 총리의 **sacking of his deputy** 부총리 해임은 **opens the door** 가능성을 보여준다 **to a protracted power struggle.** 오랫동안 끌어온 권력 투쟁의 **The economy** 경제가 **can ill-afford it.** 타격을 받을 수 있다 **Fading consumer and investor confidence** 소비자와 투자가들의 확신 감소와 **and a slumping currency** 그리고 점점 약화되는 통화는 **could mean** 의미할 수도 있다 **a long period** 앞으로 장기간 동안의 **of high interest rates,** 높은 금리 **anaemic growth** 만성적인 제자리에 머문 성장 **and soured loans.** 높은 담보 대출을

Novartis spinoff is neat cure for big pharma ills

The $275 bln Swiss pharma group is injecting three drugs-in-development into a new entity backed by UK investors. Venture capital markets can be better at valuing and nurturing small drugs than Big Pharma shareholders. With biotech markets hot, there's room for copycat deals.

Headline

Novartis spinoff is neat cure for big pharma ills

노바티스 자회사는 대형 제약회사의 문제점을 고쳐줄 수 있는 괜찮은 치료제다.

일반 표현

Separating Novatis into spinoff is a good cure for big pharma ills.

Matrix Core

헤드라인 영어문장은 기본구조로 나타낸다. ¶

Decoded Core

spin-off ⇒ 기업 분할. 한 회사가 사내 부서를 분리시켜 업무를 수행하게 하는 모기업에서 분리된 기업 ¶

Novartis spinoff ⇒ 노바티스 분리회사 ¶

Novartis ⇒ 노바티스. 스위스 바젤에 본사를 둔 다국적 제약회사 ¶

[47]

Word&Phrase

drug-in development 개발 중인 약
new entity 새로운 회사
nurture small drug 적은 약을 개발하다
with biotech market hot 바이오텍 시장이 뜨거워지고 있으므로
copycat 모방자, 유사한 행동을 하는 사람

Lead Sentence

The $275 bln Swiss pharma group is injecting three drugs-in-development into a new entity backed by UK investors. Venture capital markets can be better at valuing and nurturing small drugs than Big Pharma shareholders. With biotech markets hot, there's room for copycat deals.

2,750억 달러의 스위스 제약회사 그룹은 개발 중인 3가지 약을 이용하여 영국 투자가들의 투자를 받아 새로운 회사를 만들고 있다. 벤처 자본 시장은 대기업 주주들보다 값을 평가하고 소규모로 약품을 개발하는 능력이 더 좋다. 바이오텍 시장이 뜨거워지기 때문에 이와 유사한 거래의 가능성이 많다.

Bilingual Reading

The $275 bln Swiss pharma group 2,750억 달러의 스위스 제약회사 그룹은 **is injecting three drugs-in-development** 개발 중인 3가지 약을 이용하여 **into a new entity** 새로운 회사를 만들고 있다 **backed by UK investors.** 영국 투자가들의 투자를 받아 **Venture capital markets** 벤처 자본 시장은 **can be better** 더 좋다 **at valuing** 가격 평가와 **and nurturing small drugs** 소규모 약품 개발이 **than Big Pharma shareholders.** 대기업 주주들보다 **With biotech markets hot,** 바이오텍 시장이 뜨거워지기 때문에 **there's room for copycat deals.** 이와 유사한 거래 가능성의 여지가 있다.

Part.1 INTERNATIONAL

113

South Korea might need stronger medicine than QE

The slowest quarterly GDP growth in six years points to a malaise deeper than a virus outbreak. A weaker currency can help with faltering exports, but it won't free households from a debt trap. A bold cocktail of tax breaks, rebates and money-printing might be more effective.

Headline

South Korea might need stronger medicine than QE

한국은 양적 완화보다 좀 더 효율적인 해결책이 필요할지 모른다.

일반 표현

South Korea might need more effective remedy than quantitative easing policy.

Matrix Core

헤드라인 영어문장은 몇 개의 단어나 기본구조로 나타낸다. ¶

Decoded Core

QE ⇒ Quantitative Easing, 양적 완화 ▮ 중앙은행이 경기 부양책으로 정부의 채권이나 다른 채권을 시중으로부터 사들이고 공급을 늘리는 통화 정책을 말한다. ¶

point to a malaise ⇒ 몸에 이상이 (불안) 있음을 의미 ¶

medicine ⇒ 치료제(약), 해결책을 의미 ¶

[48]

Word&Phrase

the slowest quarterly GDP growth
분기별 최저 GDP 성장
malaise 불안, 초조, 심리적으로 몸에
이상이 있다고 느끼는 불안
faltering export 비틀거리는 수출

free households from debt trap
가구들을 부채 덫에서 구해내다
rebate 할인, 환불
bold cocktail 과감한 혼합(정책)
tax break 세금 감면

Lead Sentence

The slowest quarterly GDP growth in six years points to a malaise deeper than a virus outbreak. A weaker currency can help with faltering exports, but it won't free households from a debt trap. A bold cocktail of tax breaks, rebates and money-printing might be more effective.

지난 6년 동안 분기별 최저 GDP 성장은 바이러스 발병이라기보다 더 깊은 경제 전반에 걸친 불안이 있음을 지적한다. 통화 가치를 약화시키는 일도 비틀거리는 수출에 도움을 줄 수 있지만, 가계 부채의 덫에서 구하지는 못할 것이다. 세금 감면, 할인 그리고 통화 공급의 과감한 혼합 정책이 더욱 효과가 될 수도 있을 것이다.

Bilingual Reading

The slowest quarterly GDP growth 분기별 최저 GDP 성장은 **in six years** 지난 6년 동안 **points** 지적한다 **to a malaise deeper** 더 깊은 경제 전반에 걸친 불안이 있음을 **than a virus outbreak.** 바이러스 발병이라기보다 **A weaker currency** 통화 가치 약화는 **can help with faltering exports,** 비틀거리는 수출에 도움을 줄 수 있지만 **but it won't free households** 가계를 구하지는 못할 것이다 **from a debt trap.** 부채의 덫에서 **A bold cocktail** 과감한 혼합 정책은 **of tax breaks, rebates** 세금 감면, 할인 **and money-printing** 그리고 통화 공급의 **might be more effective.** 더욱 효과가 될 것이다.

Iran nuclear deal is huge potential step forward

The hope is that the 100-page agreement will help keep oil cheap, spur rapid growth in the Iranian economy and lead to less fighting in the Middle East. But sanctions can be revived quickly if things don't go to plan. Mistrust remains endemic. Optimists will have to be patient.

Headline

Iran nuclear deal is huge potential step forward

이란 핵 협정은 미래로 나아가기 위한 가장 이상적인 조치다.

일반 표현

Iran nuclear deal is the most idealized step to go forward.

Matrix Core

헤드라인 영어문장은 기본구조로 나타낸다. ¶

Decoded Core

potential step ⇒ 어떤 사건을 해결하기 위한 이상적인 시스템, idealized system used to model incident ¶

potential step forward ⇒ 문제를 발전시킬 이상적인 해결책 ¶

huge potential step forward ⇒ 거대한 발전을 위한 해결책 ¶

[49]

Word&Phrase

help keep cheap oil 낮은 유가 유지에 도움을 주다
lead to less fighting in the Middle East
중동지역에 분쟁을 줄이게 되다
sanctions can be revived quickly
분쟁이 빨리 살아나다
have to be patient 인내하다
things don't go to plan 일들이 계획대로 되지 않다
endemic 풍토병, 지방병, 고질적 특성

Lead Sentence

The hope is that the 100-page agreement will help keep oil cheap, spur rapid growth in the Iranian economy and lead to less fighting in the Middle East. But sanctions can be revived quickly if things don't go to plan. Mistrust remains endemic. Optimists will have to be patient.

희망 사항은 100페이지 합의가 유가를 계속 값싸게 유지시키고, 이란 경제에 빠른 성장을 유도하며, 중동지역 내 분규를 줄일 수 있을 거라는 것이다. 그러나 이란에 대한 제재 조치는 일들이 계획대로 되지 않으면 빠르게 다시 살아날 수 있다. 불신은 여전히 이 지역에 남아있다. 이란 협정에 대한 낙관론자들은 더 지켜봐야 할 것이다.

Bilingual Reading

The hope 희망은 **is that** 이런 것이다 **the 100-page agreement** 100페이지 합의가 **will help** 도움이 될 것이다 **keep oil cheap,** 석유를 계속 값싸게 유지시키고 **spur rapid growth in the Iranian economy** 이란 경제에 빠른 성장을 유도하며 **and lead to less fighting in the Middle East.** 중동지역 내 분규를 줄이는데 **But sanctions** 그러나 이란에 대한 제재 조치는 **can be revived quickly** 즉시 다시 살아날 수 있다 **if things don't go to plan.** 일들이 계획대로 되지 않으면 **Mistrust** 불신은 **remains endemic.** 여전히 이 지역에 남아있다 **Optimists will have to be patient.** 낙관론자들은 더 지켜봐야 할 것이다.

Part.1 INTERNATIONAL

Rob Cox:
The (bank) resolution will be televised

Global regulators have made great progress preparing for the technical aspects of a collapse, and resurrection, of a major financial institution. What they need to spend more time on is ensuring they can effectively communicate the process to a world consumed by financial panic.

Headline

Rob Cox:
The (bank) resolution
will be televised

Rob Cox는 방송에서 은행의 역할을 밝힐 것이다.

일반 표현

Rob Cox will come up with the bank resolution on TV.

Matrix Core

헤드라인 영어문장은 몇 개의 단어나 기본구조로 나타낸다. ¶

Decoded Core

resolution ⇒ 분쟁이나 문제점에 대한 해결책, the action of solving a problem, dispute or contentious matter ¶

Rob Cox: ⇒ Rob Cox said that, 주요한 금융관계에 대한 해결책을 Rob Cox가 방송에 나와 밝힐 것이다. ¶

Rob cox ⇒ 온라인 뉴스 ‹Breakingviews› 설립자, 칼럼니스트 ¶

[50]

Word&Phrase

make great progress 많은 발전을 하다
prepare for technical aspect of collapse 금융기관 내에 붕괴 부분을 기술적으로 준비하다
world consumed by financial panic 금융위기의 고통으로 힘이 빠진 세계
resurrection 부활, 되살아남

Lead Sentence

Global regulators have made great progress preparing for the technical aspects of a collapse, and resurrection, of a major financial institution. What they need to spend more time on is ensuring they can effectively communicate the process to a world consumed by financial panic.

글로벌 금융 규제자들은 주요 금융기관(대형 은행)의 붕괴와 회복에 대한 기술적인 면을 사전에 준비하는 데 큰 발전을 했다. 그들이 앞으로 더 많은 시간을 기울여야 하는 점은 금융위기의 고통에 의해 힘이 빠진 세계에 효율적으로 그 과정을 설명할 수 있도록 하는 일이다.

Bilingual Reading

Global regulators 글로벌 금융 규제자들은 **have made great progress preparing** 준비하는데 큰 발전을 했다 **for the technical aspects of a collapse, and resurrection,** 붕괴와 부활에 대한 기술적 측면을 **of a major financial institution.** 주요 금융기관의 **What they need to spend more time on** 그들이 앞으로 더 많은 시간을 기울여야 하는 점은 **is ensuring** 하는 일이다 **they can effectively communicate the process** 그들이 그 과정을 효율적으로 설명할 수 있도록 **to a world consumed by financial panic.** 금융위기의 고통에 의해 힘이 빠진 세계에

Part.1 INTERNATIONAL

119

Queen Elizabeth II set to become the U.K.'s longest-serving monarch

Milestones in Queen Elizabeth II's 63-year reign typically have been marked by lavish celebrations, including horse-drawn carriage processions, throngs of cheering crowds, and street parties.

Headline

Queen Elizabeth II set to become the U.K.'s longest-serving monarch

엘리자베스 2세는 영국에서 가장 오래 재임하는 군주가 되려고 한다.

일반 표현

Queen Elizabeth II has begun to become the U.K's longest-serving monarch.

Matrix Core

헤드라인 영어문장은 대체로 be 동사를 생략한다. ¶

Decoded Core

set to ⇒ **is set to** 일을 활력적으로 시작하다
여기서는 'begin doing something'의 의미로 사용했다. ¶

set to become ⇒ 하기 시작했다 ¶

ex She set to with bleach and scouring to render the bag spotless. 그 여자는 가방에 묻은 얼룩을 없애기 위해 표백을 하고 문지르기 시작했다

[51]

Word&Phrase

typically 전형적으로, 관례에 따라
lavish celebrations 화려한 경축행사
horse-drawn carriage processions 말이 끄는 마차 행렬
throngs of cheering crowds 군중들의 갈채

Lead Sentence

Milestones in Queen Elizabeth II's 63-year reign typically have been marked by lavish celebrations, including horse-drawn carriage processions, throngs of cheering crowds, and street parties.

엘리자베스 2세의 63년의 통치를 기념하는 행사는 말이 끄는 마차행렬, 수많은 인파의 갈채 그리고 길거리 파티의 화려한 행사로 치러진다.

Bilingual Reading

Milestones 축하행사는 **in Queen Elizabeth II's 63-year reign typically** 엘리자베스 2세의 63년 통치 기간을 기리는 **have been marked** 치러진다 **by lavish celebrations,** 화려한 행사로 **including horse-drawn carriage processions,** 마차행렬을 포함해서 **throngs of cheering crowds,** 수많은 인파의 갈채 속에 **and street parties.** 그리고 길거리 파티도

Part.1 INTERNATIONAL

Uber cloaks expansion announcement in secrecy, for safety's sake

A striking taxi drives past burning tyres during a national protest against car-sharing service Uber in Nice, France in June. It's pedal to the metal for Uber Technologies Inc.'s expansion plans in Europe's capital, but ongoing and sometimes violent attacks from taxi drivers forced at least one detour Thursday.

Headline

Uber cloaks expansion announcement in secrecy, for safety's sake

우버는 안전을 위해 사업 확장 계획을 비밀리에 진행했다.

일반 표현

Uber has veiled it's business expansion in secrecy for their safety's sake.

Matrix Core

헤드라인 영어문장은 완료형을 현재로 나타낸다. ¶

Decoded Core

cloak ⇒ (has) clocked ¶

Uber cloaks expansion announcement
⇒ 우버 회사는 사업 확대 발표를 은폐했다 ¶

in secrecy ⇒ 비밀리에, 기밀로 ¶

for safety's sake ⇒ 안전을 위해 ¶

[52]

Word&Phrase

pedal to metal 속력을 내다 : to make something
to go forward 무엇을 발전하게 만들다, 늘이다, 서두르는 노력
detour 우회하다

Lead Sentence

A striking taxi drives past burning tyres during a national protest against car-sharing service Uber in Nice, France in June. It's pedal to the metal for Uber Technologies Inc.'s expansion plans in Europe's capital, but ongoing and sometimes violent attacks from taxi drivers forced at least one detour Thursday.

우버의 차량 공유 서비스에 대한 전국적인 시위가 이루어진 가운데 6월 프랑스 니스에서 시위에 참가한 택시가 불타는 타이어를 지나갔다. 이것은 유럽의 수도에서 우버의 사업 확장 계획을 말해주는 시도다. 그러나 지금도 진행 중이고 때때로 폭력적인 택시 운전사들의 공격도 목요일은 우회하지 않을 수 없었다.

Bilingual Reading

A striking taxi 시위에 참가한 택시 한 대가 **drives past burning tyres** 불타는 타이어를 지나간다 **during a national protest** 전국적인 시위가 이루어진 가운데 **against car-sharing service Uber** 우버의 차량 공유 서비스에 대한 **in Nice, France in June.** 6월 프랑스 니스에서 **It's pedal to the metal** 이것은 시도다 **for Uber Technologies Inc.'s expansion plans** 우버의 사업 확장 계획을 말해주는 **in Europe's capital,** 유럽의 수도에서 **but ongoing** 그러나 지금도 진행 중이고 **and sometimes** 때때로 **violent attacks from taxi drivers** 폭력적인 택시 운전사들의 공격도 **forced at least one detour Thursday.** 목요일은 우회하지 않을 수 없었다

Cutoff of Iran's plutonium is unsung benefit of deal

Some scientists surprised Tehran gave up fuel more potent than uranium

Headline

Cutoff of Iran's plutonium is unsung benefit of deal

이란의 플루토늄 중단이 아직은 그 협정의 유익함을 보장하지 못한다.

일반 표현

Cutoff of Iran's plutonium doesn't guarantee the benefit of deal.

Matrix Core

헤드라인 영어문장은 기본구조로 나타낸다. ¶

Decoded Core

unsung ⇒ 칭찬을 받을 수 없는, 평가될 수 없는 ⁞ not lauded or praised ¶

unsung benefit ⇒ ~에 대한 혜택이 아직 평가될 수 없는 ¶

cutoff ⇒ 중단, 차단 ⁞ an act of stopping the supply of something ¶

Word&Phrase

cutoff 중단
fuel more potent than uranium 우라늄보다 더 강력한 연료를 포기하다
potent 유력한, 강력한
Tehran 이란의 수도, 이란 정부

Lead Sentence

Some scientists surprised Tehran gave up fuel more potent than uranium

일부 과학자들은 이란이 우라늄보다 더욱 강력한 연료를 포기했다는 사실에 놀랐다.

Bilingual Reading

Some scientists 일부 과학자들은 **surprised** 놀랐다 **Tehran** 이란 정부가 **gave up** 포기한데 **fuel more potent** 더욱 강력한 연료를 **than uranium** 우라늄보다

Part. 2
BUSINESS

Part 2 **BUSINESS**

INTERNATIONAL
BUSINESS
OPINION
LIFE

Global stocks end week lower after U.S. jobs data leaves Fed move unclear

Stocks on major markets fell on Friday, closing out another tough week for equity markets, after the monthly U.S. employment report failed to provide a clear signal on the likelihood of the first Federal Reserve interest rate rise for nearly a decade later this month.

Headline

Global stocks end week lower after U.S. jobs data leaves Fed move unclear

미국의 일자리 전망이 미연준의 통화정책을 불투명하게 만든 후 세계 주간 증시는 더욱 하락하며 마감했다.

일반 표현

Global stocks fell lower weekend because Fed move became unclear after U.S. job prediction had been released.

Matrix Core

헤드라인 영어문장은 완료형을 현재로 나타낸다. ¶

Decoded Core

end week ⇒ the end of week, 한 주가 끝날 무렵 ¶

leave ⇒ has left, '어떤 것을 어떤 상태로 만들다'의 의미 ¶

leave Fed move unclear ⇒ 연준의 통화정책 방향을 불투명하게 만들다 ¶

job data ⇒ employment data, 일자리 보고 자료, 일자리 수 ¶

Fed move ⇒ 미국의 연방준비위원회 통화정책 방향, 정책 움직임 ¶

Fed ⇒ 연방준비 제도(연준) ⁑ Federal Reserve System ¶

[01]

Word&Phrase

tough week 힘든 주간, 힘겨운 한 주
equity 주식, 재산
likelihood 가능성, 기회, 희망

Lead Sentence

Stocks on major markets fell on Friday, closing out another tough week for equity markets, after the monthly U.S. employment report failed to provide a clear signal on the likelihood of the first Federal Reserve interest rate rise for nearly a decade later this month.

금요일에 시장의 주요 주식이 하락했다. 미국 월별 취업 보고가 이달 말 거의 10년 만에 처음으로 연준의 금리인상 가능성에 대한 분명한 신호를 주지 못하자 주식시장이 또 어려운 한 주를 마감했다.

Bilingual Reading

Stocks on major markets fell on Friday, 시장의 주요 주식이 금요일에 하락했다 **closing out another tough week for equity markets,** 주식시장의 또 어려운 한 주를 마감하며 **after the monthly U.S. employment report** 미국 월별 취업 보고가 **failed to provide** 분명한 신호를 주지 못한 후 **a clear signal on the likelihood** 가능성에 대한 **of the first Federal Reserve interest rate rise** 처음으로 연준의 금리인상 가능성에 **for nearly a decade later this month.** 이달 말 거의 10년 만에

Part.2 BUSINESS

129

Shares edge up as global turmoil subsides

Investors were encouraged by news that the European Central Bank is ready to increase economic stimulus if inflation in the eurozone does not pick up.

Headline

Shares edge up as global turmoil subsides

글로벌 혼란이 진정되자 주가는 천천히 올라갔다.

일반 표현

Shares have picked up when global turmoil became less intense.

Matrix Core

헤드라인 영어문장은 완료형을 현재로 나타낸다. ¶

Decoded Core

Shares edge up ⇒ Shares (have) edged up 주식이 조금 오르다 ¶ **edge up** ⇒ 천천히 위로 움직이다 ⁑ move upward slowly, rise up, or pick up ¶

subside ⇒ 진정되다, 수그러들다, 가라앉다, 강도가 줄다 ⁑ become less intense ¶

They waited until the storm subsided ⇒ 그들은 태풍이 가라앉을 때까지 기다렸다 ¶

as ⇒ as soon as, when 의 의미 ¶

[02]

Word&Phrase

economic stimulus 경제 부양책
edge up 가격 등이 조금씩 오르다
pick up 어떤 전망이 높아지다

Lead Sentence

Investors were encouraged by news that the European Central Bank is ready to increase economic stimulus if inflation in the eurozone does not pick up.

투자자들은 유럽 중앙은행이 유로존 내에 인플레 전망이 높아지지 않는다면 경제 부양책을 확대할 준비가 되어있다는 소식에 고무되었다.

Bilingual Reading

Investors 투자자들은 **were encouraged** 고무되었다 **by news** 소식에 **that the European Central Bank** 유럽 중앙은행이 **is ready** 준비가 되어있다는 **to increase economic stimulus** 경제 부양책을 확대할 **if inflation in the eurozone** 유로존 내에 인플레 전망이 **does not pick up.** 높아지지 않는다면

131

Chinese plane-hire deal survives market turbulence

Bohai Leasing's $2.6 bln bid for Dublin-based Avolon confirms China's desire to grow in aircraft rental. The $31-a-share offer is slightly below Bohai's indicative bid a month ago. But rising interest rates and the falling yuan could have been reasons to drive a harder bargain.

Headline

Chinese plane-hire deal survives market turbulence

중국 기업의 항공기 임대 계약이 글로벌 시장의 혼란에도 불구하고 살아남았다.

일반 표현

Chinese Bohai Group has survived to be unaffected by global market turbulence.

Matrix Core

헤드라인 영어문장은 완료형을 현재로 나타낸다. ¶

Decoded Core

survive ⇒ has survived '살아남는다'의 의미.
즉 continue after something else died 어떤 것이 죽은 뒤에도 계속 살아남는다는 의미다. ¶

Bohai Group ⇒ 중국 보하이 그룹 ⋮ 이 기업은 항공기, 선박, 인프라 그리고 글로벌 투자를 전문적으로 해왔다. 아일랜드 두블린에 있는 아볼론 항공사 인수에 최초 입찰가는 주당 32 달러였지만 성공하지 못했고, 두 번째 시도에서 주당 31 달러를 제시하고 성공시켰다. ¶

[03]

Word&Phrase

hard bargain 어려운 합의
drive hard bargain 더욱 어려운 협상을 진행하다

Lead Sentence

Bohai Leasing's $2.6 bln bid for Dublin-based Avolon confirms China's desire to grow in aircraft rental. The $31-a-share offer is slightly below Bohai's indicative bid a month ago. But rising interest rates and the falling yuan could have been reasons to drive a harder bargain.

아일랜드 듀블린에 있는 '아볼론' 항공사를 26억 달러 매입하기 위한 입찰은 항공기 임대 사업에서도 성장하겠다는 중국의 희망을 확인시킨 것이다. 한 주당 31 달러 제안은 1개월 전 보하이 그룹이 제시한 입찰가보다 약간 밑도는 가격이다. 하지만 금리인상과 위안화 가격 하락이 협상 합의를 어렵게 만들어온 이유였을 수도 있다.

Bilingual Reading

Bohai Leasing's 보하이 임대 회사의 **$2.6 bln bid** 26억 달러 매입을 위한 입찰은 **for Dublin-based** 아일랜드 듀블린에 있는 **Avolon** 아볼론 항공사를 **confirms** 확인한 것이다 **China's desire** 중국의 희망을 **to grow in aircraft rental.** 항공기 임대 사업에서도 성장하겠다는 **The $31-a-share offer** 주식 한 주에 31 달러 제안은 **is slightly below** 약간 밑도는 가격이다 **Bohai's indicative bid** 보하이 그룹이 제시한 입찰가보다 **a month ago.** 1개월 전 **But rising interest rates** 하지만 금리인상과 **and the falling yuan** 위안화 가격 하락이 **could have been reasons** 이유였을 수도 있다 **to drive a harder bargain.** 협상 합의를 어렵게 만들어 온

Part.2 BUSINESS

133

How your emotions get in the way of smart investing

Investors think they just want to make as much money as possible. If it were only that simple. Ask investors what they want from their investments, and most will say the answer is obvious: They want profits. Their answer may be obvious, but it probably isn't true. Inside all of us are wants we don't always express or often even are aware of…

Headline

How your emotions get in the way of smart investing

당신의 예감이 가끔 현명한 투자를 방해한다.

일반 표현

How your intuition often baffles your smart investing.

Matrix Core

헤드라인 영어문장은 의문부호를 생략한다. ¶

때로 이해를 돕기 위해 뒤에서부터 읽어보자. ¶

Decoded Core

how ⇒ 어느 정도로 in how much, 의문부사를 사용하고 의문부호를 생략했다. ¶

get in the way of ⇒ ~하지 못하게 막다, 즉 '방해하다'의 의미 ¶

baffle, bar, block, cumber, allow, encourage, expedite ⇒ ~하게 하다 ¶

smart investing ⇒ 올바른 투자 ¶

[04]

Word&Phrase

baffle 방해하다, 좌절시키다, 바꾸다, 꺾어버리다
make as much money as possible 될 수 있는 대로 많은 돈을 벌다
There are wants we don't always express 우리가 표현하지 않는 욕구도 있다

Lead Sentence

Investors think they just want to make as much money as possible. If it were only that simple. Ask investors what they want from their investments, and most will say the answer is obvious: They want profits. Their answer may be obvious, but it probably isn't true. Inside all of us are wants we don't always express or often even are aware of…

투자자들은 될 수 있는 한 많은 돈을 벌고 싶을 뿐이라고 생각한다. 투가자들에게 투자로부터 그들이 원하는 것이 무엇인지 물어보라. 대부분의 사람들의 답은 분명하다, 즉 이윤을 원한다고 말할 것이다. 그들의 답은 명백할 수도 있지만 사실이 아닐 수도 있다. 우리 모두의 마음속에는 언제나 표현하지 않는 욕구도 있고 또는 흔히 잘 알고 있는 욕구도 있다…

Bilingual Reading

Investors 투자자들은 **think** 생각한다 **they just want to make** 벌고 싶을 뿐이라고 **as much money as possible.** 될 수 있는 한 많은 돈을 **If it were only that simple. Ask investors** 투자가들에게 물어보라 **what they want** 그들이 원하는 것이 무엇인지 **from their investments,** 투자로부터 **and most** 대부분은 **will say the answer is obvious:** 답이 분명하다고 말할 것이다 **They want profits.** 즉 이익을 원한다고 **Their answer** 그들의 답은 **may be obvious,** 분명할지도 모른다 **but it probably isn't true.** 하지만 사실이 아닐 수도 있다. **Inside all of us** 우리 모두의 마음속에는 **are wants we don't always express** 언제나 표현하지 않는 욕구도 있고 **or often even are aware of…** 또는 흔히 잘 알고 있는 욕구도 있다…

Asia subdued as China stocks see-saw after trading resumes

Asian stocks were subdued on Monday, lacking clear direction as Shanghai shares see-sawed in and out of the red after the Chinese markets resumed trading following a four-day long weekend.

Headline

Asia subdued as China stocks see-saw after trading resumes

증시 개장 후 중국 주식이 등락을 거듭하면서 아시아 시장도 한산했다.

일반 표현

Asian market was under control as Chinese stocks were up and down when the market reopened.

Matrix Core

헤드라인 영어문장은 대체로 be 동사를 생략한다. ¶

Decoded Core

subdued ⇒ (was) subdued ¶

China stocks see-saw ⇒ China stocks (was) see-saw ¶

subdue ⇒ 진정시키다, 가라앉히다 ⁞ moderate ¶

see-saw ⇒ 시소게임 ¶

resume ⇒ 다시 시작하다, 재개하다, begin again, reopen ¶

[05]

Word&Phrase

see saw out of the red 주가의 위험선을 넘나들다
following a four day long weekend 4일 간의 긴 주말을 보낸 뒤 : following a four day long break

Lead Sentence

Asian stocks were subdued on Monday, lacking clear direction as Shanghai shares see-sawed in and out of the red after the Chinese markets resumed trading following a four-day long weekend.

4일 간의 긴 주말을 보낸 뒤 월요일에 중국 증시가 다시 개장했을 때 상하이 주식들이 증권위원회에 의해 정해진 위험선에서 반복적 등락을 계속하자 아시아 증시들은 방향감각을 잃으면서 한산한 거래 상황을 보였다.

Bilingual Reading

Asian stocks 아시아 증시들은 **were subdued on Monday,** 월요일 진정이 되었다 **lacking clear direction** 앞으로의 확실한 방향감각을 잃으면서 **as Shanghai shares see-sawed in and out of the red** 상하이 주식들이 증권 위원회에 의해 정해진 위험선에서 반복적 등락을 계속하자 **after the Chinese markets resumed trading** 중국 시장이 다시 영업을 시작했을 때 **following a four-day long weekend.** 4일간의 긴 주말을 보낸 뒤

Microsoft gets $7.6 billion wakeup call from Nokia

The U.S. software goliath is writing off most of what it paid for the Finnish business in 2014. Microsoft's M&A-related writedowns tally $14 bln over the past three years. CEO Satya Nadella, who has already splurged on Minecraft and eyed Salesforce, should be taking the hint.

Headline

Microsoft gets $7.6 billion wakeup call from Nokia

마이크로소프트는 2014년 노키아를 인수할 때 지불한 76억 달러를 자산에서 공제하고 있다.

일반 표현

Microsoft is writing off the amount it paid for deal to Nokia.

Matrix Core

헤드라인 영어문장은 완료형을 현재로 나타낸다. ¶

Decoded Core

gets ⇒ has got ¶

wakeup call from ⇒ 충격을 준 사건, 여기서는 받을 수 없는 부채를 의미 ¶

wakeup call ⇒ '부채를 자산에서 공재하다'라는 의미
‡ write off debt ¶

Goliath ⇒ 골리앗, 거인, 거대 기업 ¶

write off ⇒ 제거하다, 탕감하다, 액수 등을 줄이거나 자산에서 공제하다(reduce or cancel) ¶

[06]

Word&Phrase

writedown 평가절하
splurge 돈 등을 물 쓰듯 사용하다, 과시
take the hint 어떤 상황을 이해하다

Lead Sentence

The U.S. software goliath is writing off most of what it paid for the Finnish business in 2014. Microsoft's M&A-related writedowns tally $14 bln over the past three years. CEO Satya Nadella, who has already splurged on Minecraft and eyed Salesforce, should be taking the hint.

마이크로소프트는 2014년 핀란드의 노키아 인수지불금 액수의 대부분을 회수하지 못하고 있다. 마이크로소프트의 M&A와 관련된 거래 손실액수는 지난 3년 동안 140억 달러이다. CEO 사트야 나델라는 '마인크라프트' 인수에 이미 많은 돈을 소비했고, 세일즈포스에도 관심을 보이고 있는 만큼 이 상황을 충분히 이해해야 할 것이다.

Bilingual Reading

The U.S. software goliath 미국 소프트웨어 거인은 **is writing off** 제거하고 있다 **most of what it paid for the Finnish business in 2014.** 2014년 핀란드에서 이루어진 비지니스(노키아 인수)에 지불한 금액의 대부분을 **Microsoft's M&A-related writedowns** 마이크로소프트의 합병 관련 손실액수는 **tally $14 bln over the past three years.** 지난 3년간 총 140억 달러이다 **CEO Satya Nadella,** CEO인 사트야 나델라는 **who has already splurged on Minecraft and eyed Salesforce,** 이미 마인크라프트 인수에 많은 돈을 소비했고 세일즈포스에도 관심을 보이고 있는 **should be taking the hint.** 힌트를 얻어야 할 것이다

China market slide turns brokers into policy tools

Authorities have enlisted securities houses to prop up stocks. As with China's banks, financial returns rank below official aims. It's a far cry from the expansion Haitong and Huatai promised as the industry raised $25 bln this year. No wonder investors are running for cover.

Headline

China market slide turns brokers into policy tools

중국 증시의 폭락은 주식 중개인들을 정책도구가 되도록 만들었다.

일반 표현

Chinese securities' decline turns brokers into situation in which they become policy tool.

Matrix Core

헤드라인 영어문장은 기본구조로 나타낸다.

Decoded Core

China market slide ⇒ 중국 증시 하락

brokers ⇒ 주식 중개인

turn into ⇒ 만들다, 바꾸다, 이용하다, make의 의미로 사용

[07]

Word&Phrase

enlist securities house 증권 중개상 등록
prop (something) up 막다, 떠받치다, 무엇으로 받쳐 넘어지지 않게 하다
far cry 불만

Lead Sentence

Authorities have enlisted securities houses to prop up stocks. As with China's banks, financial returns rank below official aims. It's a far cry from the expansion Haitong and Huatai promised as the industry raised $25 bln this year. No wonder investors are running for cover.

중국 당국은 주가 폭락을 막기 위해 증권사들을 등록시켰다. 중국 은행들과 마찬가지로 금융사들의 수익이 공식적 목표 아래 머물렀다. 이것은 올해 250억 달러 가량 성장할 거라는 화이통과 후아타이 증권사의 예상과는 거리가 먼 것이다. 투자가들이 투자한 돈을 회수하기 위해 뛰는 것은 당연하다.

Bilingual Reading

Authorities 중국 당국은 **have enlisted securities houses** 증권사들을 등록시켰다 **to prop up stocks.** 주가 폭락을 막기 위해 **As with China's banks,** 중국 은행들과 마찬가지로 **financial returns** 금융사들의 수익이 **rank below official aims.** 공식적 목표 아래 머물렀다 **It's a far cry from the expansion** 이는 확장과는 거리가 먼 것이다 **Haitong and Huatai promised** 하이통과 후아타이증권이 약속한 **as the industry raised $25 bln this year.** 올해 250억 달러를 거두어들임에 따라 **No wonder** 당연하다 **investors** 투자가들이 **are running for cover.** 투자한 돈을 회수하기 위해 뛰는 것은

Yoox glee at Net-a-Porter exit may wear thin

Shares in the upmarket online retailer popped 5 pct as Net's founder cashed out of the merger agreed in March. Terms of the severance deal with Natalie Massenet confirm that Yoox bought its rival at a bargain price.
But it is losing know-how at an important time.

Headline

Yoox glee at Net-a-Porter exit may wear thin

점점 옅어질지도 모르는 네타포르테 투자 회수에 대한 육스 사의 기쁨

네타포르테의 투자 회수에 대한 육스 사의 즐거움은 퇴색할지도 모른다.

일반 표현

Yoox could fade away their glee over Net-a-Porter exit

Matrix Core

헤드라인 영어문장은 앞의 명사가 뒤의 명사를 수식한다. ¶

뒤에서부터 읽어보는 것도 이해에 도움이 된다. ¶

Decoded Core

Yoox glee ⇒ Yoox's glee 육스 회사의 기쁨 ¶

wear thin ⇒ 점차 줄어들다, fade away, 퇴색하다 ¶

glee ⇒ 즐거움, 기쁨 ‡ exultant high spirited joy, merriment ¶

Yoox ⇒ 육스 그룹. 이탈리아 온라인 소매회사 ¶

Net-a-Porter ⇒ 네타포르테. 영국에 위치한 온라인 패션 소매 기업 ¶

[08]

Word&Phrase

upmarket online retailer
고급상품 온라인 소매상, 'Yoox'를 의미
cash out of 돈을 인출하다
severance deal 분리계약
bargain price 협상가격

know-how 전문기술

Lead Sentence

Shares in the upmarket online retailer popped 5 pct as Net's founder cashed out of the merger agreed in March. Terms of the severance deal with Natalie Massenet confirm that Yoox bought its rival at a bargain price. But it is losing know-how at an important time.

네타포르테의 창업자가 3월에 합의된 합병 기업의 주식을 매각한 후 온라인 명품시장의 주식은 5%가 뛰었다. 나탈리 마스넷(Natalie Massenet)과 맺은 퇴직금 지급 조건을 보면 육스는 그의 경쟁사를 싼값에 매입한 것이 틀림없다. 그러나 회사는 중요한 시기에 노하우를 잃고 있다.

Bilingual Reading

Shares in the upmarket online retailer 고급상품 온라인 소매상(Yoox)의 주식은 **popped 5 pct** 5%가 뛰었다 **as Net's founder** 네타포르테의 창업자가 **cashed out** 돈을 회수했을 때 **of the merger agreed in March.** 3월에 합의된 합병으로 **Terms of the severance deal** 퇴직금 지급 조건들은 **with Natalie Massenet** Natalie Massenet 네타포르테와 맺은 **confirm** 확인한 것이다 **that Yoox** 육스가 **bought its rival** 그의 경쟁사를 매입했다는 사실을 **at a bargain price.** 낮은 가격에 **But it** 그러나 육스는 **is losing** 잃어가고 있다 **know-how** 전문기술을 **at an important time.** 중요한 시기에

Wall Street's rave party feels the drop

Robert Sillerman's attempt to roll up the electronic dance music business is collapsing not long after UBS, Barclays and Jefferies helped his SFX Entertainment go public. Live Nation may once again turn out to be the buyer of a Sillerman creation, but this time will be different.

Headline

Wall Street's rave party feels the drop

월스트리트의 현란한 파티의 열기가 식어가고 있다.

월스트리트의 주식가격이 진정되고 있다.

일반 표현

Wall Street active businessman predicts the shares falling.

Matrix Core

헤드라인 영어문장은 기본구조로 나타낸다. ¶

Decoded Core

Wall Street's rave party ⇒ Wall Street enthusiastic company ¶

rave party ⇒ 매우 빠르고 현란한 음악에 맞추어 춤을 추는 파티 ¶

feel the drop ⇒ 주가 하락을 예측하다 ⁞ predict share's dropping ¶

[09]

Word&Phrase

roll up 윤곽을 갖추다, 모습을 드러내다
collapse 희망, 계획 등이 좌절하다
go public 주식을 공개(상장)하다
Sillerman creation 실러맨의 신규사업

Lead Sentence

Robert Sillerman's attempt to roll up the electronic dance music business is collapsing not long after UBS, Barclays and Jefferies helped his SFX Entertainment go public. Live Nation may once again turn out to be the buyer of a Sillerman creation, but this time will be different.

EDM(일렉트로닉 댄스음악) 사업을 추진하려는 로버트 실러의 계획은 UBS, 바클레이즈 그리고 제프리스가 그의 SFX 엔터테인먼트의 기업 공개에 투자한 지 오래지 않아 실패로 끝나고 있다. 라이브 네이션이 또 다시 실러맨 신규사업의 바이어로 판명 날지도 모르지만, 이번은 좀 다를 것이다.

Bilingual Reading

Robert Sillerman's attempt 로버트 실러의 계획은 **to roll up** 그만두려는 **the electronic dance music business** 일렉트로닉 댄스음악 사업을 **is collapsing** 실패로 끝나고 있다 **not long** 오래지 않아 **after UBS, Barclays and Jefferies** UBS(스위스 금융기업), 바클레이즈 그리고 제프리스(미국 투자은행)가 **helped his SFX Entertainment go public.** 그의 SFX 엔터테인먼트 기업 공개에 투자한 지 **Live Nation** 라이브 네이션이 **may once again turn out to be the buyer of a Sillerman creation,** 또 다시 실러맨 신규사업의 판명 날지도 모르지만 **but this time will be different.** 이번은 좀 다를 것이다.

Labor shortage pinches home builders

Delays mount as industry grapples with workload wrought by heavy demand. Home builders this year have booked their strongest sales since the recession.
A shortage of construction workers, however, is making it tough for them to deliver all those new homes on time.

Headline

Labor shortage pinches home builders

노동력 부족으로 건설업자들이 어려움을 겪고 있다

일반 표현

Home builders are suffering labor shortage.

Matrix Core

헤드라인 영어문장은 진행형을 현재로 나타낸다. ¶

Decoded Core

pinch ⇒ is pinching 어렵게 하다 ː is squeezing ¶

pinch ⇒ 꼬집다, 부담, 위기 ¶

labor shortage ⇒ 노동력(인력) 부족 ¶

home builder ⇒ 건설업자 ¶

[10]

Word&Phrase

workload 작업량
grapple with 격투하다, 해결하려고 노력하다
wrought 만들어진, 창출된
book their strongest sales 가장 많은 판매를 예약하다
on time 적기에, 시간에 맞추어

Lead Sentence

Delays mount as industry grapples with workload wrought by heavy demand. Home builders this year have booked their strongest sales since the recession. A shortage of construction workers, however, is making it tough for them to deliver all those new homes on time.

건설업계는 수요 폭등으로 어려움을 겪고 있으면서 지연이 더해지고 있다. 올해 건설업체들은 불황 이래 가장 높은 매출액을 기록할 예정이다. 하지만 건설 근로자들이 부족하여 완공을 제때에 맞추는 데 어려움을 겪고 있다.

Bilingual Reading

Delays mount 지연이 더해지고 있다 **as industry** 건설 산업계는 **grapples** 어려움을 겪고 있으면서 **with workload wrought** 창출된 작업 부하로 **by heavy demand.** 수요 폭등에 따른 **Home builders this year** 올해 건설업자들은 **have booked** 예약했다 **their strongest sales** 가장 큰 판매를 **since the recession.** 불황 이래 **A shortage of construction workers,** 건설 근로자들이 부족하여 **however,** 하지만 **is making it tough** 어렵게 한다 **for them** 그들로 하여금 **to deliver** 제공하기가 **all those new homes on time.** 새집을 제 때에 맞추어

147

With strong new backer, Olam gets what Noble needs

Mitsubishi is backing a Singapore-listed trader bashed by short-sellers, paying $1.1 bln at a big premium. Noble needs such a vote of confidence. But the Japanese group is actually endorsing Olam—a firm supported by Temasek that has been spared the worst of the commodity rout.

Headline

With strong new backer, Olam gets what Noble needs

새로운 강력한 후원자를 등에 엎은 올람은 노블 그룹이 필요한 것을 획득했다.

일반 표현

Olam Group with strong new backer takes what Noble needs.

Matrix Core

헤드라인 영어문장은 앞의 명사가 뒤의 명사를 수식한다. ¶

Decoded Core

with strong new backer ⇒ Olam 식품업체를 수식 ¶

Olam with strong new backer ⇒ 주어가 너무 길기 때문에 with strong new backer(형용사구)를 주어 Olam 앞에 놓았다. ¶

backer ⇒ 후원자, 지지자, 돈을 거는 사람 ¶

Noble ⇒ 노블 그룹. 텍사스에 위치한 에너지와 농산물 공급업체 ¶

Olam ⇒ 올람. 싱가포르에 위치한 동남아 최대 식품업체 ¶

[11]

Word&Phrase

vote of confidence 신임투표. 다른 사람이나 어떤 대상에 대해 보여주는 신뢰
bash 강타하다, 공격하다, 충돌하다, 축제 소동
endorse 보증하다, 배서하다, 승인하다, 돕고 있다
: be behind, approve of

commodity 생필품, 원자재, 상품
Temasek 테마섹 홀딩스, 싱가포르 투자회사
short seller 자기 소유가 아닌 주식을 팔고 그 상품의 주가가 떨어지면 다시 매입을 하는 주식 브로커를 가리키는 주식 용어

Lead Sentence

Mitsubishi is backing a Singapore-listed trader bashed by short-sellers, paying $1.1 bln at a big premium. Noble needs such a vote of confidence. But the Japanese group is actually endorsing Olam – a firm supported by Temasek that has been spared the worst of the commodity rout.

미쓰비시는 주식 브로커들에 의해 많은 타격을 받은 싱가포르의 한 상장기업을 후원하면서 주식 프리미엄으로 11억 달러를 지급했다. 노블 그룹은 신임투표가 필요하다. 하지만 실제로 일본 그룹(미쓰비시)은 최악의 상품 혼란을 겪어낸 테마섹의 후원을 받고 있는 올람을 돕고 있다.

Bilingual Reading

Mitsubishi 미쓰비시는 **is backing** 밀고 **a Singapore-listed trader bashed** 많은 타격을 받은 싱가포르에 한 상장기업을 **by short-sellers,** 주식 브로커들에 의해 **paying $1.1 bln at a big premium.** 주식 프리미엄으로 11억 달러를 지급했다 **Noble** 노블 그룹은 **needs such a vote of confidence.** 신임투표가 필요하다 **But** 그러나 **the Japanese group** 일본의 미쓰비시 그룹이 **is actually endorsing Olam** 실제적으로 올람을 돕고 있다 **–a firm** 이 회사는 **supported by Temasek** 테마섹이 후원하고 있다 **that has been spared the worst of the commodity rout.** 최악의 상품혼란을 겪어낸 회사다

Part.2 BUSINESS

149

Tesco's global hopes can survive Korea sale

Britain's biggest grocer is close to selling its supermarkets in South Korea, reports say. The mooted 4.3 bln stg proceeds would cut net debt in half and relieve operational headaches. Yet an exit need not be the end of Tesco's international ambitions.

Headline

Tesco's global hopes can survive Korea sale

테스코의 국제시장에 대한 희망은 한국의 유통매장을 매각한 뒤에도 생존할 수 있는 것이다.

일반 표현

Tesco's global ambitions are hopping for being unaffected by Korea sale.

Matrix Core

헤드라인 영어문장은 기본구조로 나타낸다. ¶

Decoded Core

survive ⇒ 살아남다, 계속 유지하다 ⁑ continue in existence ¶
hopes ⇒ 희망, 기대, 야심 ⁑ expectation, ambitions ¶
Tesco ⇒ 테스코. 영국 최대 소매 유통기업 ¶
Korea sale ⇒ 한국에 있는 슈퍼마켓 매각 ¶

[12]

Word&Phrase

moot 이론상의, 가설적인, 의제로 삼다, 토론의 여지가 있는
bln: billion 10억
stg: sterling 파운드화

would cut net debts in half 순 부채를 반으로 줄이다
relieve operational headache 영업적 두통거리를 덜어버리다
exit 나가다, 퇴출하다, 종료하다

Lead Sentence

Britain's biggest grocer is close to selling its supermarkets in South Korea, reports say. The mooted 4.3 bln stg proceeds would cut net debt in half and relieve operational headaches. Yet an exit need not be the end of Tesco's international ambitions.

보고에 의하면 영국에서 가장 큰 식료품 유통기업인 테스코는 한국에 있는 슈퍼마켓을 곧 매각하게 될 것으로 보인다. 43억 파운드로 추정되는 판매대금은 기업의 부채를 반으로 줄이고 영업 분야의 두통거리를 덜어버리게 될 것이다. 그러나 투자 회수가 반드시 테스코가 국제적 야심을 포기한다는 뜻은 아니다.

Bilingual Reading

Britain's biggest grocer 영국 최대 유통기업은 **is close to selling its supermarkets in South Korea,** 한국에 있는 슈퍼마켓을 곧 매각하게 될 것 같다고 **reports say.** 보고는 전한다 **The mooted 4.3 bln stg proceeds** 추정금액 43억 파운드 판매대금은 **would cut net debt in half** 부채를 반으로 줄이고 **and relieve operational headaches.** 영업 분야의 두통거리를 덜어버리게 될 것이다 **Yet an exit** 이렇게 종료하더라도 **need not be the end** 포기하는 것은 아닐 것이다 **of Tesco's international ambitions.** 테스코의 국제적 야심을

Silicon Valley rule of thumb points right way

In a land that fetishizes revenue growth over profitability, there's a new sanity check for software firms to see if the two rates add up to at least 40 pct. A Breakingviews analysis suggests it can be a useful guideline. Investors should just be wary of extrapolating too much.

Headline

Silicon Valley rule of thumb points right way

실리콘밸리에서 그동안 경험을 통해 얻은 정확한 사업원칙이 앞으로 나아가야 할 올바른 길을 제시하고 있다.

일반 표현

The first guide of Silicon Valley shows right way.

Matrix Core

헤드라인 영어문장을 기본구조로 나타낸다. ¶

Decoded Core

rule of thumb ⇒ 광범위한 지침, 방법 또는 원칙을 의미 ‡ broadly accurate principle based on experience ¶

point right way ⇒ 올바른 방법을 가리키다 ¶

Silicon Valley ⇒ 실리콘 밸리. 샌프란시스코 남부 지역 기술 회사들을 의미 ¶

[13]

Word&Phrase

fetishize 맹목적으로 숭배하다
revenue 매출, 수입, 수익, 세입, 순이익
profitability 수익성, 수익률
extrapolate 기존 자료에 기초하여 추정하다 : predict by known data

sanity check 결과를 놓고 사실 여부를 빠르게 평가하는 것, 명백한 실수가 없었는지 확인하기 위한 점검

Lead Sentence

In a land that fetishizes revenue growth over profitability, there's a new sanity check for software firms to see if the two rates add up to at least 40 pct. A Breakingviews analysis suggests it can be a useful guideline. Investors should just be wary of extrapolating too much.

이윤율보다 이익 증가에 집착하는 나라에서는 소프트웨어회사를 평가할 때 두 비율의 합계가 40%에 달하는가를 확인하는 새로운 점검 테스트가 있다. 〈브레이킹뷰〉의 분석가는 이것이 매우 유용한 가이드라인이라고 말한다. 투자자들은 지금까지의 기본 자료에 너무 의존하는 것은 조심해야 한다.

Bilingual Reading

In a land that fetishizes revenue growth 이익 증가를 맹목적으로 따르는 나라에는 **over profitability,** 이익을 원칙으로 **there's a new sanity check** 새로운 점검 방법이 있다 **for software firms to see** 소프트웨어회사를 두고 보는 **if the two rates add up** 2개의 평가 합계가 **to at least 40 pct.** 적어도 40%에 달하는가를 **A Breakingviews analysis** 브레이킹뷰 평가회사 분석은 **suggests** 제시한다 **it can be a useful guideline.** 이것이 매우 유용한 가이드라인이라고 **Investors** 투자가들은 **should just be wary** 조심해야 한다 **of extrapolating too much.** 지금까지의 기본 자료에 너무 의존하는 것을

153

Slowing growth exposes Chinese banks' debt debris

Dodgy credits on the balance sheets of China's four biggest lenders rose 28 pct in the first half of the year-much faster than the banks replenished provisions. Though overall bad debt levels remain low, continued deterioration threatens to reverse years of profit growth.

Headline

Slowing growth exposes Chinese banks' debt debris

경제 성장 둔화는
중국 은행 부채의 결과이다.

일반 표현

Slowing growth shows bad consequence from Chinese banks' dead.

Matrix Core

헤드라인 영어문장은 기본구조로 나타낸다. ¶

Decoded Core

slowing growth ⇒ the growth's slowing down, 성장 둔화 ¶

expose ⇒ 보여주다, 의미하다 ⁑ to make something visible, reveal ¶

debris ⇒ 결과, 영향 ⁑ consequence, ramification (development that complicates a situation) ¶

[14]

Word&Phrase

dodgy 속임수를 잘 쓰는 사기의, 위험한, 서투른, 약한
dodgy credits 정직하지 못한 신용
balance sheet 대차대조표
lender 대출자, 빌려주는 사람
replenish 다시 채우다, 보충하다, 보급하다

provision 조항, 규정, 대비, 지원
deterioration 악화, 저하, 타락
reverse 반대의, 뒤집다, 바꾸다, 되돌리다

Lead Sentence

Dodgy credits on the balance sheets of China's four biggest lenders rose 28 pct in the first half of the year-much faster than the banks replenished provisions. Though overall bad debt levels remain low, continued deterioration threatens to reverse years of profit growth.

중국 4대 은행들의 대차대조표에 기록된 부실해 보이는 신용거래 수치는 올 상반기에 28%나 올랐는데, 이것은 해당 은행들이 비축분을 쌓는 것보다 훨씬 더 빠른 속도였다. 전반적인 부실 채권의 정도는 아직 낮은 편이지만, 계속적인 악화는 수 년 동안의 이익 성장을 뒤집어놓을 정도이다.

Bilingual Reading

Dodgy credits 정직하지 못한 수치는 **on the balance sheets** 대차대조표에 기록된 **of China's four biggest lenders** 중국 4대 은행들의 **rose 28 pct** 28%나 올랐는데 **in the first half of the year** 올 상반기에 **-much faster** 훨씬 더 빠른 속도였다 **than the banks replenished provisions.** 은행들이 비축분을 채우기보다 **Though overall** 전반적인 **bad debt levels** 부실 채권의 수준은 **remain low,** 아직 낮은 편이지만 **continued deterioration** 계속된 악화는 **threatens** 위협하고 있다 **to reverse years of profit growth.** 수 년 동안의 이익성장을 뒤집을 정도로

Ben Bernanke and a global monetary plague

Ever since the collapse of Lehman Brothers, the Federal Reserve has engaged in financial experimentation that has delivered the weakest rebound on record while spreading deleterious effects around the globe that author Brendan Brown, in a forthcoming book, likens to a plague.

Headline

Ben Bernanke and a global monetary plague

벤 버냉키는 연준 의장으로 있는 동안 글로벌 금융재난을 가져왔다.

일반 표현

Ben Bernamke has delivered a global monetary plague in his office.

Matrix Core

헤드라인 영어문장은 몇 개의 단어로 축약하여 나타낸다.

Decoded Core

Ben Bernanke ⇒ Ben Bernanke has delivered '버냉키가 가져왔다'의 의미

plague ⇒ 질병 : disease that affects humans

Ben Bernanke ⇒ 벤 버냉키, 전 연준 의장(2차례 연임)이자 경제학자

[15]

Word&Phrase

Federal Reserve 미국 연방준비은행
rebound 반동, 되튀다
spread 퍼지다, 확산되다, 유포시키다
deleterious 해로운, 유독한
plague 전염병, 괴롭히다

Lead Sentence

Ever since the collapse of Lehman Brothers, the Federal Reserve has engaged in financial experimentation that has delivered the weakest rebound on record while spreading deleterious effects around the globe that author Brendan Brown, in a forthcoming book, likens to a plague.

리만 브라더스 금융회사의 도산 이래로 미국 연준(U.S. Federal Reserve Board)은 전 세계적으로 유해한 영향을 끼친 반면 경기 회복은 아주 낮은 수준밖에 기록하지 못한 금융 실험을 벌였는데, 작가 브렌든 브라운은 곧 출간될 자신의 저서에서 이를 끔찍한 전염병에 비유했다.

Bilingual Reading

Ever since the collapse of Lehman Brothers, 리만 브라더스 금융서비스 회사의 도산 이래 **the Federal Reserve** 미국 연준은 **has engaged in financial experimentation** 금융실험을 했다 **that has delivered the weakest rebound on record** 기록적인 최저의 경기회복을 가져온 **while spreading deleterious effects** 유해한 효과를 퍼트린 **around the globe** 전 세계로 **that author Brendan Brown,** 작가 브레덴 브라운은 **in a forthcoming book,** 그의 출판을 앞두고 있는 저서에서 **likens to a plague.** 질병에 비유했다

Part. 2 BUSINESS

157

Google EU antitrust spat riddled with holes

The search giant's robust response to a European challenge over price comparison tools ratchets up a complex theoretical battle over what makes a monopoly. Yet the dispute misses a broader point: it's hard to see how any likely outcome will make a massive difference to consumers.

Headline

Google EU antitrust spat riddled with holes

구글과 EU의 반독점법 싸움은 여러 가지 어려운 상황으로 점철되어 있다.

일반 표현

Anti-trust spat between Google and EU is riddled with many difficult situations.

Matrix Core

헤드라인 영어문장은 대체로 be 동사를 생략한다. ¶

Decoded Core

spat riddled with ⇒ spat (is) riddled with, 갈등이 ~로 채워졌다 ¶

Google EU ⇒ between Google and EU ¶

riddle ⇒ 채워지다, 영향을 주다 ⁝ to fill or affect with something ¶

hole ⇒ 어려운 상황 ⁝ difficult situation ¶

antitrust ⇒ 독점 금지 ¶

spat ⇒ 갈등, 승강이하다 ⁝ argue, fight ¶

[16]

Word&Phrase

robust 강건한, 튼튼한, 활기 있는, 힘이 드는, 풍부한
ratchet 미늘 톱니바퀴
ratchet up 단계적으로 증가시키다, 강화
monopoly 독점, 전매
broader point 광범위한 면, 일반적인 관점

Lead Sentence

The search giant's robust response to a European challenge over price comparison tools ratchets up a complex theoretical battle over what makes a monopoly. Yet the dispute misses a broader point: it's hard to see how any likely outcome will make a massive difference to consumers.

가격 비교 방법에 대한 EU의 도전을 둘러싸고 대형 검색사이트의 강력한 대응책은 무엇이 독점인가에 대한 복잡한 이론 싸움을 가져왔다. 하지만 그 논쟁은 더 넓은 핵심을 놓치고 있다. 즉, 발생될 결과가 고객들에게 어떤 영향을 줄 것인지 파악하기 어렵다는 점이다.

Bilingual Reading

The search giant's robust response 대기업의 강력한 대응책은 **to a European challenge** EU의 도전에 대한 **over price comparison tools** 가격 비교 방법에 대한 **ratchets up** 증가시킨다 **a complex theoretical battle** 복잡한 이론 싸움을 **over what makes a monopoly.** 무엇이 독점인가에 대한 **Yet** 하지만 **the dispute** 그 논쟁은 **misses a broader point:** 더 넓은 핵심을 놓치고 있다, 즉 **it's hard to see** 파악하기 어렵다는 **how any likely outcome** 가능성 있는 결과가 **will make a massive difference** 어떤 영향을 줄 지 **to consumers.** 고객들에게

Coke's sparkling H₂O talk is a bit too fizzy

The soft-drinks giant has done more than many corporations to nurture water resources. Now CEO Muhtar Kent reckons he can hit Coke's goal of replenishing every liter it uses five years early. But the company's claim that it will be water neutral doesn't yet pass the taste test.

Headline

Coke's sparkling H₂O talk is a bit too fizzy

코카콜라의 그럴듯한 물 사업 구상 이야기는 현실성이 별로 없다.

일반 표현

Coke's convincing water talk is somewhat off reality.

Matrix Core

헤드라인 영어문장을 기본구조로 나타낸다.

Decoded Core

a bit too fizzy ⇒ 현실성이 별로 없다는 의미

sparkling ⇒ 활기에 넘친, 발포성의, 반짝이는, 불꽃을 내는

fizzy ⇒ 발포성의, 거품 이는, 탄산을 녹인

[17]

Word&Phrase

nurture 양육하다, 키우다
reckon 전망하다, 계산하다, 간주하다, 세다 : think, calculate, count
replenish 보충하다, 다시 채우다 : to fill or build up (something) again

Lead Sentence

The soft-drinks giant has done more than many corporations to nurture water resources. Now CEO Muhtar Kent reckons he can hit Coke's goal of replenishing every liter it uses five years early. But the company's claim that it will be water neutral doesn't yet pass the taste test.

거대한 청량음료 기업(코카콜라)은 물 자원을 아끼기 위해 다른 많은 업체들보다 더 많은 노력을 기울여왔다. 무탈 켄트 현 CEO는 사용하는 물을 모두 다시 채우는 Coke 사의 목표를 5년 더 일찍 달성할 수 있을 거라고 전망한다. 하지만 중성수가 될 것이라는 업체의 주장은 아직 관능검사를 통과하지 못했다.

Bilingual Reading

The soft-drinks giant 음료수 Coke 기업은 **has done more** 더 많은 일을 해왔다 **than many corporations** 많은 업체들보다 **to nurture water resources.** 물 자원을 아끼기 위해 **Now CEO Muhtar Kent** 지금 CEO 무탈 켄트는 **reckons** 생각하고 있다 **he can hit Coke's goal of replenishing** 다시 채우는 코크의 목표를 달성할 수 있다고 **every liter it uses** 그 회사가 사용하는 매 리터의 물을 **five years early.** 5년 일찍 **But the company's claim** 하지만 코크 회사의 주장인 **that it will be water neutral** 코크 회사의 물은 중성워터가 된다는 이야기는 **doesn't yet pass the taste test.** 아직 Coke의 맛 시험을 통과하지 않았다

Britain losing its competitive edge in banking, trade group warns

The British government needs to take "urgent action" to address concerns about its regulatory and tax environment if London is to remain a global financial center and if lenders based in Britain are to remain competitive internationally, according to a banking trade group.

Headline

Britain losing its competitive edge in banking, trade group warns

영국은 금융업계의 국제적, 경쟁적 우위를 상실하고 있다고 금융업계에서 경고하고 있다.

일반 표현

Trade Group warns that Britain will be no more competitive in financial sector.

Matrix Core

헤드라인 영어문장은 be 동사를 생략하고 나타낸다. ¶

Decoded Core

Britain losing ⇒ Britain (is) losing ¶

competitive edge ⇒ 경쟁적 우위 ¶

banking ⇒ financial sector 금융계, 금융업 ¶

[18]

Word&Phrase

environment 금융업계의 환경, 분위기
lender 대출인, 은행
indicative bid 제시한 입찰가
urgent action 긴급조치
regulatory 규제

Lead Sentence

The British government needs to take "urgent action" to address concerns about its regulatory and tax environment if London is to remain a global financial center and if lenders based in Britain are to remain competitive internationally, according to a banking trade group.

런던이 앞으로도 계속 국제 금융의 중심지로 남고 영국 내에 있는 은행들이 국제적으로 경쟁력을 계속 유지하기 위해서는 영국 정부가 시행하고 있는 규제, 세금에 관한 문제점을 해결할 수 있는 긴급 조치를 취할 필요가 있다고 영국 금융업계가 밝혔다.

Bilingual Reading

The British government 영국 정부가 **needs to take "urgent action"** 긴급 조치를 취할 필요가 있다 **to address concerns** 문제점을 해결할 수 있는 **about its regulatory and tax environment** 시행하고 있는 규제, 세금에 관한 **if London** 런던이 **is to remain a global financial center** 앞으로도 계속 국제 금융 중심지로 남고 **and if lenders based in Britain** 영국 내에 있는 은행들이 **are to remain competitive internationally,** 국제적으로 경쟁력을 계속 유지하기 위해서는 **according to a banking trade group.** 영국 금융업계가 밝혔다

163

Monsanto leaves Syngenta facing awkward questions

The world's largest seed maker has given up pursuit of its Swiss rival. The $46 bln deal required aggressive assumptions and carried risks. Syngenta's management now needs to prove its reluctance to talk was worth it.

Headline

Monsanto leaves Syngenta facing awkward questions

몬산토는 신젠타로 하여금 어려운 문제점에 직면하게 만들었다.

일반 표현

Monsanto left Syngenta with difficult question.

Matrix Core

헤드라인 영어문장은 몇 개의 단어나 기본구조로 나타낸다. ¶

Decoded Core

leave ⇒ 어떤 상태가 되게 하다 ⁑ let stay or be as specified
leave+object (목적어)+동명사 ⇒ leave Syngenta facing awkward question 신젠타 회사를 어려운 문제점에 부딪치게 하다 ¶

awkward ⇒ 다루기 힘든, 곤란한, 골치 아픈 ⁑ well not planned ¶

Monsanto ⇒ 몬산토, 미국 세인트루이스에 본사를 둔 생화학 제조 다국적 기업 ¶

Syngenta ⇒ 신젠타, 스위스 바젤에 본사를 둔 농업부문 글로벌 기업 ¶

[19]

Word&Phrase

seed maker 종자 제조사
pursuit 추격, 쫓음
assumption 인수
reluctance 주저, 꺼림

Lead Sentence

The world's largest seed maker has given up pursuit of its Swiss rival. The $46 bln deal required aggressive assumptions and carried risks. Syngenta's management now needs to prove its reluctance to talk was worth it.

세계 최대 종자 메이커 몬산토는 자신들의 스위스 경쟁사를 따라잡을 계획을 포기했다. 460억 달러 상당의 인수 거래는 도전적이기도 했고 위험부담도 있었다. 신젠타 회사는 이제 협상을 꺼려한 것이 그만한 가치가 있었는지 입증해야 한다.

Bilingual Reading

The world's largest seed maker 세계 최대 종자 메이커 몬산토는 **has given up** 포기했다 **pursuit of its Swiss rival.** 그의 스위스 경쟁사를 따라잡을 계획을 **The $46 bln deal** 460억 달러 인수거래는 **required aggressive assumptions** 도전적이기도 했고 **and carried risks.** 위험부담도 있었다 **Syngenta's management now** 신젠타 회사는 이제 **needs to prove** 입증할 필요가 있다 **its reluctance to talk was worth it.** 협상 주저가 그만한 가치가 있었다는 것을

165

As some hedge funds sink, the challenge buoys others

The closure of macro hedge funds run by Bain Capital and Fortress Investment does not mean bad news for the industry. Lesser-known funds have had double-digit growth.

Headline

As some hedge funds sink, the challenge buoys others

일부 헤지펀드 수익률은 떨어졌지만, 그 영향은 다른 산업체에게 경기부양을 가져다주었다.

일반 표현

Even if some hedge funds fell, its impact uplifted other industries.

Matrix Core

헤드라인 영어문장은 완료형을 현재로 나타낸다. ¶

Decoded Core

sink ⇒ had sunk, had fallen off(값이 추락하다: 과거완료를 현재로 표현) ¶

buoy ⇒ buoyed 증가시키다(support: 과거를 현재로 표현) ¶

[20]

Word&Phrase

closure 주식 등을 폐쇄하다
macro hedge fund 대형 헤지펀드
Lesser-known fund 덜 알려져 있는 펀드회사, 소규모 펀드

Lead Sentence

The closure of macro hedge funds run by Bain Capital and Fortress Investment does not mean bad news for the industry. Lesser-known funds have had double-digit growth.

베인캐피털과 포트레스인베스트먼트 사가 운영했던 대형 헤지펀드의 폐쇄는 산업계에 나쁜 소식만 의미하지는 않는다. 소형 펀드들은 두 자리 성장을 기록했다.

Bilingual Reading

The closure of macro hedge funds run 대형 헤지펀드의 운영 폐쇄는 **by Bain Capital and Fortress Investment** 베인캐피털과 포트레스인베트스먼트 사에 의한 **does not mean bad news** 나쁜 소식을 의미하지 않는다 **for the industry.** 산업계에 **Lesser-known funds** 소형 펀드들은 **have had double-digit growth.** 두 자리 성장을 기록했다

Buyout Barons like the sound of a blank check

David Bonderman's TPG and Alec Gores' eponymous firm are the latest to jump on the shell-company bandwagon. A cutthroat M&A scene and the success enjoyed by the likes of Martin Franklin have amplified the siren call. Not all acquisition is necessarily the same, however.

Headline

Buyout Barons like the sound of a blank check

기업인수를 하는 대기업들은 백지수표의 소리에도 솔깃해 한다.

일반 표현

M&A businessmen have been enticed the bandwagon.

Matrix Core

헤드라인 영어문장은 기본구조로 나타낸다. ¶

Decoded Core

buyout ⇒ 매입
Baron ⇒ 남작, 봉건 영주
buyout Baron ⇒ 기업인수 기업인
blank check ⇒ 백지수표
sound of a blank check ⇒ 백지수표의 (유혹적인) 소리

[21]

Word&Phrase

eponymous 이름을 딴
bandwagon 인기 편승, 요란한 선전
cutthroat M&A scene 치열한 기업인수 현장
amplify 확대하다, 증폭하다
siren call 유혹

enticing 꾀다 : appeal of something alluring

Lead Sentence

David Bonderman's TPG and Alec Gores' eponymous firm are the latest to jump on the shell-company bandwagon. A cutthroat M&A scene and the success enjoyed by the likes of Martin Franklin have amplified the siren call. Not all acquisition is necessarily the same, however.

데이비드 본더만의 TPG와 창업자의 이름을 딴 알렉 고레스 사는 최근 껍질만 남은 회사들의 요란한 선전에 편승하고 있다. 치열한 M&A 현장과 마틴 프랭클린과 같은 사람들이 누린 성공은 많은 기업들을 유혹했다. 그러나 모든 기업 인수가 반드시 똑같은 것은 아니다.

Bilingual Reading

David Bonderman's TPG 데빗 번더만의 TPG와 **and Alec Gores' eponymous firm** 알렉 골스 이름을 단 회사는 **are the latest to jump** 최근 가담한 회사들이다 **on the shell-company bandwagon.** 껍질만 남은 회사의 요란한 선전에 **A cutthroat M&A scene** 치열한 M&A 현장과 **and the success enjoyed by the likes of Martin Franklin** 마틴 프랭클린과 같은 사람들이 누린 성공은 **have amplified the siren call.** 유혹을 증폭시켰다 **Not all acquisition is necessarily the same, however.** 그러나 모든 기업인수가 반드시 똑같은 것은 아니다.

Idealism that may leave shareholders wishing for pragmatism

Laureate Education is going public as a so-called public benefit corporation, but a screen of lofty ideals could leave shareholders out.

Headline

Idealism that may leave shareholders wishing for pragmatism

이상주의가 실용주의를 희망하는 주주들을 떠나게 할 수도 있다.

실용주의를 희망하는 주주들을 떠나게 만들 수 있는 이상주의

일반 표현

Idealism may lead shareholders to turning to pragmatism.

Matrix Core

헤드라인 영어문장은 몇 개의 단어나 기본구조로 나타낸다. ¶

Decoded Core

Idealism that may leave ⇒ idealism may leave로 이해. cause는 cause someone to do의 패턴으로 쓰고 leave 동사는 목적어+ing 동명사 패턴으로 사용 ¶

[22]

Word&Phrase

go public 주식을 상장하다
leave someone out ~를 떠나게 하다

Lead Sentence

Laureate Education is going public as a so-called public benefit corporation, but a screen of lofty ideals could leave shareholders out.

로리엇 교육재단은 이른바 '사회적기업'이란 타이틀로 증시에 상장될 예정이다. 그러나 높은 이상의 은막은 주주들을 다 떠나게 할 수도 있다.

Bilingual Reading

Laureate Education 로리엇 교육재단은 **is going public** 증시에 주식 상장될 예정이다 **as a so-called public benefit corporation,** 사회적기업이란 이름으로 **but** 그러나 **a screen of lofty ideals** 높은 이상의 은막은 **could leave shareholders out.** 주주들을 다 떠나게 할 수도 있다

Hedge fund wobbles hand ammunition to FeeFighters

Big names from Greenlight to Pershing to Third Point have taken a pounding from recent market turmoil. It's just a month's bad performance. But if high-priced managers can't provide a hedge to regular investments, it lends extra weight to Calpers and others who are ditching them.

Headline

Hedge fund wobbles hand ammunition to FeeFighters

헤지 펀드가 피파이터스(FeeFighters)에게 소액의 자금을 빌려주고 비틀거렸다.

일반 표현

Hedge fund wobbled by giving small amount of fund to FeeFighters.

Matrix Core

헤드라인 영어문장은 과거를 현재로 나타낸다.

Decoded Core

Hedge fund wobbles ⇒ Hedge fund wobbled
wobble ⇒ 비틀거리다, 불안하게 옆으로 움직이다 ⋮ to be unsteady

hand ammunition ⇒ 가지고 있는 적은 자금

ammunition ⇒ 탄약, 무기, 명분

hand ammunition to FeeFighters ⇒ 적은 자금을 FeeFighters에게 빌려주다

FeeFighters ⇒ 중소기업인을 위해 신용 카드 거래를 해결해주는 웹사이트로 시작하였지만, 2013년 Groupon에 인수되었다.

[23]

Word&Phrase

pounding 큰 타격, 고동, 치는 것, 대패, 완패
turmoil 소란, 혼란, 불안, 동요
Greenlight 그린라이트캐피털(Greenlight Capital), 데이비드 아이혼이 이끄는 대형 헤지펀드
Pershing 퍼싱스퀘어캐피털(Pershing Square Capital Management), 빌 애크먼이 이끄는 대형 헤지펀드
Third Point 서드포인트, 대니엘 로브가 창업한 대형 헤지펀드
Calpers 캘리포니아공무원연금(The California Public Employees' Retirement System)

Lead Sentence

Big names from Greenlight to Pershing to Third Point have taken a pounding from recent market turmoil. It's just a month's bad performance. But if high-priced managers can't provide a hedge to regular investments, it lends extra weight to Calpers and others who are ditching them.

그린라이트를 비롯하여 퍼싱, 서드포인트에 이르는 대형 헤지펀드들은 최근 시장 혼란에서 엄청난 손해를 보았다. 한 달째 실적이 좋지 못했다. 그러나 높은 월급을 받는 펀드 매니저들이 정규적인 투자자들에게 어떤 자금 방어책을 제공해주지 못한다 하더라도 이는 캘퍼스나 많은 손해를 보고 있는 주식 투자자들에게 힘을 실어주고 있다.

Bilingual Reading

Big names from 대형 기업들 **Greenlight** 그린라이트에서 **to Pershing** 퍼싱까지 **to Third Point** 서드포인트까지 **have taken a pounding** 엄청난 손해를 보았다 **from recent market turmoil.** 최근 시장혼란에서 **It's just a month's bad performance.** 한 달째 실적이 좋지 못했다 **But if high-priced managers** 그러나 높은 월급을 받는 펀드 매니저들이 **can't provide a hedge** 자금 방어책을 제공해주지 못한다 하더라도 **to regular investments,** 정규 투자자들에게 **it lends extra weight** 힘을 실어주고 있다 **to Calpers** 캘퍼스(캘리포니아공무원연금) **and others** 그리고 다른 주식투자자들에게 **who are ditching them.** 많은 손해를 보고 있는

In a flurry of deals, the beginning of the end?

Mergers and acquisitions are on track for a record year, with nearly $3.5 trillion worth of transactions. And that may signal the beginning of the end of a bull market.

Headline

In a flurry of deals, the beginning of the end?

바빠진 업체 간 통합 계약은 시장의 주가 상승 거래가 끝났음을 의미하는가?

일반 표현

Does busy deals mean the beginning of the end of mergers and acquisitions?

Matrix Core

헤드라인 영어문장은 대체로 be 동사를 생략한다. ¶

Decoded Core

in a flurry of deals ⇒ Deals are busy의 의미로 표현. deal을 주어로 보는 것이 좋다. ¶

flurry ⇒ 눈보라, 돌풍, 몸부림 ¶

the beginning of the end ⇒ 기업체 간 합병 인수 종료의 시작 ¶

[24]

Word&Phrase

on track 궤도에 진입한
for a record year 연 대비 최고로
bull market 강세시장

Lead Sentence

Mergers and acquisitions are on track for a record year, with nearly $3.5 trillion worth of transactions. And that may signal the beginning of the end of a bull market.

기업 합병 인수가 거의 3조 5천억 달러로 연 대비 최고기록이다. 이것은 주식 강세시장이 끝나간다는 것을 의미하는 지도 모른다.

Bilingual Reading

Mergers and acquisitions 기업 합병 인수가 **are on track for a record year,** 연 대비 최고기록이다 **with nearly $3.5 trillion worth of transactions.** 거의 3조 5천억 달러 거래로 **And that** 이것은 **may signal the beginning** 시작을 의미하는 지도 모른다 **of the end of a bull market.** 주식 강세시장 끝의

Focus Media relisting defies China's market rout

The advertising group is trying to list again in Shenzhen after a previous attempt in June fell through. But despite the stock market slump, Focus Media's $7.2 bln valuation is unchanged. Other U.S.-listed companies eyeing a return to the mainland may need to be more realistic.

Headline

Focus Media relisting defies China's market rout

뉴욕 증시를 떠났던 중국의 광고업체가 중국시장에 다시 상장하는 것은 침체된 중국시장에 완전히 도전하는 것이다.

일반 표현

Focus Media attempts to return to Chinese domestic market.
Focus Media challenges to China's market rout.

Matrix Core

헤드라인 영어문장은 몇 개의 단어나 기본구조로 나타낸다. ¶

Decoded Core

defy ⇒ 도전하다, challenge의 의미 ¶

Focus Media relisting ⇒ 포커스미디어의 상장 ¶

relist ⇒ 증시에 다시 이름을 올리다 ¶

rout ⇒ 침체 ¶

Focus Media ⇒ 포커스미디어 ‡ 중국의 광고업체. 2년 전 의혹사건으로 나스닥을 떠났다가 근래 다시 중국 내에서 영업활동을 재개했다 ¶

[25]

Word&Phrase

advertising group 광고 회사
slump 폭락, 쓰러짐, 급락, 감퇴, 평이 나쁨
eyeing 주시, 쳐다보다 : look, glance, attention
realistic 실질적인, 현실적인, 사실적인

Lead Sentence

The advertising group is trying to list again in Shenzhen after a previous attempt in June fell through. But despite the stock market slump, Focus Media's $7.2 bln valuation is unchanged. Other U.S.-listed companies eyeing a return to the mainland may need to be more realistic.

이 광고 그룹은 6월에 상장을 하려다가 실패한 후 중국 선전에서 다시 상장을 시도하고 있다. 중국 주식시장이 침체되고 있지만, 포커스미디어의 시장가격은 72억 달러로서 변함이 없다. 중국으로 돌아갈 기회를 엿보는 미국상장 회사들은 이제 더욱 현실적 정책이 필요한지 모른다.

Bilingual Reading

The advertising group 광고 그룹은 **is trying to list again** 다시 주식상장을 하려고 노력하고 있다 **in Shenzhen** 선전에서 **after a previous attempt in June fell through.** 6월에 상장을 하려다가 실패한 후 **But despite the stock market slump,** 중국 주식시장이 침체되고 있지만 **Focus Media's $7.2 bln valuation** 포커스미디어의 시장가격은 72억 달러로서 **is unchanged.** 변함이 없다 **Other U.S.-listed companies** 미국상장 회사들이 **eyeing a return to the mainland** 중국으로 돌아갈 기회를 엿보는 **may need to be more realistic.** 더욱 현실적 정책이 필요한지 모른다.

Alibaba still looks pricey despite selloff

Less than a year after its $25 bln offering, the web giant's shares have fallen below their $68 IPO price. Growth worries have afflicted all technology stocks and Chinese ones in particular. But Alibaba's core e-commerce business is still highly valued compared with its rivals.

Headline

Alibaba still looks pricey despite selloff

알리바바 주식이 대량매각되었지만 여전히 높은 가격을 자랑한다.

일반 표현

Alibaba stocks have been sold out, but still high priced.

Matrix Core

헤드라인 영어문장은 몇 개의 단어나 기본구조로 나타낸다. ¶

Decoded Core

Alibaba still looks pricey ⇒ Alibaba's stocks still have a high price although they have been sold off.
pricey ⇒ 값비싼 ‡ expensive
selloff ⇒ 대량 매각, 매각하다
Alibaba ⇒ 알리바바 ‡ 중국 항저우에 본사를 둔 세계 최대 규모 온라인 쇼핑몰

[26]

Word&Phrase

offering 주식 상장
afflict 괴롭히다, 가하다, 지게 하다
e-commerce 전자 상거래, 온라인 상거래

Lead Sentence

Less than a year after its $25 bln offering, the web giant's shares have fallen below their $68 IPO price. Growth worries have afflicted all technology stocks and Chinese ones in particular. But Alibaba's core e-commerce business is still highly valued compared with its rivals.

250억 달러의 주식이 상장된 지 채 1년도 되지 않아 이 거대 온라인몰의 주식은 상장가격 68달러 선 아래로 떨어졌다. 성장 불확실에 관한 우려가 모든 기술주와 특히 중국 기술주에 악영향을 주었다. 그러나 알리바바의 핵심 전자 상거래 사업주식은 다른 경쟁사들과 비교해서 여전히 높다.

Bilingual Reading

Less than a year 일 년도 되지 않아 **after its $25 bln offering,** 250억 달러의 주식이 상장된 지 **the web giant's shares** 이 웹 자이언트의 주식은 **have fallen below their $68 IPO price.** 상장가격 68달러 선 아래로 떨어졌다 **Growth worries** 성장 불확실에 관한 우려가 **have afflicted** 악영향을 주었다 **all technology stocks** 모든 기술주와 **and Chinese ones in particular.** 특히 중국 기술주에 **But** 그러나 **Alibaba's core e-commerce business** 알리바바의 핵심 전자 상거래 사업주식은 **is still highly valued** 여전히 높다 **compared with its rivals.** 다른 경쟁사들과 비교해서

Southern's $12 bln deal could find true north

The hefty 38 pct premium it's paying for AGL looks rich for the utility sector. Though Southern isn't giving a synergy figure, hacking out over 6 percent of costs would help justify the price. Previous mergers like Duke's acquisition of Progress at least suggest it's achievable.

Headline

Southern's $12 bln deal could find true north

서든의 120억 달러 합병이 성공하면 이 회사는 런던 북쪽 지역까지 운행할 수 있다.

일반 표현

If Southern's $12 bln acquisition deal is achieved, it can find true north.

Matrix Core

헤드라인 영어문장에서 could는 미래 가능성을 나타낸다. ¶

Decoded Core

Southern's $12bln deal could find true north ⇒
Southern could find north의 의미. 서든 철도회사는 런던 남쪽지역만 운행하고 있으나 이번 120억 달러 합병이 이루어지면 런던 북쪽지역까지 운행을 할 수도 있다. ¶

Southern ⇒ 영국 철도회사, South London Metro area, 런던에서 브라이튼까지 운행 ¶

[27]

Word&Phrase

hefty 크고 튼튼한, 육중한
utility sector 공공요금 부분
synergy 협동, 상승효과
hack 난도질하다, 마구 자르다

Duke Energy 노스캐롤라이나 샬롯에 본부를 둔 미국 최대 전력회사
AGL Energy 호주 전력회사

Lead Sentence

The hefty 38 pct premium it's paying for AGL looks rich for the utility sector. Though Southern isn't giving a synergy figure, hacking out over 6 percent of costs would help justify the price. Previous mergers like Duke's acquisition of Progress at least suggest it's achievable.

이 회사가 지급하는 엄청난 38%의 프리미엄은 공공사업 분야치고는 꽤 높은 액수로 보인다. 이 회사는 시너지효과 숫자는 밝히지 않고 있지만 운임가격을 6% 이상 할인해주면 그 가격을 정당화하는 역할을 할 것이다. 듀크의 프로그래스 합병인수와 같은 이전 사례를 보면 불가능한 일은 아니다.

Bilingual Reading

The hefty 38 pct premium 엄청난 38% 프리미엄은 **it's paying for AGL** 호주전력회사를 위해 이 회사가 지급하는 **looks rich** 꽤 높은 액수로 **보인다** **for the utility sector.** 공공사업 분야로서 **Though Southern** 서든이 비록 **isn't giving** 밝히지 않고 있지만 **a synergy figure,** 시너지효과 숫자를 **hacking out over 6 percent of costs** 이 회사는 운임가격을 6% 이상 할인해주면 **would help justify the price.** 그 가격을 정당화하는 역할을 할 것이다 **Previous mergers like Duke's acquisition of Progress at least** 듀크의 프로그래스 합병인수와 같은 이전 합병들은 **suggest it's achievable.** 이것이 가능한 일이라고 말하고 있다.

Autoworkers said to veto Fiat Chrysler contract

Hourly workers at Fiat Chrysler Automobiles appear to have soundly rejected a proposed new union contract that set no limit on the number of lower-paid workers and that contained no mechanism to move them up to top-wage status.

Headline

Autoworkers said to veto Fiat Chrysler contract

자동차 제조 근로자들은 피아트 크라이슬러와의 계약을 거부할 것으로 전해진다.

일반 표현

It is said that autoworkers will veto Fiat Chrisler contract.

Matrix Core

헤드라인 영어문장은 be 동사를 생략하고 to로 미래를 나타낸다. ¶

Decoded Core

autoworkers said to veto ⇒ autoworkers (are) said to veto ¶

veto ⇒ 거절하다, 거부권을 행사하다 ‡ refuse ¶

to veto ⇒ will veto, 거부할 것이다 ¶

[28]

Word&Phrase

soundly 굳건하게, 확고하게
lower-paid 저임금
mechanism 체계, 방법, 장치

Lead Sentence

Hourly workers at Fiat Chrysler Automobiles appear to have soundly rejected a proposed new union contract that set no limit on the number of lower-paid workers and that contained no mechanism to move them up to top-wage status.

피아트 크라이슬러의 시간제 근로자들은 저임금 근로자 수에 대한 제한을 정하지 않고 또한 자신들을 최고임금까지 끌어올려줄 방법도 포함시키지 않은 새로운 노조안건을 강력하게 거절했다.

Bilingual Reading

Hourly workers 시간제 근로자들은 **at Fiat Chrysler Automobiles** 피아트 크라이슬러 자동차에서 일하는 **appear to have soundly rejected** 강력하게 거절한 것으로 보인다 **a proposed new union contract** 새로운 노조안건을 **that set no limit** 제한을 정하지 않은 **on the number of lower-paid workers** 저임금 근로자 수에 대한 **and** 또한 **that contained no mechanism** 메커니즘도 포함시키지 않은 **to move them up to top-wage status.** 그들을 최고임금까지 끌어올려줄

Investors to scrutinize India's tech company earnings

Investors will, in the next week, be looking for signs of their ability to thrive as cloud computing, and other forces reshape the industry.

Headline

Investors to scrutinize India's tech company earnings

투자가들은 인도의 기술회사의 수입을 조사할 것이다.

일반 표현

Investors will plan to inspect India's tech company income.

Matrix Core

헤드라인 영어문장은 대체로 be 동사를 생략한다. ¶

Decoded Core

investors to scrutinize ⇒ investors (are) to scrutinize ¶

scrutinize ⇒ 조사하다 ‡ probe ¶

[29]

Word&Phrase

reshape ~을 다시 만들다, 고치다, 새 형태로 만들다
thrive 확장하다, 무성하다

Lead Sentence

Investors will, in the next week, be looking for signs of their ability to thrive as cloud computing, and other forces reshape the industry.

투자가들은 지속적으로 번창할 수 있는 가능성이 있는지에 대해서 클라우드 컴퓨팅으로써 다음 주 중 조사할 것이며 다른 세력들은 회사의 내부를 재조직하고 있다.

Bilingual Reading

Investors 투자가들은 **will, in the next week, be looking** 다음 주 중 조사를 할 것이며 **for signs of their ability to thrive** 지속적으로 번창할 수 있는 능력의 조짐에 대해 **as cloud computing,** 클라우드 컴퓨팅으로써 **and** 그리고 **other forces** 다른 세력들은 **reshape the industry.** 회사의 내부를 재조직하고 있다

Fed officials seem ready to deploy negative rates in next crisis

Federal Reserve officials now seem open to deploying negative interest rates to combat the next serious recession even though they rejected that option during the darkest days of the financial crisis in 2009 and 2010.

Headline

Fed officials seem ready to deploy negative rates in next crisis

금융위기가 다시 오면 미국 연방준비제도(연준)은 마이너스 금리를 적용할 가능성이 있다.

일반 표현

Federal Reserve System is likely to turn to negative interest rate if financial crisis comes again.

Matrix Core

헤드라인 영어문장은 대체로 be 동사를 생략한다. ¶

Decoded Core

seem ready ⇒ seem (to be) ready ¶

to deploy ⇒ 적용하다, 활용하다 ¶

turn to ⇒ 전환하다 ¶

resort ⇒ 의존하다 ¶

negative rate ⇒ negative (interest) rate, 마이너스 금리 ¶

Fed ⇒ Federal Reserve system, 연방준비제도, 미국 중앙은행 ¶

[30]

Word&Phrase

deploy 알맞게 사용하다, 전개하다, 배치하다
recession 경기 침체, 불황, 후퇴

Lead Sentence

Federal Reserve officials now seem open to deploying negative interest rates to combat the next serious recession even though they rejected that option during the darkest days of the financial crisis in 2009 and 2010.

미국 연방준비제도 관리들은 2009~2010년 금융위기의 어려웠던 시기에도 꺼내지 않았던 마이너스 금리 카드를 다음에 올 가능성 있는 심각한 불황과 싸우기 위해 사용할 가능성이 있는 것으로 보인다.

Bilingual Reading

Federal Reserve officials 미국 연방 준비제도 관리들은 **now seem open** 가능성이 있는 것으로 보인다 **to deploying negative interest rates** 마이너스 금리를 사용할 **to combat the next serious recession** 다음에 올 가능성 있는 심각한 불황과 싸우기 위해 **even though they rejected** 그들이 사용하지 않았지만 **that option** 그 선택은 **during the darkest days** 어려웠던 시기 동안에도 **of the financial crisis in 2009 and 2010.** 2009~2010년 금융위기의

ABN Amro's IPO could prove sweetly timed

The Dutch bank's second-quarter earnings doubled to 600 mln euros, justifying state zeal for a reprivatisation. ABN's first sale may end up a third below the government's in-price, like the UK's selloff of RBS. But with the domestic economy firing, pressing ahead makes sense.

Headline

ABN Amro's IPO could prove sweetly timed

ABN Amro 은행이 지금 주식상장을 한다면 시기적으로 상당히 적절한 것으로 평가할 수 있다.

일반 표현

ABN Amro's IPO proves to be well-timed.

Matrix Core

헤드라인 영어문장은 조동사로 가능성을 나타낸다.

Decoded Core

could prove sweetly timed ⇒ 시기적으로 적절했다고 판명될 수도 있다.

ABN Amro ⇒ 네덜란드 암스텔담에 본부를 둔 은행, 완전한 금융상품과 서비스를 내놓고 있다.

IPO ⇒ 기업 공개, 신규 상장 ‡ Initial Public Offering

sweetly ⇒ 제대로, 제때에

[31]

Word&Phrase

second-quarter earnings 2/4 분기 수입
zeal 열의, 노력, 목표
reprivatisation 재사유화
selloff 대량매각, 처분

Lead Sentence

The Dutch bank's second-quarter earnings doubled to 600 mln euros, justifying state zeal for a reprivatisation. ABN's first sale may end up a third below the government's in-price, like the UK's selloff of RBS. But with the domestic economy firing, pressing ahead makes sense.

네덜란드 ABN Amro 은행의 2/4 분기 수입은 두 배로 늘어나서 6억 유로가 되었고, 정부의 재사유화 목표의 정당한 이유가 되었다. ABN의 첫 번째 매각은 영국의 RBS 매각과 마찬가지로 정부의 제시 가격을 밑도는 1/3 가격으로 끝날지도 모른다. 그러나 국내 경기가 다시 활성화됨으로 해서 앞으로 매각 압력은 더 가열될 것이다.

Bilingual Reading

The Dutch bank's second-quarter earnings 네덜란드 은행의 2/4 분기 수입은 **doubled to 600 mln euros,** 두 배로 늘어나서 6억 유로달러가 되었고 **justifying state zeal for a reprivatisation.** 정부의 재사유화 목표의 정당한 이유가 되었다 **ABN's first sale** ABN의 첫 번째 매각은 **may end up** 끝날지도 모른다 **a third below the government's in-price,** 정부 제시가격을 밑도는 1/3 가격으로 **like the UK's selloff of RBS.** 영국의 RBS 매각과 마찬가지로 **But with the domestic economy firing,** 그러나 국내 경기가 다시 활성화됨으로 해서 **pressing ahead makes sense.** 앞으로 매각 압력은 더 가열될 것이다.

The tangle of loose lending to tight oil

A few weeks ago, a big hedge fund manager in New York asked a major Wall Street bank what was happening to energy sector loan. The answer was sobering.
"They said that the covenants on 72 out of 74 loans to the oil and gas sector has recently been modified."

Headline

The tangle of loose lending to tight oil

자금 사정이 어려운 석유회사를 대상으로 완화된 대출조건

일반 표현

The loose lending to tight oil brings confusion.

Matrix Core

헤드라인 영어문장은 몇 개의 단어로 나타낸다. ¶

Decoded Core

tangle ⇒ 어려움, 혼란상태 ¶

loose ⇒ 완화된 ⁞ not strict ¶

tight oil ⇒ 자금 사정이 어려운 ⁞ oil company under very strict control ¶

[32]

Word&Phrase

sober 냉정한, 진지한, 술을 끊다, 정신이 든
covenant 계약, 서약, 계약하다
modify 완화시키다 **:** loose

Lead Sentence

A few weeks ago, a big hedge fund manager in New York asked a major Wall Street bank what was happening to energy sector loan. The answer was sobering. "They said that the covenants on 72 out of 74 loans to the oil and gas sector has recently been modified."

몇 주 전 뉴욕에 있는 해지펀드 이사가 월스트리트에 있는 한 대형 은행에 에너지 분야 대출에 변화가 있느냐고 묻자 의미 있는 대답이 돌아왔다. "74건의 대출 중에서 72건에 대한 대출 합의 조건들이 최근 많이 완화되었다고 말했다."

Bilingual Reading

A few weeks ago, 몇 주 전 **a big hedge fund manager in New York** 뉴욕에 있는 해지펀드 이사가 **asked** 물었다 **a major Wall Street bank** 월스트리트에 있는 한 대형은행에게 **what was happening to energy sector loan.** 에너지 분야 대출에 발생한 것을 **The answer was sobering.** 그 대답은 정신이 번쩍 들게 하는 것이었다. **"They said** 그들은 대답했다 **that the covenants on 72 out** 72건에 대한 대출 합의 조건들이 **of 74 loans** 74건의 대출 중에서 **to the oil and gas sector** 석유와 가스 분야에 대한 **has recently been modified."** 최근 많이 완화되었다고

Glaxo sale comes with cheeky earnings side effect

UK pharmaceutical firm GlaxoSmithKline is selling a multiple sclerosis drug to Novartis for up to $1 bln. It's a logical move and Glaxo gets a good price. The quirk: it will include proceeds from the one-off as part of underlying revenue. Pharma investors need to watch their core.

Headline

Glaxo sale comes with cheeky earnings side effect

신경에 거슬릴 정도로 엄청난 동맥경화증 글락소 판매 약값이 부작용을 동반했다.

일반 표현

Side effect of nervy earning follows glaxo sale.

Matrix Core

헤드라인 영어문장은 기본구조로 나타낸다. ¶

Decoded Core

come with ⇒ 가져오다, 동반하다, 뒤따르다 ⁑ accompany, follow ¶

cheeky earning side effect ⇒ the side effect of cheeky earning 엄청난 수입 부작용, 신경에 거슬리는 수입에 따른 부작용

cheeky ⇒ 엄청난, 놀라운 ⁑ huge, nervy ¶

side effect ⇒ 후유증, 부작용 ¶

Glaxo SmithKline ⇒ 글락소스미스클라인, 영국 다국적 제약회사 ¶

[33]

Word&Phrase

sclerosis 경화, 경변
Novartis 스위스 다국적 제약회사
logical move 합리적 행동
quirk 버릇, 변덕, 일격
multiple sclerosis 다발성경화증

Lead Sentence

UK pharmaceutical firm GlaxoSmithKline is selling a multiple sclerosis drug to Novartis for up to $1 bln. It's a logical move and Glaxo gets a good price. The quirk: it will include proceeds from the one-off as part of underlying revenue. Pharma investors need to watch their core.

영국 제약회사 글락소스미스클라인(Glaxo SmithKline)은 다발성경화증 약품을 노바티스 제약사에 10억 달러 값에 팔고 있다. 이것은 합리적인 행동이며 글락소는 높은 이익을 얻는 것이다. 이상한 점은 실제적인 총수입의 일부로서 단 한 차례의 거래에서 받은 판매대금이라는 것이다. 이 제약사의 투자가들은 핵심내용을 지켜볼 필요가 있다.

Bilingual Reading

UK pharmaceutical firm GlaxoSmithKline 영국 제약회사 **Glaxo SmithKline**은 **is selling** 팔고 있다 **a multiple sclerosis drug** 다발성경화증 약을 **to Novartis** 노바티스 제약사에 **for up to $1 bln.** 10억 달러 값에 **It's a logical move** 이것은 합리적인 판매행동이며 **and Glaxo gets a good price.** 글락소는 비싼 값을 받는다 **The quirk:** 이상한 점은 즉, **it will include proceeds** 판매대금이라는 것이다 **from the one-off** 단 한 차례의 거래에서 받은 **as part of underlying revenue.** 실제적인 총수입의 일부로서 **Pharma investors** 이 제약사의 투자가들은 **need to watch their core.** 그들의 핵심내용을 지켜볼 필요가 있다.

193

Public markets are great equalizers in an age of inequality

Markets are some of the few remaining places where people of different economic classes still interact. Union Square is one of those rare places left in Manhattan where just about anyone has business being. And, for that matter, shopping.

Headline

Public markets are great equalizers in an age of inequality

시장은 불평등 시대에 많은 계층의 사람들이 모여 서로 동등하게 활동하는 곳이다.

일반 표현

Market is a place where different classes are together and interact.

Matrix Core

헤드라인 영어문장은 기본구조로 나타낸다. ¶

Decoded Core

equalizer ⇒ 균등하게 만들어 주는 사람, 균등하게 만드는 장치 ¶

age of inequality ⇒ 불균등시대 ¶

[34]

Word&Phrase

equalizer 균형을 잡아주는 사람, 장치
interact 상호작용하다, 상호 교류하다
classes 계층
Union Square 유니언스퀘어, 뉴욕 맨해튼의 한 구역

Lead Sentence

Markets are some of the few remaining places where people of different economic classes still interact. Union Square is one of those rare places left in Manhattan where just about anyone has business being. And, for that matter, shopping.

시장은 다른 계층의 사람들이 여전히 서로 상호 작용하는 아직 남아있는 몇 개 안 되는 장소 중의 하나다. 뉴욕 맨해튼에 있는 유니언 스퀘어는 모든 사람이 볼일이 있는 곳, 즉 쇼핑을 하는 그런 곳이다.

Bilingual Reading

Markets 시장은 **are some of the few remaining places** 아직 남아있는 몇 개 안 되는 장소 중의 하나다 **where people of different economic classes** 다른 경제 계층의 사람들이 **still interact.** 아직 서로 상호 작용하는 **Union Square** 유니언 스퀘어는 **is one of those rare places** 드문 장소 중의 하나다 **left in Manhattan** 뉴욕 맨해튼에 있는 **where just about anyone has business being.** 모든 사람이 볼일이 있는 **And, for that matter,** 그런 면에서는 **shopping.** 쇼핑이다

Part.2 BUSINESS

195

Coming soon to checkouts: microchip-card payment systems

Retailers are racing to meet an Oct. 1 deadline set by credit card networks to switch to the more secure payment technology that is common in most of the world except the United States.

Headline

Coming soon to checkouts: microchip-card payment systems

마이크로칩 카드 지불 제도가 곧 계산대에서 사용될 예정이다.

일반 표현

Microchip-card payment system is coming soon to checkout.

Matrix Core

헤드라인 영어문장은 몇 개의 단어나 기본구조로 나타낸다. ¶

Decoded Core

coming soon to checkouts ⇒ 계산대에 곧 나타나다, 계산대에서 곧 사용되다 ¶

microchip-card payment systems ⇒ 주어 ¶

checkouts ⇒ 계산대 ¶

[35]

Word&Phrase

switch to the more secure payment technology 좀 더 안전한 지불 기술
switch to ~로 전환하다

Lead Sentence

Retailers are racing to meet an Oct. 1 deadline set by credit card networks to switch to the more secure payment technology that is common in most of the world except the United States.

소매상들은 미국 외에 다른 나라에서도 일반적인 좀 더 안전한 지불 기술로 전환하기 위해 신용카드사들이 정해놓은 10월 1일 기한일을 지키기 위해 애쓰고 있다.

Bilingual Reading

Retailers 소매상들은 **are racing** 애쓰고 있다 **to meet an Oct. 1 deadline** 10월 1일 기한일을 지키기 위해 **set by credit card networks** 신용카드사들이 정해놓은 **to switch** 전환하기 위해 **to the more secure payment technology** 좀 더 안전한 지불 기술로 **that** 그것은 **is common** 일반적이다 **in most of the world except the United States.** 미국 이외 다른 나라에서

Amazon offers One Less Reason to shop elsewhere: hot food delivery

Amazon.com Inc. is trying to give consumers yet another reason to shop only on its site amid a torrent of competition.

Headline

Amazon offers One Less Reason to shop elsewhere: hot food delivery

아마존은 다른 곳에서 쇼핑하면 '한 가지 부족한 이유가 있음'을 제시했다. 즉 자신들은 뜨거운 음식을 배달한다는 것이다.

일반 표현

Amazon offers a less convincing reason why you should shop at Amazon; hot food delivery

Matrix Core

헤드라인 영어문장을 기본구조로 나타낸다. ¶

Decoded Core

One Less Reason ⇒ Band 그룹의 이름 ⁑ 이 밴드는 대단한 인기가 있었던 "Everyday Life" 앨범을 내었다. 이 헤드라인은 이 그룹의 이름만 이용했다. ¶

one less reason to shop ⇒ 문장의 내용은 재치가 들어 있는 구문 ¶

less ~ to ⇒ ~을 하기에 부족한 ¶

one less reason to shop elsewhere ⇒ 다른 곳에서 쇼핑하기에는 한 가지 부족한 이유 ¶

[36]

Word&Phrase

amid torrent of competition 경쟁이 치열한 가운데
another reason 또 하나의 다른 이유

Lead Sentence

Amazon.com Inc. is trying to give consumers yet another reason to shop only on its site amid a torrent of competition.

아마존은 경쟁이 치열한 가운데 왜 아마존이 아닌 다른 곳에서 쇼핑해서는 안 되는지 이유를 내놓았다. 바로 아마존에서는 뜨거운 음식을 배달한다는 것이다.

Bilingual Reading

Amazon.com Inc. 아마존.com 기업은 **is trying** 노력하고 있다 **to give consumers** 소비자들에게 내놓으려고 **yet another reason** 또 하나의 이유를 **to shop only** 쇼핑해야만 되는 **on its site** 오직 아마존 사이트에서만 **amid a torrent of competition.** 경쟁이 치열한 가운데

Judge's ruling offers peek into private equity's secret world

Infiltrating the supersecret world of private equity is difficult, so any glimpse into how these firms operate is worth highlighting. A bankruptcy judge in Manhattan ruled that Apax Partners and TPG Capital will go to trial next year over fraud allegations in a 2006 deal involving Hellas Telecommunications.

Headline

Judge's ruling offers peek into private equity's secret world

판사의 판결문을 들여다보면 개인회사의 비밀 세계를 알 수 있다.

일반 표현

Judge's ruling offers enables us to look into private equity's secret world.

Matrix Core

헤드라인 영어문장은 기본구조로 나타낸다. ¶

Decoded Core

peek into ⇒ 슬그머니 무언가를 들여다 보다 ≒ look into something furtively ¶

Judge's ruling offers ⇒ 판사의 판결문 권고안 ¶

private equity ⇒ 개인회사 ¶

[37]

Word&Phrase

bankrupcy judge 파산담당 판사
go to trial 재판을 받다
is worth highlighting 이야기할 만하다

Lead Sentence

Infiltrating the supersecret world of private equity is difficult, so any glimpse into how these firms operate is worth highlighting. A bankruptcy judge in Manhattan ruled that Apax Partners and TPG Capital will go to trial next year over fraud allegations in a 2006 deal involving Hellas Telecommunications.

개인회사의 최고 비밀 속으로 침투해 들어가기는 어렵다. 그래서 이들 회사가 어떻게 운영되는가를 잠깐 들여다보면 이야기를 해볼 만하다. 맨해튼 파산담당 판사는 에이펙스파트너스와 TPG캐피털이 2006년 헬라스텔레커뮤니케이션스와의 거래에서 연루된 사기혐의로 내년에 재판을 받게 될 것이라고 판결했다.

Bilingual Reading

Infiltrating 침투해 들어가기는 **the supersecret world of private equity** 개인회사의 최고 비밀 속으로 **is difficult,** 어렵다 **so any glimpse into how these firms operate** 그래서 이 회사들이 어떻게 운영되는지 엿보기는 **is worth highlighting.** 이야기를 해볼 만하다 **A bankruptcy judge in Manhattan** 맨해튼 파산 판사는 **ruled** 판결했다 **that Apax Partners** 에이펙스파트너스와 **and TPG Capital** TPG캐피털이 **will go to trial next year** 내년에 재판을 받게 된다고 **over fraud allegations** 사기혐의로 **in a 2006 deal involving Hellas Telecommunications.** 2006년 헬라스텔레커뮤니케이션스와의 거래에서 연루된

Rocket venture aims to boost nonmilitary business

United Launch Alliance seeks new clients amid dwindling Pentagon satellite launches. Responding to dwindling Pentagon satellite launches, a Boeing Co. and Lockheed Martin Corp. joint venture is seeking to boost its share of commercial and nonmilitary government rocket business.

Headline

Rocket venture aims to boost nonmilitary business

로켓 벤처업체들은 비군사분야의 사업을 확대시키려고 한다.

일반 표현

Rocket Venture would increase nonmilitary business.

Matrix Core

헤드라인 영어문장은 몇 개의 단어나 기본구조로 나타낸다. ¶

Decoded Core

boost ⇒ increase의 의미. 뉴스 헤드라인에는 주로 increase 동사보다 boost를 더 자주 사용 ¶

aim to ⇒ 목표로 하다 ¶

United Launch Alliance ⇒ 미국 최대 방위산업체 록히드마틴과 보잉의 디펜스, 우주, 안보 사업부(BDS: Boeing Defense, Space & Security)의 합작투자 업체 ¶

[38]

Word&Phrase

dwindling 규모가 줄어들고 있는
commercial and non military business 민간부분과 비군사 부분 사업

Lead Sentence

United Launch Alliance seeks new clients amid dwindling Pentagon satellite launches. Responding to dwindling Pentagon satellite launches, a Boeing Co. and Lockheed Martin Corp. joint venture is seeking to boost its share of commercial and nonmilitary government rocket business.

유나이티드 런치 얼라이언스는 펜타곤이 인공위성 발사 횟수를 줄이고 있는 가운데 새로운 고객을 찾고 있다.
횟수가 줄고 있는 인공위성 발사에 대응책으로 태어난 보잉과 록히드마틴의 합작투자 회사는 상업용과 비군사용 정부 로켓 사업부분을 늘리기 위해 노력 중이다.

Bilingual Reading

United Launch Alliance 유나이티드 런치 얼라이언스는 **seeks new clients** 새로운 고객을 찾고 있다 **amid dwindling Pentagon satellite launches** 펜타곤이 인공위성 발사 횟수를 줄이고 있는 가운데 **Responding to dwindling Pentagon satellite launches,** 횟수가 줄고 있는 펜타곤 인공위성 발사에 대응으로 **a Boeing Co. and Lockheed Martin Corp. joint venture** 보잉과 록히드마틴의 합작투자 회사는 **is seeking to boost** 늘리기 위해 노력 중이다 **its share of commercial and nonmilitary government rocket business.** 상업용과 비군사용 정부 로켓 사업부분을

Part 2 BUSINESS

203

Yahoo's plan for tax-free Alibaba spinoff faces IRS setback

Yahoo plans to spin off some $23 billion worth of shares in Alibaba. The federal government dealt a setback to Yahoo Inc.'s tax-free plan to spin off some $23 billion worth of shares in Alibaba Group Holding Ltd., potentially jeopardizing one of Chief Executive Marissa Mayer's defining moves in…

Headline

Yahoo's plan for tax-free Alibaba spinoff faces IRS setback

비과세 알리바바 자회사 분할을 시도한 야후의 계획은 미 연방 국세청의 거부에 부딪쳤다.

일반 표현

Yahoo's plan to found its spinoff for tax-free share in Alibaba faces IRS's denial.

Matrix Core

헤드라인 영어문장은 기본구조로 나타낸다. ¶

Decoded Core

face IRS setback ⇒ 미국 국세청의 반대에 부딪치다 ¶

Yahoo's plan for tax-free Alibaba spinoff ⇒ 분할회사(spinoff)를 설립하여 알리바바의 주식 230억 달러 지분을 처리하게 함으로써 세금을 내지 않겠다는 야후의 계획 ¶

spinoff ⇒ 기업분할, 회사분리 ¶

Alibba ⇒ 알리바바. 중국의 전자거래회사, Chinese e-commerce Company ¶

IRS ⇒ 미국 국세청, Internal Revenue Service ¶

[39]

Word&Phrase

deal setback 거절하다

Lead Sentence

Yahoo plans to spin off some $23 billion worth of shares in Alibaba. The federal government dealt a setback to Yahoo Inc.'s tax-free plan to spin off some $23 billion worth of shares in Alibaba Group Holding Ltd., potentially jeopardizing one of Chief Executive Marissa Mayer's defining moves in…

야후는 알리바바 주식 230억 달러 규모의 회사 분할을 계획하고 있다. 연방정부는 야후의 알리바바 회사의 230억 달러 규모의 분할 회사 설립 관련 비과세계획을 거절했고, 이는 CEO 마리사 메이어의 획기적 사업 중 하나를 좌절하게 했다…

Bilingual Reading

Yahoo plans 계획하고 있다 **to spin off** 분할회사 신설을 **some $23 billion worth of shares in Alibaba.** 알리바바 주식 약 230억 달러 **The federal government** 연방정부는 **dealt a setback** 거절했다 **to Yahoo Inc.'s tax-free plan** 야후의 세금 회피 계획을 **to spin off some $23 billion worth of shares** 230억 달러 주식 가치의 **spinoff** 회사 설립을 **in Alibaba Group Holding Ltd.,** 알리바바 회사의 **potentially jeopardizing** 좌절하게 만들면서 **one of Chief Executive Marissa Mayer's defining moves CEO in…** 마리사 메이어의 획기적 사업 중 하나를…

205

Oil price slide complicates life for central banks

Brent is back down at $50 a barrel. Bond prices show this is eroding investor confidence that inflation will pick up. Central banks usually ignore the temporary impact of commodity price swings, but can't afford to be complacent with inflation and policy rates already so low.

Headline

Oil price slide complicates life for central banks

유가 하락이 미연준과 유럽 중앙은행의 골칫거리가 되고 있다.

일반 표현

Oil price falling is becoming a headache for central banks.

Matrix Core

헤드라인 영어문장은 기본구조로 나타낸다. ¶

Decoded Core

complicate ⇒ 복잡하게 만들다 ⁝ make hard to deal with ¶

slide ⇒ 하락 ⁝ falling
oil price slide ⇒ 석유값 하락 ⁝ falling of the oil price ¶

life for central banks ⇒ 중앙은행들의 업무에 골칫거리, 까다로운 문제 ¶

[40]

Word&Phrase

brent 브렌트 석유, 런던에서 거래되는 북해산 석유
Inflation will pick up 인플레이션 가능성이 높아질 것이다 : the outlook for inflation will rise
to be complacent with inflation 인플레이션에 대해 마음 놓다
policy rate 인플레이션을 막기 위한 금리

Lead Sentence

Brent is back down at $50 a barrel. Bond prices show this is eroding investor confidence that inflation will pick up. Central banks usually ignore the temporary impact of commodity price swings, but can't afford to be complacent with inflation and policy rates already so low.

브렌트유 가격이 배럴 당 50달러로 다시 떨어졌다. 인플레이션 가능성이 높을 거라는 것이 투자가들의 자신감을 좀먹어가고 있음을 보여주고 있다. 보통 미 연준이나 유럽 중앙은행은 상품가격 변동이 가져오는 일시적인 영향은 무시하는 경향이 있다. 그러나 인플레이션에 대해서는 마음을 놓을 수도 없고, 인플레이션을 방지하기 위한 금리가 이미 너무 낮은 상태이다.

Bilingual Reading

Brent 브렌트유 가격이 **is back down** 다시 떨어졌다 **at $50 a barrel.** 배럴 당 50달러로 **Bond prices** 국채 가격은 **show** 보여준다 **this** 이것이 **is eroding** 좀먹어가고 있음을 **investor confidence** 투자가들의 자신감을 **that inflation** 인플레이션 가능성이 **will pick up.** 높을 거라는 **Central banks** 유럽 중앙은행은 **usually** 보통 **ignore the temporary** 무시하는 경향이 있다 **impact of commodity price swings,** 상품가격 변동이 가져오는 일시적인 영향은 **but** 그러나 **can't afford to be complacent** 마음을 놓을 수도 없고 **with inflation** 인플레이션에 대해서는 **and** 그리고 **policy rates** 인플레이션을 방지하기 위한 금리가 이미 **already so low.** 너무 낮은 상태에 와있다

BP is making the best of a bad situation

Underlying profit at the UK oil major fell 64 percent. The lower oil price is the main culprit. Costs and capital expenditure are coming down, and operating cashflow remains resilient. But with the oil price falling again, BP has more challenges than opportunities.

Headline

BP is making the best of a bad situation

BP는 좋지 못한 상황을 더욱 어렵게 만들고 있다.

영국 석유회사(BP)의 석유 유출에 대한 서투른 대응책은 상황을 최악으로 만들었다.

일반 표현

BP is making the situation worse.

Matrix Core

헤드라인 영어문장은 기본구조로 나타낸다.

Decoded Core

the best of a bad situation ⇒ worst situation

make the best of bad situation ⇒ 좋지 못한 상황을 더욱 어렵게 만들다

BP is making the best of a bad situation ⇒ BP's clumsy response to oil spill has made the situation worse

oil spill of Gulf of Mexico by BP ⇒ BP 사의 멕시코 만 석유 유출 사건

[41]

Word&Phrase

underlying profit 순 수익
main culprit 주요 범인, 원인
cash expenditure 현금 지출
operating cashflow 현금유동성

Lead Sentence

Underlying profit at the UK oil major fell 64 percent. The lower oil price is the main culprit. Costs and capital expenditure are coming down, and operating cashflow remains resilient. But with the oil price falling again, BP has more challenges than opportunities.

영국 석유회사 BP의 순이익이 64%나 떨어졌다. 수익을 어렵게 만든 주범은 유가 하락이다. 인건비와 현금 지출도 줄이고 현금유동성도 여전히 탄력적이다. 그러나 석유 값이 다시 떨어지는 상황에서 BP는 기회보다 어려운 도전이 더 많다.

Bilingual Reading

Underlying profit 순 수익이 **at the UK oil major** 영국 석유회사 BP의 **fell 64 percent.** 64%나 떨어졌다 **The lower oil price** 석유값 하락이 **is the main culprit.** 수익을 어렵게 만든 주요 범인이다 **Costs** 인건비와 **and capital expenditure** 현금지출도 **are coming down,** 줄이고 **and operating cashflow** 현금유동성도 **remains resilient.** 여전히 탄력적이다 **But with the oil price falling again,** 그러나 석유 값이 다시 떨어지는 상황에서 BP 비피는 **has more challenges** 어려운 도전이 더 많다 **than opportunities.** 기회보다

Financial logic in $1.3 bln FT buy is paper thin

Japanese media group Nikkei is taking a bold step with its purchase of the Financial Times. The price equates to 35 times adjusted operating income. Sure, Nikkei gets a bucketload of kudos. But the tag is around three times higher than the multiple enjoyed by quoted media peers.

Headline

Financial logic in $1.3 bln FT buy is paper thin

일본 니케이 그룹의
FT 13억 달러 매입은
금융적으로 볼 때 좀 회의적이다.

일반 표현

Nikei's buy of FT for $1.3 bln is financially skeptic.

Matrix Core

헤드라인 영어문장은 기본구조로 나타낸다. ¶

Decoded Core

financial logic ⇒ 금융적 논리, 이론 ¶

paper thin ⇒ 회의적, skeptic의 의미. 일본의 언론 그룹 티케이가 영국의 ‹파이낸셜 타임스(FT)›를 피어스 그룹(Pearson)으로부터 13억 달러에 매입한 기업인수 기사 ¶

[42]

Word&Phrase

equate 같게 하다
A equates B: A와 B는 같다
bucketload 많은 수량 : a large quantity
price quoted by media peers 언론 경쟁사들이 부른 가격

Lead Sentence

Japanese media group Nikkei is taking a bold step with its purchase of the Financial Times. The price equates to 35 times adjusted operating income. Sure, Nikkei gets a bucketload of kudos. But the tag is around three times higher than the multiple enjoyed by quoted media peers.

일본 미디어 그룹 니케이는 ‹파이낸셜 타임스›를 매입함으로써 대담한 행동을 하고 있다. 그 값은 예상수입에 35배에 해당된다. 확실한 것은 니케이는 이미 '쿠도스'를 인수한 무거운 짐을 안고 있다. (쿠도스를 인수할 때는 예상수입 보다 35배의 가격을 지불했다) 그러나 이번 FT의 인수가격표는 다른 경쟁자이 부른 액수의 3배 되는 가격이다.

Bilingual Reading

Japanese media group 일본 미디어 그룹 **Nikkei** 니케이는 **is taking a bold step** 대담한 행동을 하고 있다 **with its purchase of the Financial Times.** 파이낸셜 타임스를 매입 함으로서 **The price** 그 값은 **equates** 해당된다 **to 35 times adjusted operating income.** 예상수입에 35배에 **Sure,** 확실한 것은 **Nikkei** 니케이는 **gets a bucketload of kudos.** 이미 '쿠도스'를 인수한 무거운 짐을 안고 있다 **But** 그러나 **the tag** 이번 인수가격표는 **is around three times higher** 3배되는 가격이다 **than the multiple enjoyed by quoted media peers.** 다른 경쟁자들이 부른 액수의

211

Barclays investment bank is hardest to turn round

The UK lender, Credit Suisse and Deutsche Bank have all changed chief executives this July. Each has a distinct investment banking challenge. The Swiss bank is capital-light, Deutsche needs to cut costs. Yet Barclays' shrinking top line suggests its revamp will be the toughest.

Headline

Barclays investment bank is hardest to turn round

바클레이스 투자은행은 정상적인 상태로 돌아가는 데 가장 어려운 도전에 직면하고 있다.

일반 표현

Barclay faces the biggest challenge to its normality.

Matrix Core

헤드라인 영어문장은 기본구조로 나타낸다. ¶

Decoded Core

turn round ⇒ 적자 상태에서 흑자로 전환하다 ‡ to stop being unsuccessful and start being successful
  ex EU's aid to the country will help the country turn round
       EU의 지원은 국가 경제를 돌려놓는데 도움을 줄 것이다 ¶

Barclays PLC ⇒ 바클레이스. 영국에 본사를 둔 글로벌 금융서비스 기업 ¶

[43]

Word&Phrase

top line 기업의 총 판매액이나 수입을 말한다
the company is growing its top line 회사는 수익을 늘리고 있다
shrinking top line 줄어드는 회사 수입

Lead Sentence

The UK lender, Credit Suisse and Deutsche Bank have all changed chief executives this July. Each has a distinct investment banking challenge. The Swiss bank is capital-light, Deutsche needs to cut costs. Yet Barclays' shrinking top line suggests its revamp will be the toughest.

영국은행(바클레이스), 크레딧 스위스, 그리고 도이체방크(독일은행)는 모두 금년 7월에 CEO를 교체했다. 각 은행들은 모두 투자은행으로서의 분명한 어려움을 가지고 있다. 스위스은행은 자본이 충분하지 않고, 독일은행은 임금을 줄여야 한다. 하지만 바클레이스의 줄어드는 영업 수입은 이 회사의 개조가 가장 어렵다는 것을 말해준다.

Bilingual Reading

The UK lender, Credit Suisse and Deutsche Bank 영국은행(바클레이스), 크레딧스위스 그리고 도이체방크는 **have all changed chief executives** 그들의 CEO를 모두 바꾸었다 **this July.** 금년 7월에 **Each** 각 은행들은 **has a distinct investment banking challenge.** 투자은행으로서의 분명한 어려움을 가지고 있다 **The Swiss bank** 스위스 은행은 **is capital-light,** 자본이 충분하지 않고 **Deutsche needs to cut costs.** 도이체방크는 임금을 줄여야 한다 **Yet Barclays' shrinking** 하지만 바클레이스의 줄어드는 영업 수입은 **top line suggests** 말해준다 **its revamp** 이 회사의 개조가 **will be the toughest.** 가장 어렵다는 것을

213

Part. 3
OPINION

Part. 3 OPINION

INTERNATIONAL
BUSINESS
OPINION
LIFE

America is still great, and immigration is still why

Immigrants' rights advocates in San Francisco. Immigrants commit fewer crimes than the native-born and are assimilating as fast as ever, according to a new report.

Headline

America is still great, and immigration is still why

미국은 여전히 위대하고, 이민은 여전히 조용하다.

일반 표현

America is still great, and immigrants are quiet. What is the reason?

Matrix Core

헤드라인 영어문장은 몇 개의 단어나 기본구조로 나타낸다. ¶

Decoded Core

still ⇒ 부사 '여전히'의 의미와 형용사 '조용한'의 의미가 있다. ¶

America is still great ⇒ 미국은 여전히 위대하다 ¶

immigration is still ⇒ 이민은 조용하다 ¶

why ⇒ 왜 그런가? ¶

[01]

Word&Phrase

immigrant's right advocate 이민변호사
commit fewer crimes 범죄를 보다 적게 저지르다
native-born 본토박이
assimilate ~에 동화되다

Lead Sentence

Immigrants' rights advocates in San Francisco. Immigrants commit fewer crimes than the native-born and are assimilating as fast as ever, according to a new report.

샌프란시스코의 이민변호사들의 주장에 의하면 이민자들의 범죄율은 미국 출생자보다 낮으며 꾸준히 빠르게 사회에 동화되고 있다고 밝혔다.

Bilingual Reading

Immigrants' rights advocates 이민변호사 **in San Francisco.** 샌프란시스코에서 **Immigrants** 미국으로 들어온 이민자들은 **commit fewer crimes** 범죄율이 더 낮고 **than the native-born** 미국 출생자보다 **and are assimilating** 사회에 동화되고 있다 **as fast as ever,** 이전보다 빠르게 **according to a new report.** 새로운 보고에 따르면

Why it's a bad idea for China to prop up its stock market

Regulators say they will keep supporting stocks. That unwise pledge is the high price of being a financial free rider. Like many governments, China's authorities found the easy gains from a rising market irresistible, and have ended up its slaves.

Headline

Why it's a bad idea for China to prop up its stock market

왜 국내 증시를 지원하겠다는 중국의 약속은 현명하지 못한가?

일반 표현

China's pledges to support its stock market is unwise.

Matrix Core

헤드라인 영어문장은 의문 부호를 생략한다. ¶

Decoded Core

Why it's a bad idea ⇒ why is it?
의문부호를 생략하고 도치 형태 Why it is로 나타냈다. ¶

prop up ⇒ 일반 문장에서는 주로 **support**를 사용한다. 떠받치다, 지원하다 ¶

a bad idea ⇒ 현명하지 못한 ‡ unwise ¶

[02]

Word&Phrase

regulators 증권 감독원
end up its slave 결국 노예가 되어버리다
financial free rider 금융시장에 무임승차인, 무임승차 하는 사람

Lead Sentence

Regulators say they will keep supporting stocks. That unwise pledge is the high price of being a financial free rider. Like many governments, China's authorities found the easy gains from a rising market irresistible, and have ended up its slaves.

증권감독원이 앞으로도 계속 주가를 지원하겠다고 말하고 있다. 그와 같은 현명하지 못한 약속은 금융계 무임승차비로 높은 가격을 지불하는 것이다. 많은 정부와 마찬가지로 중국 당국은 통제할 수 없을 정도로 값이 오르는 시장으로부터 쉽게 이익을 찾을 수가 있었고 결국은 그 시장의 노예가 되어 버렸다.

Bilingual Reading

Regulators 증권 감독원이 **say** 말한다 **they** 그들이 **will keep supporting stocks.** 계속 주가를 지원하겠다고 **That unwise pledge** 그와 같은 현명하지 못한 약속은 **is the high price** 높은 가격을 지불하는 것이다 **of being a financial free rider.** 금융계 무임승차비로 **Like many governments,** 많은 정부와 마찬가지로 **China's authorities** 중국 당국은 **found** 알았다 **the easy gains** 쉽게 이익을 찾을 수가 있었고 **from a rising market irresistible,** 통제할 수 없을 정도로 값이 오르는 시장으로부터 **and have ended up its slaves.** 그리고 결국은 그 시장의 노예가 되어 버렸다는 것을

Malaysia mess puts Goldman Sachs in the hot seat

The Wall Street firm raised lots of money very quickly for state-backed 1MDB. Though the deals earned Goldman outsized fees, a brewing political scandal involving the fund leaves the bank exposed and raises questions about its processes for vetting reputational risk.

Headline

Malaysia mess puts Goldman Sachs in the hot seat

말레이시아의 정치적 스캔들은 미국의 골드만삭스를 곤란하게 만들었다.

일반 표현

Malaysian political scandal has thrown Goldman Sachs into a very difficult position.

Matrix Core

헤드라인 영어문장은 완료형을 현재로 나타낸다. ¶

Decoded Core

put ⇒ has put, 상태에 놓이게 하다 ¶

mess ⇒ 어수선한 상태, 혼란 상태 ⋮ state of confusion or disorder ¶

put someone in hot seat ⇒ 어떤 사람을 상당히 어려운 상태에 빠트리다 ¶

Malaysia mess ⇒ 말레이시아의 정치적 스캔들 ¶

1MDB ⇒ 2009년 설립된 말레이시아 정부 산하 투자개발사 ¶

[03]

Word&Phrase

state-backed 1MDB 정부지원 1MDB 자금
outsized fee 거대한 자금
brew 끓이다, 일으키다
vet 검사, 수사하다, 진료하다

Lead Sentence

The Wall Street firm raised lots of money very quickly for state-backed 1MDB. Though the deals earned Goldman outsized fees, a brewing political scandal involving the fund leaves the bank exposed and raises questions about its processes for vetting reputational risk.

월스트리트 회사는(골드만삭스 투자은행) 정부 지원의 1MDB에 대한 투자를 위해 단기간에 많은 자금을 모았다. 이 거래로 대단한 액수의 수수료를 벌었지만, 해당 자금을 둘러싸고 발생한 정치적 스캔들이 골드만삭스를 노출시켰고 신용의 위험부담을 조사하는 과정에서 문제점을 야기했다.

Bilingual Reading

The Wall Street firm 월스트리트 회사는(Goldman Sachs 투자은행) **raised lots of money very quickly** 빠르게 많은 돈을 모았다 **for state-backed** 정부가 지원하는 **1MDB.** 말레이시아 개발 자금 추진을 위해 **Though the deals** 비록 그 협상은 **earned Goldman** 골드만삭스에게 가져다 주었지만 **outsized fees,** 대단한 액수의 수수료를 **a brewing political scandal** 발생한 정치적 스캔들은 **involving the fund** 그 자금을 둘러싸고 **leaves** 남게 했다 **the bank** 그 투자은행 골드만삭스를 **exposed** 노출시켰고 **and raises questions** 의문점을 제기했다 **about its processes for vetting reputational risk.** 신용의 위험부담을 조사하는 과정에서

221

Review: Dealmaking when lives are at stake

Financiers like to compare their negotiations to military strategy. Yet the art of the deal matters far more when those talking also kill. Jonathan Powell's "Terrorists at the Table" is a primer like few others, by a worldly ex-diplomat of stubborn hope. It's also darkly funny.

Headline

Review: Dealmaking when lives are at stake

금융인들은 주로
위험에 처할 때 협상을 한다.

일반 표현

Financiers tend to make deal when they are at stake.

Matrix Core

헤드라인 영어문장은 동명사로 습관적 상황을 나타낸다. ¶

Decoded Core

review ⇒ 평론 ¶

dealmaking ⇒ 협상하기, 주어와 동사가 하나의 동명사로 표현 ¶

dealmaking ⇒ 사람은 협상을 하다 ⁝ people make deals ¶

at stake ⇒ 위기에 처할 때, 위기에서 ⁝ to be at risk ¶

lives ⇒ 사람, 주로 금융인들을 의미 ⁝ Financier ¶

222

[04]

Word&Phrase

the art of deal matters far more than those talking kills
대화자들이 서로 죽고 사는 문제가 달렸을 때 협상의 기술은 더욱 중요하다
darkly funny 좋지 못한 것을 재미있게 묘사한

Lead Sentence

Financiers like to compare their negotiations to military strategy. Yet the art of the deal matters far more when those talking also kill. Jonathan Powell's "Terrorists at the Table" is a primer like few others, by a worldly ex-diplomat of stubborn hope. It's also darkly funny.

금융인들은 자신들의 협상을 군사 전략과 비교하기를 좋아한다. 하지만 협상의 기술은 협상 당사자들이 서로 죽고 사는 문제가 달렸을 때 더욱 중요하다. 조나단 포엘의 «협상 테이블에 나온 테러리스트»라는 책은 고집스러울 정도로 희망을 포기하지 않으며 협상을 잘하는 전직 외교관이 쓴 몇 안 되는 교본과 같다. 이 책은 어두운 사건들을 재미있게 다루어 놓았다.

Bilingual Reading

Financiers 금융인들은 **like** 좋아한다 **to compare their negotiations** 그들의 협상을 비교하기 **to military strategy.** 군의 전략에 **Yet the art of the deal** 하지만 협상의 기술은 **matters far more** 더욱 중요하다 **when those talking also kill.** 서로 죽고 사는 문제가 달렸을 때 **Jonathan Powell's** 조나단 포엘의 **"Terrorists at the Table"** «협상 테이블에 나온 테러리스트»는 **is a primer like few others,** 몇 안 되는 교본과 같다 **by a worldly ex-diplomat** 희망을 포기하지 않는 협상을 잘하는 전직 외교관이 쓴 **of stubborn hope.** 고집스러울 정도로 **It's also darkly funny.** 이 책은 어두운 사건들을 재미있게 다루어 놓았다.

An aging population, without the doctors to match

WE talk a lot these days about what constitutes a good way to die. There's also much discussion about the art of healthy aging. But largely absent from the conversation are all the people between the two. People who aren't dying but who grow more frail. People who have significant health concerns. People who suddenly find themselves in need of care.

Headline

An aging population, without the doctors to match

돌봐줄 적합한 의사가 없는 노년층

일반 표현

Aged people have to do without the doctors to match.

Matrix Core

헤드라인 영어문장은 동사를 생략하여 명사구로 표현한다. ¶

Decoded Core

An aging population ⇒
An aging population has to do~ 노인층은 ~해야만 한다 ¶

to match ⇒ 적절한
agree with ⇒ 맞는 ¶

without the doctors to match ⇒ 질환에 적합한 의사도 없이 ¶

[05]

Word&Phrase

constitute 형성하다, 제시하다, 나타내다
art of healthy aging 노년기 건강법
absent from the conversation 대화에서 빠지다, 끼지 못하다

Lead Sentence

WE talk a lot these days about what constitutes a good way to die. There's also much discussion about the art of healthy aging. But largely absent from the conversation are all the people between the two. People who aren't dying but who grow more frail. People who have significant health concerns. People who suddenly find themselves in need of care.

최근 우리는 잘 죽는 법을 제시하는 것에 대해 많이 이야기한다. 노년기 건강법에 관해서도 역시 많은 이야기가 나온다. 하지만 그런 대화에 끼지 못하는 대부분의 사람들은 다음 두 경우에 해당되는 모든 사람들이다. 하나는 죽지는 않지만 몸이 점점 허약해져 가는 사람이고, 다른 하나는 심각한 건강문제를 갖고 있는 사람이다.

Bilingual Reading

WE talk 우리는 이야기 한다 **a lot these days** 최근 많이 **about what constitutes a good way to die.** 좋은 죽는 방법을 제시하는 것에 관해 **There's also much discussion** 역시 많이 이야기를 한다 **about the art of healthy aging.** 노년 건강 방법에 대해서도 **But** 하지만 **largely absent from the conversation** 그런 대화에 끼지 못하는 대부분은 **are all the people** 모든 사람들이다 **between the two.** 두 경우에 해당되는 **People who aren't dying** 죽지는 않지만 **but who grow more frail.** 몸이 점점 허약해져 가는 사람들 **People who have significant health concerns.** 심각한 건강문제를 갖고 있는 사람들 **People who suddenly find themselves in need of care.** 갑자기 보호를 받아야 하는 사람들

Part.3 OPINION

225

As Germany welcomes migrants, some wonder how to make acceptance last

Although Germans have met waves of newcomers with an outpouring of generosity, the country has also experienced a formidable backlash against the migrants.

Headline

As Germany welcomes migrants, some wonder how to make acceptance last

독일인들은 이민자들을 환영하지만 일부 사람들은 그와 같은 환영을 어떻게 오래 지속시킬지 궁금해 한다.

일반 표현

German welcomes migrants, but some wonder if such acceptance would last.

Matrix Core

헤드라인 영어문장은 접속사를 as로 나타낸다. ¶

Decoded Core

접속부사 as ⇒ although의 의미 ¶

last ⇒ 오래 지속하다 ː to go on, to continue or remain ¶

make acceptance last ⇒ 이민 유입 정책을 계속 유지하다 ¶

[06]

Word&Phrase

waves of newcomers 새로운 사람들의 유입
outpouring 넘쳐흐르는
generosity 관용
formidable backlash 무서운 반발

Lead Sentence

Although Germans have met waves of newcomers with an outpouring of generosity, the country has also experienced a formidable backlash against the migrants.

독일 사람들은 새로운 사람들의 파도를 넘쳐흐르는 관용으로 받아들였지만, 한편으로 이민자들을 상대로 한 무서운 반발 역시 경험했다.

Bilingual Reading

Although Germans 비록 독일 사람들은 **have met** 받아들였지만 **waves of newcomers** 새로운 사람들의 파도를 **with an outpouring of generosity,** 넘쳐흐르는 관용으로 **the country** 독일은 **has also experienced** 또한 경험했다 **a formidable backlash** 무서운 반발을 **against the migrants.** 이민자들에 대한

Oil exports should be paired with clean energy tax breaks

The oil industry and its friends in Congress, mostly Republicans, want to get rid of restrictions on exports of crude oil that were established 40 years ago during the energy crisis. President Obama and most Democratic lawmakers are rightly opposed to such measures, at least in their current form.

Headline

Oil exports should be paired with clean energy tax breaks

석유 수출도 청정에너지 세금 감면과 같은 조치가 주어져야 한다.

일반 표현

Oil exports should be given same benefit as clean energy tax breaks.

Matrix Core

헤드라인 영어문장은 기본구조로 나타낸다. ¶

Decoded Core

oil export ⇒ 석유 수출 회사 ¶

paired with ⇒ 짝을 짓다 ¶

pair something with something else ⇒ 어떤 것을 다른 것과 하나로 묶다 ¶

clean energy ⇒ 청정에너지, 태양열 에너지, 전기 등 공기를 오염시키지 않는 에너지 ¶

tax break ⇒ 세금 감면 ¶

[07]

Word&Phrase

the oil industry and its friends in congress 석유업계와 국회에 있는 석유업계 친구들
at least in their current form 적어도 그들의 현 입장에서는
get rid of restrictions 규제를 폐지하다

Lead Sentence

The oil industry and its friends in Congress, mostly Republicans, want to get rid of restrictions on exports of crude oil that were established 40 years ago during the energy crisis. President Obama and most Democratic lawmakers are rightly opposed to such measures, at least in their current form.

석유업계와 국회에 있는 석유업계의 친구들 중 대부분은 공화당 의원들로서 40년 전 석유위기 때에 제정된 원유 수출 제한규정을 폐지하기를 원하고 있다. 오바마 대통령과 대부분의 민주당 의원들은 적어도 현 상태로서는 그와 같은 조치를 반대하고 있다.

Bilingual Reading

The oil industry 석유업계와 **and its friends in Congress,** 국회에 있는 석유업계 친구들 **mostly Republicans,** 대부분이 공화당 의원들로서 **want to get rid of restrictions** 폐지하기를 원하고 있다 **on exports of crude oil** 원유 수출 제한규정을 **that were established 40 years ago during the energy crisis.** 40년전 석유위기 때에 제정된 **President Obama** 오바마 대통령과 **and most Democratic lawmakers** 대부분의 민주당 의원들은 **are rightly opposed** 적당히 반대하고 있다 **to such measures,** 그와 같은 조치를 **at least in their current form.** 적어도 현 상태로서는

229

Opening City Hall's wallets to innovation

Cities are challenging a wide range of companies to imagine new ways to solve local problems, rather than just inviting familiar contractors to bid on brain-dead repair jobs.

Headline

Opening City Hall's wallets to innovation

시의 재정을 풀어 문제점을 해결하려 한다.

혁신을 위해 시의 재정을 열 것이다.

일반 표현

City wants to open its wallets to bring in innovation.

Matrix Core

헤드라인 영어문장은 몇 개의 단어로 나타낸다. ¶

Decoded Core

City Hall ⇒ 주어 ¶

to innovation ⇒ 문제를 혁신하다 ⁑ to innovate local problem ¶

[08]

Word&Phrase

a wide range of companies 다양한 회사들
brain-dead 뇌사 상태, 머리를 쓰지 않는
bid on ~에 입찰하다
familiar contractor 잘 알려진

Lead Sentence

Cities are challenging a wide range of companies to imagine new ways to solve local problems, rather than just inviting familiar contractors to bid on brain-dead repair jobs.

시 정부들은 지역적 난제를 해결할 수 있는 새로운 방법을 생각해내기 위해 단순히 기존의 익숙한 계약업체들을 뇌사 상태에 빠진 개선 작업에 입찰하도록 하는 대신 다양한 회사들을 고려하고 있다.

Bilingual Reading

Cities 시 정부들은 **are challenging** 도전하고 있다 **a wide range of companies** 다양한 회사들에 **to imagine new ways** 새로운 방법을 생각해 내기 위해 **to solve local problems,** 지역적 문제를 해결할 수 있는 **rather than just inviting familiar contractors** 잘 알려진 계약자들을 초청하기보다 **to bid** 입찰하도록 **on brain-dead repair jobs.** 뇌사 상태의 개선 업무에

231

Is the bar too low to get into law school?

Room for Debate asks what it means for the legal profession when an increasing number of graduates are failing the exam that allows them to practice their trade.

Headline

Is the bar too low to get into law school?

변호사 시험의 합격이 어려워 로스쿨 입학을 꺼려하는 것인가?

일반 표현

Is the bar exam is losing its vitality to get into law school?

Matrix Core

헤드라인 영어문장은 기본구조로 나타낸다. ¶

Decoded Core

the bar ⇒ 변호사 시험
the bar exam ⇒ 사법고시 ¶
low ⇒ 침체된, 활력을 잃어버린 ⁞ depressed, lacking vitality ¶
too ~ to 패턴 ⇒ 너무 ~해서 ~하지 못하다 ¶
law school ⇒ 로스쿨, 법대 ¶

[09]

Word&Phrase

legal profession 법조계
the bar exam 변호사 시험
practice their trade 변호사 업무를 개업하다

Lead Sentence

Room for Debate asks what it means for the legal profession when an increasing number of graduates are failing the exam that allows them to practice their trade.

토론방(전문가들)에서는 변호사 업무를 개업할 수 있도록 허락하는 시험에 실패하는 졸업생들의 숫자가 점점 늘어나는 상황이 법조계에 어떤 의미인지 묻는다.

Bilingual Reading

Room for Debate 토론방(전문가들)은 **asks** 묻는다 **what it means for the legal profession** 법조계에 어떤 의미가 있는지 **when an increasing number** 숫자가 점점 늘어나는 상황에 **of graduates are failing the exam** 시험에 실패하는 졸업생들의 **that allows them** 그들을 허가하는 **to practice their trade.** 변호사 업무를 할 수 있도록

Farewell to the era of no fences

Europe's openness rests on America's strength. You can't have one without the other. This was supposed to be the Era of No Fences. No walls between blocs. No borders between countries. No barriers to trade. Visa-free tourism. The single market. A global Internet. Frictionless transactions and seamless exchanges. In the early 1990s, Israel's then-Foreign Minister Shimon Peres published a book called…

Headline

Farewell to the era of no fences

담이 없는 시대는
더 이상 존재하지 않을 것이다.

담이 없는 시대의 결별

일반 표현

The era of no fence will exist no longer.

Matrix Core

헤드라인 영어문장 가운데 오피니언에서는 리드보다 서두문장으로 시작한다. ¶

Decoded Core

farewell ⇒ 작별을 고하다 ¶

to the era of no fence ⇒ 담장이 없는 시대.
지금까지 국가 간 담이 없는 시대에서 서로 담장을 치는 그런 시대가 되었다. ¶

[10]

Word&Phrase

rest on ~에 놓여 있다
frictionless 마찰이 없는
transaction 거래
seamless 솔기가 없는, 이음매가 없는, 끊긴 데 없는
This is supposed to be the era of no fences 담이 없는 시대가 되어야만 한다.

Lead Sentence

Europe's openness rests on America's strength. You can't have one without the other. This was supposed to be the Era of No Fences. No walls between blocs. No borders between countries. No barriers to trade. Visa-free tourism. The single market. A global Internet. Frictionless transactions and seamless exchanges. In the early 1990s, Israel's then-Foreign Minister Shimon Peres published a book called…

유럽의 개방은 미국의 힘에 달려 있다. 한쪽이 없으면 다른 쪽도 가질 수 없다. 지금은 벽이 없는 시대가 되어야 한다. 구역 간에 벽도 없어야 한다. 국가 간에 국경선도 없어야 한다. 통상에 장애물이 없어야 하고 관광에 비자가 없어야 한다. 다시 말해, 단일 시장이 되어야 한다. 한 개의 글로벌 인터넷. 분열이 없는 거래 그리고 이음새가 없는 교류. 1990년대 초 당시 이스라엘이던 총리 시몬은 책 한 권을 편찬했다. 책의 제목은…

Bilingual Reading

Europe's openness 유럽의 개방은 **rests on America's strength.** 미국의 힘에 달려 있다 **You can't have one** 하나도 가질 수 없다 **without the other.** 다른 것이 없으면 **This** 지금은 **was supposed to be the Era of No Fences.** 벽이 없는 시대가 되어야 한다 **No walls** 벽도 없어야 한다 **between blocs.** 구역 간에 **No borders** 국경선도 없어야 한다 **between countries.** 국가 간에 **No barriers** 장애물이 없어야 하고 **to trade.** 통상에 **Visa-free** 비자가 없어야 한다 **tourism.** 관광에 **The single market.** 단일 시장이 되어야 한다 **A global Internet.** 한 개의 글로벌 인터넷 **Frictionless transactions** 분열이 없는 거래 **and seamless exchanges.** 그리고 이음새가 없는 교류 **In the early 1990s,** 1990년대 초 **Israel's then-Foreign Minister Shimon Peres** 이스라엘 총리 시몬 페레는 **published a book called…** 책을 편찬했다. 제목은…

Use medicare's muscle to lower drug prices

Medicaid has ways to get big rebates from drug manufacturers; Medicare should be given similar powers.

Headline

Use medicare's muscle to lower drug prices

메디케어 대상자들에게도 약값 보조가 이루어져야 한다.

일반 표현

Drug prices may be lowered by medicare.

Matrix Core

헤드라인 영어문장은 긴 문장을 짧은 단어를 이용해 나타낸다. ¶

Decoded Core

use medicare's muscle ⇒ 의료보험을 이용해 약값을 줄이다 ⁝ if using medicare's system ¶

medicare ⇒ 미국에서 65세 이상 고령자에게 적용되는 노인의료보험제도 ¶

medicaid ⇒ 미국에서 저소득층을 위한 의료비 보조금 제도 ¶

muscle ⇒ 파워, 힘 ¶

[11]

Word&Phrase

get big rebates 크게 할인을 받다
ways to get big rebate 큰 할인을 받을 수 있는 방법

Lead Sentence

Medicaid has ways to get big rebates from drug manufacturers; Medicare should be given similar powers.

메디케이드 대상자는 약품 제조회사로부터 할인을 받을 수 있는 방법을 가지고 있다. 메디케어 대상자에게도 같은 권한이 부여되어야 한다.

Bilingual Reading

Medicaid 메디케이드는 **has ways** 방법을 가지고 있다 **to get big rebates** 할인을 받을 수 있는 **from drug manufacturers;** 약품 제조사로부터 **Medicare** 메디케어에도 **should be given similar powers.** 같은 힘이 부여되어야 한다

Part.3 OPINION

237

California's right-to-die bill

The governor should sign into law a bill that would allow some terminally ill patients to hasten their death.

Headline

California's right-to-die bill

캘리포니아 주가 환자의 죽을 수 있는 권리법안을 추진하다.

일반 표현

California has proposed a bill allowing right to die.

Matrix Core

헤드라인 영어문장은 몇 개의 단어로 나타낸다. ¶

Decoded Core

right to die bill ⇒ 죽을 수 있는 법안. 캘리포니아 주에는 말기환자의 안락사 법안을 추진하고 있다. ¶

sign into law a bill ⇒ 법안을 서명하여 입법으로 만들다 ¶

[12]

Word&Phrase

sign into law 서명하여 입법으로 만들다
terminally ill patients 말기 환자
hasten their death 죽음을 서두르게 하다
allow someone to 누가 ~하도록 허용하다

Lead Sentence

The governor should sign into law a bill that would allow some terminally ill patients to hasten their death.

캘리포니아 주지사는 말기 환자의 죽음을 앞당겨줄 수 있는 법안에 서명하여 입법시켜야 한다.

Bilingual Reading

The governor 캘리포니아 주지사는 **should sign** 서명해야 한다 **into law** 법을 만들도록 **a bill** 법안으로 **that would allow** 허용하는 **some terminally ill patients** 말기 환자의 **to hasten their death.** 죽음을 앞당겨줄 수 있는

Europe's threat from within

ON Oct. 13, 1765, the writer James Boswell arrived in Corsica to meet the nationalist hero Pasquale Paoli. The trip was remarkable in part because the island-home to a wild people fighting one another when not fighting off foreign conquerors-had never before been explored by someone from England. It was no less remarkable because Boswell, though a resident of London, was not English, but rather a Scot.

Headline

Europe's threat from within

유럽은 유럽 내부로부터 위협 받고 있다.

일반 표현

Europe is suffering a threat from its within.

Matrix Core

헤드라인 영어문장은 주어와 목적어만 사용했다. ¶

Decoded Core

Europe's threat ⇒ Europe is suffering a threat 유럽은 위협을 겪고 있다 ¶

within ⇒ within Europe을 의미 ¶

from within ⇒ 유럽 내부로부터 ¶

[13]

Word&Phrase

nationalist hero 민족주의 영웅
remarkable 주목 받는, 의미 있는
had never before been explored by
이전에는 일찍이 탐험된 적이 없었다

no less remarkable 적지 않게 주목 받다
Corsica 프랑스 남동부 코르시카 섬

Lead Sentence

ON Oct. 13, 1765, the writer James Boswell arrived in Corsica to meet the nationalist hero Pasquale Paoli. The trip was remarkable in part because the island–home to a wild people fighting one another when not fighting off foreign conquerors–had never before been explored by someone from England. It was no less remarkable because Boswell, though a resident of London, was not English, but rather a Scot.

1765년 10월 13일 작가 제임스 보즈웰은 민족주의자 영웅 파스칼레 파올리를 만나기 위해 코르시카 섬에 도착했다. 이 여행은 나름의 의미가 있었는데, 외부에서 쳐들어온 정복자와 싸우지 않으면 서로 싸우기 일쑤였던 흉폭한 민족이 살았던 그 섬에 일찍이 영국의 어떤 탐험가도 간 적이 없었기 때문이다. 보즈웰은 런던에 살기는 했지만 영국 사람이 아니고 스코틀랜드 사람이었지만, 그 사실이 이 여행의 가치를 낮추지는 않았다.

Bilingual Reading

ON Oct. 13, 1765, 1765년 10월 13일에 **the writer James Boswell** 작가 제임스 보즈웰은 **arrived in Corsica** 코르시카에 도착했다 **to meet the nationalist hero Pasquale Paoli.** 민족주의자 영웅 파스칼레 파올리를 만나기 위해 **The trip was remarkable in part** 그 여행은 어떤 점에서 중요한 의미가 있었다 **because** 왜냐하면 **the island** 그 섬은 **–home to a wild people fighting one another** 서로 싸웠던 난폭한 민족이 살았던 곳 **when not fighting off foreign conquerors** 외국 정복자들과 싸움을 하지 않았던 시절에 **–had never before been explored** 결코 이전에 탐험된 적이 없었다 **by someone from England.** 영국 사람에 의해 **It was no less remarkable** 그 여행은 덜 주목 받은 건 아니다 **because** 왜냐하면 **Boswell, though a resident of London,** 보즈웰은 런던 주민이기는 했지만 **was not English,** 영국 사람이 아닌 **but rather a Scot.** 스코틀랜드 사람이었기 때문에

China slowdown could end upbeing good for U.S.

China's economic slowdown and Beijing's fumbling policy response have battered U.S. markets recently. But a slower-growing China, over the long haul, could be a plus for the U.S.

Headline

China slowdown could end up being good for U.S.

중국의 침체는 결국 미국에게 좋은 일이 될 수 있다.

일반 표현

China slowdown eventually turns out to be good for U.S.

Matrix Core

헤드라인 영어문장은 조동사로 가능성을 나타낸다. ¶

Decoded Core

could ⇒ 미래의 어떤 가능성을 의미. 즉, '될 수도 있다'를 의미 ¶

end up ⇒ 계획하지 않았던 일이 그렇게 되어 버리다 ¶

could end up being good ⇒ 좋은 일이 될 수도 있다 ¶

[14]

Word&Phrase

end up 결국은 ~되다 **:** become eventually turn out to be
fumble 어떤 일을 어설프게 다루다
over the long haul 오랜 기간 동안
could be a plus for the U.S. 미국에게는 플러스가 될 수 있다

Lead Sentence

China's economic slowdown and Beijing's fumbling policy response have battered U.S. markets recently. But a slower-growing China, over the long haul, could be a plus for the U.S.

중국의 경제 침체와 서투른 정책 대응은 최근 미국 시장을 계속 파괴시켰다. 그러나 이전보다 더욱 저성장 하고 있는 상황은 장기적으로 볼 때 미국에게 플러스가 될 수 있다.

Bilingual Reading

China's economic slowdown 중국의 경제 침체와 **and Beijing's fumbling policy response** 서투른 정책 대응은 **have battered U.S. markets recently.** 최근 미국 시장을 계속 파괴시켰다 **But a slower-growing China, over the long haul,** 그러나 이전보다 더욱 저성장 하고 있는 중국은 **could be a plus for the U.S.** 장기적으로 볼 때 미국에게 플러스가 될 수 있다.

Silicon Valley's new philanthropy

THE enduring credo of Silicon Valley is that innovation, not money, is its guiding purpose and that world-changing technology is its true measure of worth.

Headline

Silicon Valley's new philanthropy

실리콘밸리 회사들의
새로운 신념은 자선이다.

일반 표현

Silicon Valley has adopted its new credo.
Silicon Valley's credo is new philanthropy.

Matrix Core

헤드라인 영어문장은 몇 개의 단어로 나타낸다. ¶

Decoded Core

philanthropy ⇒ 자선, 박애, 인류애, 자선 활동 ¶

Silicon Valley ⇒ 샌프란시스코 남부 지역에 위치한 기술 회사 ¶

[15]

Word&Phrase

credo 신조, 신념
business credo 기업정신
enduring 어려움에도 굴하지 않고 이겨내는 : suffer without yielding
guiding purpose 지침이 되는 목표
true measure of worth 가치의 진정한 척도

Lead Sentence

THE enduring credo of Silicon Valley is that innovation, not money, is its guiding purpose and that world-changing technology is its true measure of worth.

돈이 아닌 혁신이라는 실리콘밸리의 영구적인 기업정신은 실리콘밸리의 최우선 목표이며, 세계를 바꾸는 기술이 실리콘밸리의 진정한 가치 척도다.

Bilingual Reading

THE enduring credo of Silicon Valley 실리콘밸리의 영구적인 기업 신념은 **is that innovation,** 혁신이라는 **not money,** 돈이 아닌 **is its guiding purpose** 실리콘밸리의 제일의 목적이며 **and that world-changing technology** 세계를 바꾸는 기술이 **is its true measure of worth.** 실리콘밸리의 진정한 가치 척도다.

Part.3 OPINION

A better way to bring 'Elites' into line

The only good answer is a federal government that stops mass-producing so many vested interests. A rebellion against failed elites-that's the thoughtful explanation of the Donald Trump phenomenon. And it's probably true in some sense. Necessary to add, though, is that "rebelling against elites" is a term to dignify 60-year-olds shaking their fists at Mommy and Daddy.

Headline

A better way to bring 'Elites' into line

미국의 모든 '엘리트'도 다른 계층의 사람들과 동일하게 처우를 받게 만들 수 있는 방법은 무엇인가?

일반 표현

What is a better way to make elites even paid?

Matrix Core

헤드라인 영어문장은 몇 개의 단어로 나타낸다. ¶

Decoded Core

elite ⇒ 여기서는 미국의 노동조합(노조)과 그들의 정치적 후원 기득권자들을 의미 ¶

elite ⇒ 일반적으로 정치적 또는 사회적 면에서 많은 부를 가지고 있는 소수 집단 ¶

bring someone or something into line ⇒ 다른 사람과 비슷하게 만들다 ‡ to force someone to be similar with someone else

[16]

Word&Phrase

mass produce 대량 생산을 하다
mom and daddy 여기서는 '미국 정부'를 의미
dignify 위험을 부여하다, 그럴듯하게 꾸미다

rebellion against failed elites
실패한 기득권자들에 대한 반란
vested interest 기득권

Lead Sentence

The only good answer is a federal government that stops mass-producing so many vested interests. A rebellion against failed elites–that's the thoughtful explanation of the Donald Trump phenomenon. And it's probably true in some sense. Necessary to add, though, is that "rebelling against elites" is a term to dignify 60-year-olds shaking their fists at Mommy and Daddy.

유일한 대답은 다수의 기득권자들을 양산시키는 것을 중단하는 연방정부 구성이다. 실패한 기득권자에 대한 반란– 이것이 바로 도널드 트럼프(미국 공화당 대선주자) 현상에 대한 통찰력 있는 설명이 될 것이다. 그리고 어떤 의미에서는 사실일지 모른다. 그럼에도 '실패한 기득권자에 대한 반란'은 연방정부를 향해 주먹을 흔들어 대는 60대 노인들을 그럴듯하게 꾸민 말이라는 사실은 짚고 넘어가야겠다.

Bilingual Reading

The only good answer 유일한 대답은 **is a federal government** 연방정부다 **that stops** 중단 시키는 **mass-producing so many vested interests.** 많은 기득권자들 양산을 **A rebellion against failed elites** 실패한 기득권자에 대한 반란은 **–that's the thoughtful explanation** 즉, 가져온 생각이 깊은 설명이다 **of the Donald Trump phenomenon.** 도널드 트럼프의 현상이 **And it's probably true in some sense.** 어떤 의미에서는 사실일지 모른다 **Necessary to add, though,** 하지만 첨가할 필요가 있는 것은 **is that "rebelling against elites" is a term** 엘리트에 대한 반란은 **to dignify 60-year-olds shaking their fists** 그들의 주먹을 흔들어 대는 60대 노인들을 그럴듯하게 꾸민 말이다 **at Mommy and Daddy.** 연방정부를 향해

The terrorists have no gun problem

If Europe's antigun laws are so effective, how is it that an immigrant who was on the terrorist watch list in three different countries was able to obtain an AK-47 automatic weapon and a pistol?

Headline

The terrorists have no gun problem

테러리스트들은 총을 구입하는 데 어려움이 없다.

일반 표현

Terrorists have little trouble in obtaining gun.

Matrix Core

헤드라인 영어문장은 리드 문장에서 압축된 의미가 풀린다. ¶

Decoded Core

이해하기 위해 배경을 알면 도움이 된다. 배경을 알지 못할 경우에 헤드라인 문장을 이해하기 위해서 리드 문장을 참조한다.
⇒ 유럽에 총기 단속법이 시행되고 있는데도 테러리스트들은 총을 구입하는 데 어려움이 없다. 왜 그런가? ¶

[17]

Word&Phrase

have no gun problem 총기를 구입하는 데 어려움이 없다
how is it that~ 왜 그런가? ≒ why is it that~?

Lead Sentence

If Europe's antigun laws are so effective, how is it that an immigrant who was on the terrorist watch list in three different countries was able to obtain an AK-47 automatic weapon and a pistol?

유럽의 총기 단속법이 제대로 실효성 있게 시행되고 있다면 3개의 다른 나라에서 테러리스트 명단에 올라 있던 한 이민자가 어떻게 AK-47 자동소총과 권총을 한 자루씩 구입할 수 있었던 것인가?

Bilingual Reading

If Europe's antigun laws 유럽의 총기 단속법이 **are so effective,** 대단히 효과적으로 시행이 되고 있다면 **how is it that an immigrant who was on the terrorist watch list** 어떻게 테러리스트 명단에 올라있던 한 이민자가 **in three different countries** 3개의 다른 나라에서 **was able to obtain** 구입할 수 있었는가 **an AK-47 automatic weapon and a pistol?** AK-47 자동소총 한 자루와 권총 한 자루를

Part. 3 OPINION

Hiding on the internet

Last year a European court discovered a "right to be forgotten" on the Internet, allowing Europeans to demand that search engines remove links in search results to news stories and other accurate information that these people don't want discovered.

Headline

Hiding on the internet

모든 사람은 인터넷 검색 엔진에서 잊혀질 권리를 갖는다.

인터넷 상에서 잊혀지기.

일반 표현

Everyone has a right to be forgotten in search results of internet.

Matrix Core

헤드라인 영어문장 가운데 오피니언은 서론으로 전개된다. ¶

Decoded Core

이해를 위해 배경 지식이 필요하다.
⇒ 2014년에 한 스페인 변호사가 자신을 검색하면 예전에 어려운 경제상황으로 집을 내놓는다는 기사가 검색된다며 구글을 상대로 소송을 했을 때, 유럽사법재판소가 구글에게 이 링크를 인터넷에서 다 제거하라며 원고 승소 판결을 내렸다. '모든 사람은 인터넷에서 잊혀질 수 있는 권리가 있다'고 판결을 내린 기사에서 나온 헤드라인. ¶

[18]

Word&Phrase

impose 부과하다, 짐을 지우다 ; force something unwelcome to be accepted
Google search engine 구글의 검색엔진
search results 검색결과

Lead Sentence

Last year a European court discovered a "right to be forgotten" on the Internet, allowing Europeans to demand that search engines remove links in search results to news stories and other accurate information that these people don't want discovered.

작년에 한 유럽사법재판소는 인터넷에서 "잊혀질 권리"를 인정했고, 검색엔진에 대해 자신에 대한 뉴스와 다른 정보들에 대한 링크를 삭제해 달라는 유럽인들의 요구를 허용했다.

Part.3 OPINION

Bilingual Reading

Last year a European court 작년에 한 유럽사법재판소는 **discovered** 찾아냈고 **a "right to be forgotten"** "잊혀질 권리"를 **on the Internet,** 인터넷 검색엔진에서 **allowing Europeans to demand** 유럽인들의 요구를 허용했다 **that search engines** 검색엔진이 **remove links** 링크를 제거하는 **in search results** 검색결과 내에서 **to news stories** 새로운 이야기에 **and other accurate information** 그리고 다른 축적된 정보를 **that these people don't want discovered.** 사람들이 밝히기를 원치 않는

251

Maybe CEOs aren't pessimistic enough

In the middle of the debate over corporate 'short-termism,' one company bows to investor fears about a rocky future. Short-termism! That's the accusation shrieked at public companies by everyone from Hillary Clinton to Marty Lipton, the famed corporate lawyer who recently proposed that the Securities and Exchange Commission stop requiring companies to file quarterly reports.

Headline

Maybe CEOs aren't pessimistic enough

CEO들은
단기성 이익을 내기에 주력한다.

일반 표현

Maybe most CEOs do not want any business unhopeful.

Matrix Core

헤드라인 영어문장은 기본구조로 나타낸다. ¶

Decoded Core

aren't pessimistic enough ⇒ '충분히 비관적이지 못하다(단기성 이익에)'의 의미 ¶

여기서 함축하는 의미 ⇒ 기업의 CEO들은 단기성 이익에만 집중한다, CEOs focus on short-termism. ¶

[19]

Word&Phrase

short-termism 단기주의, 장기적인 이익을 포기하고 지나칠 정도로 단기적인 이익만 추구하는 노력, 즉, 단기성 이익 추구

quarterly reports 분기별 보고

Lead Sentence

In the middle of the debate over corporate 'short-termism,' one company bows to investor fears about a rocky future. Short-termism! That's the accusation shrieked at public companies by everyone from Hillary Clinton to Marty Lipton, the famed corporate lawyer who recently proposed that the Securities and Exchange Commission stop requiring companies to file quarterly reports.

기업들의 단기성 이익추구에 대한 토론 중에 한 회사는 투자자들의 험난한 미래에 대한 우려에 굴복했다. 단기성 이익추구! 힐러리 클린턴에서부터 미국 증권위원회는 모든 회사로 하여금 분기별 실적보고를 제출하도록 요구하는 일을 중단해야 한다고 제안한 유명한 기업 변호사 마티 립턴에 이르기까지 모든 사람이 공기업에서 부르짖었던 비난의 소리다.

Bilingual Reading

In the middle of the debate 토론 중에 **over corporate 'short-termism,'** 기업 단기성 이익추구에 대한 **one company bows** 한 회사는 굴복했다. **to investor fears about a rocky future.** 투자자들의 험난한 미래에 대한 우려에 **Short-termism!** 단기성 이익추구! **That's the accusation** 그것은 비난이다 **shrieked at public companies** 공기업에서 부르짖었던 **by everyone** 모든 사람에 의한 **from Hillary Clinton** 힐러리 클린턴에서부터 **to Marty Lipton,** 마티 립턴에 이르기까지 **the famed corporate lawyer** 그는 유명한 기업 변호사로 **who recently proposed** 최근 요구했다 **that the Securities and Exchange Commission** 미국 증권위원회는 **stop requiring** 요구를 중단해야 한다고 **companies to file quarterly reports.** 모든 회사로 하여금 분기별 실적보고를 제출하도록 하는

Part.3 OPINION

253

Making government logical

Obama is requiring government to use behavioral insights to simplify forms and reduce burdens.

Headline

Making government logical 합리적인 정부를 만들다.

일반 표현

Obama wants U.S government to be logical.

Matrix Core

헤드라인 영어문장은 이해를 돕기 위해 뒤에서부터 읽어보기도 한다. ¶

Decoded Core

Making government logical ⇒ logical government making, 합리적인 정부 만들기 ¶

logical ⇒ 합리적인 ¶

Word&Phrase

require government to use behavioral insight 행동적 통찰력을 발휘하다
simplify 간소화하다
reduce burdens 부담을 줄이다

Lead Sentence

Obama is requiring government to use behavioral insights to simplify forms and reduce burdens.

오바마 대통령은 행정양식을 간소화하고 부담을 줄이기 위해 정부가 행동적 통찰력을 발휘해줄 것을 요구하고 있다.

Bilingual Reading

Obama 오바마는 **is requiring** 요구하고 있다 **government** 정부가 **to use behavioral insights** 행동적 통찰력을 발휘해줄 것을 **to simplify forms** 행정양식을 간소화하고 **and reduce burdens.** 부담을 줄이기 위해

My tax overhaul to unleash 4% growth

Three income-tax rates: 10%, 25% and 28%, plus a 20% corporate rate and immediate expensing on new investment. Under President Obama, Americans have now endured six years of tax increases, endless regulation, vast new federal programs and $8 trillion in added debt. The president told us this "stimulus" would jump-start the economy. Instead, we got an anemic economy growing at barely 2% a year.

Headline

My tax overhaul to unleash 4% growth

4% 인상된 세금을 내려면 나의 세금내역이 충분히 검토되어야 한다.

일반 표현

My tax should be overhauled to unleash 4% hike.

Matrix Core

헤드라인 영어문장은 조동사를 생략하고 단순시제를 쓴다. ¶

Decoded Core

overhaul ⇒ should be overhauled, 충분히 검토되어야 한다 ¶

overhaul ⇒ 검토하다 ¶

unleash ⇒ 석방시키다, 주머니에서 내어놓다 ※ set free ¶

4% grow ⇒ 세금이 4% 인상되었다는 의미 ¶

[21]

Word&Phrase

income-tax 소득세
corporate rate 법인세
immediate expensing (공장 또는 장비) 무형 자산세

Lead Sentence

Three income-tax rates: 10%, 25% and 28%, plus a 20% corporate rate and immediate expensing on new investment. Under President Obama, Americans have now endured six years of tax increases, endless regulation, vast new federal programs and $8 trillion in added debt. The president told us this "stimulus" would jump-start the economy. Instead, we got an anemic economy growing at barely 2% a year.

소득세에는 세 종류가 있다. 10%, 25% 그리고 28%, 거기에 법인세 20%, 그리고 새로운 투자에 대한 무형 자산세(공장 또는 장비). 오바마 정부 하에서 지난 6년 동안 미국인들은 세금 인상, 끝없는 규제, 엄청난 연방정부 프로그램 그리고 8조 달러의 추가 부채를 미국인들은 참아왔다. 대통령은 이런 부양책이 경기를 활성화 시킬 것으로 말을 해왔다. 하지만 실제로는 일 년에 겨우 2%라는 허약한 성장율을 기록했다.

Bilingual Reading

Three income-tax rates: 3종류의 소득세가 있다 **10%, 25% and 28%, plus a 20% corporate rate** 10%, 25% 그리고 28%, 거기에 법인세 20% **and immediate expensing on new investment.** 그리고 새로운 투자에 대한 무형 자산세(공장 또는 장비). **Under President Obama,** 오바마 정부 하에서 **Americans have now endured** 미국인들은 참아왔다 **six years of tax increases,** 지난 6년 동안의 세금 인상 **endless regulation,** 끝없는 규제 **vast new federal programs** 엄청난 연방정부 프로그램 **and $8 trillion in added debt.** 그리고 8조 달러 상당의 추가 부채를 **The president** 대통령은 **told us** 우리에게 말을 해왔다 **this "stimulus"** 이런 경기 부양책은 **would jump-start the economy.** 경기를 활성화 시킬 것으로 **Instead,** 하지만 **we** 우리는 **got an anemic economy growing** 허약한 성장을 했다 **at barely 2% a year.** 일 년에 겨우 2%라는

Trump and China give opposing lessons in failure

Presidential hopeful Donald Trump says bankruptcy in America is no reason to be embarrassed. In debt-laden China it's different: the state throws money at avoiding failure. Both positions end in the same place. If going bust brings too much pain or too little, disaster follows.

Headline

Trump and China give opposing lessons in failure

트럼프와 중국은 실패에 대해서 서로 반대의 교훈을 내놓았다.

일반 표현

Trump and China have come up with opposing lesson in failure.

Matrix Core

헤드라인 영어문장은 완료형을 현재로 나타낸다. ¶

Decoded Core

give ⇒ have given ¶

opposing lesson ⇒ 반대되는 ¶

give opposing lessons ⇒ come up with opposing lesson ¶

[22]

Word&Phrase

no reason to be embarrassed 당황할 이유가 없는
debt-laden 많은 부채를 지고 있는 : owing a lot money
going bust 진행되고 있는 실패

Lead Sentence

Presidential hopeful Donald Trump says bankruptcy in America is no reason to be embarrassed. In debt-laden China it's different: the state throws money at avoiding failure. Both positions end in the same place. If going bust brings too much pain or too little, disaster follows.

대통령 후보인 도널드 트럼프는 미국에서의 파산은 부끄러워할 이유가 없다고 말한다. 많은 부채를 안고 있는 중국에서의 파산은 좀 다르다. 중국은 실패를 피하기 위해 돈을 뿌리고 있다. 두 가지 입장이 모두 같은 입장이다. 현재 이 파산이 너무 많은 고통을 가져다주든지 또는 너무 적은 고통을 가져다준다 하더라도 재난은 그 뒤에 따라온다.

Bilingual Reading

Presidential hopeful Donald Trump 대통령 후보 도널드 트럼프는 **says** 말한다 **bankruptcy in America** 미국의 파산은 **is no reason to be embarrassed.** 당황할 이유는 없다고 **In debt-laden China** 많은 부채를 안고 있는 중국은 **it's different:** 좀 다르다 즉, **the state** 그 국가는 **throws money** 돈을 뿌리고 있다 **at avoiding failure.** 실패를 피하기 위해 **Both positions** 두 가지 입장이 **end in the same place.** 모두 같은 입장이다 **If going bust** 현재 이 파산이 **brings too much pain** 너무 많은 고통을 가져다주든지 **or too little,** 또는 너무 적은 고통을 가져다준다 하더라도 **disaster follows.** 재난은 그 뒤에 따라온다.

Part.3 OPINION

Singapore at 50 ought to loosen up

Pragmatic policy and hard work helped the city-state attain a level of prosperity unimaginable five decades ago. Future success depends on dialling back state capitalism and paternalism, and spawning more entrepreneurs. Few will bet against Singapore continuing to defy the odds.

Headline

Singapore at 50 ought to loosen up

건국 50주년이 된 싱가포르는 이제 긴장을 풀어야 한다.

일반 표현

Singapore of 50 years needs to be less tight.

Matrix Core

헤드라인 영어문장은 몇 개의 단어나 기본구조로 나타낸다. ¶

Decoded Core

Singapore at 50 ⇒ 건국 50주년이 된 싱가포르 ¶

ought ⇒ 해야 한다, 필요하다, need의 의미 ¶

loosen up ⇒ 긴장을 풀다 ⁝ become loose, become less tight ¶

ought to loosen up ⇒ 관용적으로 '긴장을 풀다'의 의미 ¶

[23]

Word&Phrase

immigrant's right advocate 이민변호사
commit fewer crimes 범죄를 보다 적게 저지르다
native-born 본토박이
assimilate ~에 동화되다

Lead Sentence

Pragmatic policy and hard work helped the city-state attain a level of prosperity unimaginable five decades ago. Future success depends on dialling back state capitalism and paternalism, and spawning more entrepreneurs. Few will bet against Singapore continuing to defy the odds.

실용 정책과 노력이 이 도시국가에 50년 전에는 상상할 수 없었던 높은 수준의 번영을 가져왔다. 미래의 성공은 국가가 관리하는 자본주의와 가부장주의의 강도를 줄이고 더 많은 기업가를 배출하는 데 달렸다. 미래에는 성공의 가능성을 거부하는 싱가포르에 투자하는 사람은 별로 없을 것이다.

Bilingual Reading

Pragmatic policy and hard work 실용 정책과 노력이 h**elped the city-state** 그 도시국가에 **attain** 가져오게 했다 **a level of prosperity** 높은 수준의 번영을 **unimaginable five decades ago.** 50년 전에는 상상할 수 없었던 **Future success** 미래의 성공은 **depends on** 달렸다 **dialling back** 강도를 줄이는 데 **state capitalism** 국가가 관리하는 자본주의와 **and paternalism,** 가부장주의의 **and spawning** 그리고 배출하는 데 **more entrepreneurs.** 더 많은 기업가를 **Few will bet** 투자하는 사람은 별로 없을 것이다 **against Singapore** 싱가포르에 **continuing** 거부하는 **to defy the odds.** 미래에는 성공의 가능성을

Asia's sly austerity makes debt challenge worse

The region's companies and households are nursing a debt hangover. Blame China's credit binge and cheap Western money. But tight fiscal policies are pushing the region in the wrong direction by worsening an economic slowdown. It's time for governments to loosen the purse strings.

Headline

Asia's sly austerity makes debt challenge worse

아시아 국가들의
어설픈 긴축이 독약이 되었다.

일반 표현

Asia's austerity turns into poison.

Matrix Core

헤드라인 영어문장은 기본구조로 나타낸다. ¶

Decoded Core

debt challenge ⇒ 빠르게 늘어나는 부채, 부채 문제
⁝ debt problem ¶

sly ⇒ 은밀한, clandestine이나 unofficial도 사용 가능 ¶

[24]

Word&Phrase

credit binge 신용담보 대출 건 확대
cheap western money 이율이 낮은 유럽이나 미국에서 들어온 돈
blame 비난하다, 원인을 누구에게 돌리다
hangover 숙취, 약 등의 부작용

Lead Sentence

The region's companies and households are nursing a debt hangover. Blame China's credit binge and cheap Western money. But tight fiscal policies are pushing the region in the wrong direction by worsening an economic slowdown. It's time for governments to loosen the purse strings.

아시아의 회사와 가계들이 부채 후유증을 겪고 있다. 중국의 신용대출 환대 그리고 값싼 미국과 유럽 발 자금이 그 원인이다. 그러나 긴축 금융 정책들은 경제적 침체를 악화시킴으로써 이 지역을 완전히 잘못된 방향으로 내몰고 있다. 지금은 각 정부들이 지갑의 끈을 풀 때다.

Bilingual Reading

The region's companies and households 그 지역의 회사와 가계들이 **are nursing a debt hangover.** 부채 후유증을 맞이하고 있다 **Blame** 원인은 **China's credit binge** 중국의 신용대출 확대와 **and cheap Western money.** 값싼 서구세력의 돈이다 **But tight fiscal policies** 그러나 긴축 금융 정책들은 **are pushing** 내몰고 있다 **the region** 이 지역을 **in the wrong direction** 잘못된 방향으로 **by worsening an economic slowdown.** 경제적 침체를 악화시킴으로써 **It's time** 지금은 **for governments** 각 정부들이 **to loosen the purse strings.** 지갑의 끈을 풀 때다.

Part. 3 OPINION

Singapore could use a fresh approach to water

The city-state built its economic success partly on carefully managing scarce H_2O and reducing reliance on foreign sources. Now Singapore wants to be self-sufficient. But with the population set to double, the quest for water independence risks becoming a distracting pipe dream.

Headline

Singapore could use a fresh approach to water

싱가포르는 일찍이 물 관리 정책을 수립했다.

일반 표현

Singapore could use early focus on fresh water.

Matrix Core

헤드라인 영어문장은 리드 문장에서 압축된 의미가 풀린다. ¶

Decoded Core

배경을 알면 이해하기 쉽다.
⇒ 싱가포르는 일찍부터 H_2O 관리(물 관리)에 신경을 기울여 왔다. ¶

fresh approach to water ⇒ Early focus on water, 일찍이 말레이시아가 강물을 막았던 까닭에 물 관리를 철저히 함으로써 오늘의 경제적 성공을 가져올 수 있었다. ¶

[25]

Word&Phrase

Carefully managing scarce H₂O 조심스럽게 부족한 물 관리를 하다
foreign sources 외국 수원(말레이시아로부터 흐르는 강물)
pipe dream 몽상, 꿈같은 이야기
distract 관심이 멀어지다, 주의를 빼앗다

Lead Sentence

The city-state built its economic success partly on carefully managing scarce H₂O and reducing reliance on foreign sources. Now Singapore wants to be self-sufficient. But with the population set to double, the quest for water independence risks becoming a distracting pipe dream.

이 도시국가는 조심스럽게 부족한 물을 관리하고 외국으로부터 오는 수원에 대한 의존도를 줄임으로써 경제적 성공을 이룩했다. 이제 싱가포르는 자급자족을 원하고 있다. 그러나 인구가 두 배로 늘어나면서 물 자급 추구는 몽상으로 끝날 위기에 있다.

Bilingual Reading

The city-state 이 도시국가는 **built its economic success** 경제적 성공을 이룩했다 **partly** 어느 정도 **on carefully managing scarce H₂O** 조심스럽게 부족한 물을 관리하고 **and reducing reliance on foreign sources.** 외국의 수원 의존도를 줄임으로써 **Now Singapore** 이제 싱가포르는 **wants to be self-sufficient.** 자급자족을 원하고 있다 **But with the population set to double,** 그러나 인구가 두 배로 늘어남으로써 **the quest for water independence** 물 자급 추구는 **risks** 위기에 있다 **becoming a distracting pipe dream.** 혼미한 몽상이 되는

265

Edward Hadas: Nikkei joins demographic denial cult

Nikkei is the latest Japanese company to look for growth outside the shrinking domestic market. Its Financial Times purchase may work out, but the approach is flawed. Few companies can profitably escape their demographic destiny. It may be better to accept steady decline.

Headline

Edward Hadas: Nikkei joins demographic denial cult

일본의 인구가 줄어들고 있으므로 ‹파이낸셜 타임스› 매입은 잘못된 것이다.

일반 표현

Nikei has made a wrong acquisition of Financial Times thanks to decling population.

Matrix Core

헤드라인 영어문장은 리드 문장에서 압축의 의미가 풀린다. ¶

Decoded Core

이해를 돕기 위해 배경지식이 필요하다. ⇒ 니케이는 영국 ‹파이낸셜 타임스›를 최근 매입했다. 그러나 인구 유입률과 출생률이 낮아지면서 세대 당 인구가 약 30%씩 줄고 있다. 많은 회사들은 이제 해외시장으로 나가기를 원한다. 이런 시기에 니케이가 ‹파이낸셜 타임스›를 매입한 것은 인구 숫자를 감안할 때 잘못된 생각이다. ¶

demographic denial cult ⇒ 현재 통계학적 인구 수가 잘못되었다는 전반적인 생각 ¶

joins ⇒ has joined ¶

Edward Hadas ⇒ 온라인 뉴스 ‹Breakingviews›의 칼럼니스트 ¶

[26]

Word&Phrase

cult 숭배, 광신
demographic 연령별 인구 집단
flaw 결함, 흠

Lead Sentence

Nikkei is the latest Japanese company to look for growth outside the shrinking domestic market. Its Financial Times purchase may work out, but the approach is flawed. Few companies can profitably escape their demographic destiny. It may be better to accept steady decline.

니케이는 규모가 줄어드는 국내시장 밖에서 성장을 찾아야 하는 마지막 일본 기업이다. ‹파이낸셜 타임스› 의 매입은 성공할 수 있을지 모른다. 그러나 그 접근 방법은 잘못된 것이다. 어떤 회사도 줄어드는 인구를 무시하고 이익을 내기는 어렵다. 점차적으로 줄어드는 운명을 받아들이는 것이 좋을지도 모른다.

Bilingual Reading

Nikkei 니케이는 **is the latest Japanese company** 마지막 일본 기업이다 **to look for growth outside** 밖에서 성장을 찾아야 하는 **the shrinking domestic market.** 규모가 줄어드는 국내시장 **Its Financial Times purchase** 파이낸셜 타임스의 매입은 **may work out,** 성공할 수 있을지 모른다 **but the approach is flawed.** 그러나 그 접근 방법은 잘못된 것이다 **Few companies** 어떤 회사도 **can profitably** 이익을 내기는 어렵다 **escape their demographic destiny.** 줄어드는 인구를 무시하고 **It may be better** 더 나을지 모른다 **to accept steady decline.** 점차적으로 줄어드는 운명을 받아들이는 것이

I am paying for your expensive medicine

We need to evaluate whether new drugs are really worthwhile, because the costs are widely, although perhaps invisibly, shared.

Headline

I am paying for your expensive medicine

당신의 값비싼 약값을 내가 지불하고 있다.

일반 표현

Some portion of medicine cost is also on me.

Matrix Core

헤드라인 영어문장은 몇 개의 단어나 기본구조로 나타낸다. ¶

헤드라인 영어문장은 진행형으로 상황이 진행되고 있음을 나타낸다. ¶

Decoded Core

am paying for ⇒ 지불하고 있다
현재 진행형을 사용하여 실제 진행되고 있는 상황을 나타낸다. ¶

expensive medicine ⇒ 값비싼 약값 ¶

your expensive medicine ⇒ 타인의 비싼 약값 ¶

[27]

Word&Phrase

although 부사구를 수동형 동사구 사이
즉 are widely와 shared 중간에 삽입한 독특한 문장 형태다.
evaluate 평가하다
invisibly 눈에 안 보이는

Lead Sentence

We need to evaluate whether new drugs are really worthwhile, because the costs are widely, although perhaps invisibly, shared.

우리는 새로운 약이 실제적으로 그만한 가치가 있는지 평가할 필요가 있다. 왜냐하면 약값은 전반적으로 비록 눈에 드러나지 않지만 소비자 모두가 분담하고 있기 때문이다.

Bilingual Reading

We need to evaluate 우리는 평가할 필요가 있다 **whether new drugs** 새로운 약이 **are really worthwhile,** 실제적으로 그만한 가치가 있는지 아닌지 **because** 왜냐하면 **the costs** 약값은 **are widely,** 전반적으로 **although perhaps invisibly,** 비록 눈에 보이지는 않지만 **shared.** 소비자 모두가 분담하고 있기 때문이다.

Part. 4
LIFE

INTERNATIONAL BUSINESS OPINION LIFE

Part.4 LIFE

Attitudes shift on paid leave: Dads sue, too

As more men take time off work when a baby is born, many are also filing lawsuits and complaints about how much time they can take and setbacks they endure when they return to work.

Headline

Attitudes shift on paid leave: Dads sue, too

유급휴가에 대한 인식이 바뀌고 있다: 아버지들은 소송도 한다.

일반 표현

Dads shift their attitude on paid leave and sue, too.

Matrix Core

헤드라인 영어문장은 대체로 be 동사를 생략한다. ¶

Decoded Core

shift ⇒ are shifting 바꾸고 있다
Dads are shifting their attitudes on paid leave.
아버지들은 유급휴가에 대한 태도를 바꾸고 있다. ¶

Dads sue, too ⇒ 아버지들은 소송까지 한다
Dads are suing too when they return to work 휴가를 마치고 회사로 돌아온 후 소송까지 한다. ¶

[01]

Word&Phrase

take time off work 직장에서 시간을 내다
file lawsuit 소송하다
complaints 불만, 불평
setback 불이익, 좌절

Lead Sentence

As more men take time off work when a baby is born, many are also filing lawsuits and complaints about how much time they can take and setbacks they endure when they return to work.

남성들이 육아휴직을 신청하는 추세가 높아지면서 관련 소송을 제기하는 이들의 숫자도 늘어나고 있는데, 이는 사용 가능한 휴가 일수와 복직 후 감당해야 하는 불이익에 관한 불만으로 인한 것이다.

Bilingual Reading

As more men 더 많은 남성들이 **take time off work** 회사에서 휴가를 냄으로 인해 **when a baby is born,** 아기가 태어날 때 **many** 많은 사람들은 **are also filing lawsuits** 소송을 제기하기도 하고 **and complaints** 불평하기도 한다 **about how much time they can take** 그들이 얻을 수 있는 시간이 얼마나 되며 **and setbacks they endure** 그들이 겪어야 하는 불이익에 관해 **when they return to work.** 그들이 돌아왔을 때

What Venture Capital and Art Have in Common

A unicorn appeared at a Silicon Valley event Wednesday night-in a screen print by the British artist Mark Wallinger. Unicorns of the tech type-startups with a valuation over $1 billion-also were discussed at a cocktail party on the top floor of the Epiphany Hotel in Palo Alto.

Headline

What Venture Capital and Art Have in Common

벤처 자본과 예술 사이의 공통점은 무엇인가?

일반 표현

What is something common venture capital has with art?

Matrix Core

헤드라인 영어문장은 의문부호를 생략한다. ¶

Decoded Core

have in common ⇒ ~와 공통점을 가지다 ⁞ have (something) in common (with someone) ¶

What venture capital and art have in common ⇒ **v**enture capital has (what) in common with art. 즉 벤처자본은 예술과 어떤 공통점을 가지고 있는가? ¶

[02]

Word&Phrase

unicorn 최근 투자 산업에서 소개된 용어, 전자화폐
Unicorns 유니콘 사, 최근 회사 가치가 10억 달러로 치솟은 기업
startup 신생기업

Lead Sentence

A unicorn appeared at a Silicon Valley event Wednesday night-in a screen print by the British artist Mark Wallinger. Unicorns of the tech type-startups with a valuation over $1 billion-also were discussed at a cocktail party on the top floor of the Epiphany Hotel in Palo Alto.

유니콘 전자화폐가 수요일 저녁 실리콘밸리 이벤트에 영국 예술가 마크 월링거가 도안한 스크린프린트로 모습을 나타내었다. 10억 달러 이상 가치의 신생기업인 테크 타입의 유니콘 사는 팔로 알토에 있는 에피파니 호텔 옥상에서 있었던 칵테일파티에서도 많은 이들의 입에 오르내렸다.

Bilingual Reading

A unicorn 유니콘 전자화폐가 **appeared** 모습을 나타내었다 **at a Silicon Valley event Wednesday night** 수요일 저녁 실리콘밸리 이벤트에 **-in a screen print** 스크린프린트로 **by the British artist Mark Wallinger.** 영국 예술가 마크 월링거가 도안한 **Unicorns of the tech type** 테크 타입의 유니콘 사는 **-startups with a valuation over $1 billion** 10억 달러 이상 가치의 신생기업으로 **-also were discussed** 역시 많이 거론되었다 **at a cocktail party** 칵테일파티에서도 **on the top floor of the Epiphany Hotel in Palo Alto.** 팔로 알토에 있는 에피파니 호텔 옥상에서 있었던

'The Odyssey' takes a populist turn as a musical

Professional actors like Brandon Victor Dixon and amateur entertainers combine to turn this adaptation of Homer's poem into a vibrant tapestry.

Headline

'The Odyssey' takes a populist turn as a musical

뉴욕 뮤지컬 '오디세이'는 포퓰리스트 장면을 뮤지컬로 각색했다.

일반 표현

The Odyssey has adapted a populist turn into a musical.

Matrix Core

헤드라인 영어문장은 완료형을 현재로 나타낸다. ¶

Decoded Core

take ⇒ has taken ¶

take a populist turn as a musical ⇒ 포퓰리스트 장면을 뮤지컬로 각색하다 ¶

take something turn as ~ ⇒ 무엇을 ~으로 바꾸다 ¶

[03]

Word&Phrase

tapestry 양탄자, 다른 물건, 다른 사람, 그리고 다른 색깔로 만들어진 작품

Lead Sentence

Professional actors like Brandon Victor Dixon and amateur entertainers combine to turn this adaptation of Homer's poem into a vibrant tapestry.

브랜든 빅터 딕슨 같은 전문 배우들과 아마추어 연예인들이 연합해 호머의 시를 개작하여 생생한 작품으로 만들었다.

Bilingual Reading

Professional actors 직업배우들과 **like Brandon Victor Dixon** 브랜든 빅터 딕슨 같은 **and amateur entertainers** 아마추어 연예인들이 **combine** 결합하여 **to turn this adaptation of Homer's poem** 호머의 시를 개작하여 **into a vibrant tapestry.** 생생한 작품으로 만들었다

Pluto and pentaquarks boost non-profit science

NASA's distant mission has gone viral, while European researchers have accidentally proven a 50-year-old theory about matter. Open-ended research at, say, Google is valuable, but government-funded basic science offers unmatched intellectual gains and unexpected practical benefits.

Headline

Pluto and pentaquarks boost non-profit science

명왕성과 펜타쿼크는 기초 과학의 수준을 크게 발전시켰다.

일반 표현

Pluto and pentaquarks hiked up basic science.

Matrix Core

헤드라인 영어문장은 발생한 사실을 현재로 나타낸다. ¶

Decoded Core

boost ⇒ 끌어올리다
elevate, hike, elevate, develop 단어를 일반적으로 사용한다. ¶

non-profit ⇒ 비영리 ¶

pentaquark ⇒ 펜타쿼크, 최근 발견된 새로운 소립자 ¶

[04]

Word&Phrase

Pluto 명왕성
quarks 원자보다 작은 입자
basic science 기초과학

Lead Sentence

NASA's distant mission has gone viral, while European researchers have accidentally proven a 50-year-old theory about matter. Open-ended research at, say, Google is valuable, but government-funded basic science offers unmatched intellectual gains and unexpected practical benefits.

나사의 원거리 임무는 입소문을 통해 빠르게 퍼졌고, 한편 유럽의 과학자들도 이 물질에 대한 50년 된 이론을 우연히 입증했다. 말하자면 구글의 개방적인 연구도 값지지만, 정부 지원 기초과학은 비할 데 없는 지적 유익과 기대되지 않았던 유익을 주고 있다.

Bilingual Reading

NASA's distant mission 나사의 원거리 임무는 **has gone viral,** 입소문을 통해 빠르게 퍼졌고 **while European researchers** 한편 유럽의 과학자들도 **have accidentally proven** 우연히 입증했다 **a 50-year-old theory about matter.** 이 물질에 대한 50년 된 이론을 **Open-ended research** 개방적인 연구도 **at, say, Google is valuable,** 말하자면 구글의 값진 연구지만 **but government-funded basic science** 정부 지원 기초과학은 **offers unmatched intellectual gains** 비할 데 없는 지적 유익과 **and unexpected practical benefits.** 기대되지 않았던 유익을 주고 있다

Tactic born as a coaching trick is in Vogue

The inside-out forehand, once seen as a sign of a shaky player, has become "the most devastating shot in the game."

Headline

Tactic born as a coaching trick is in Vogue

'인사이드아웃 포핸드' 기술이 유행이다.

일반 표현

Inside-out forehand tactic is in vogue.

Matrix Core

헤드라인 영어문장은 기본구조로 나타낸다. ¶

Decoded Core

tactic born as a coachinbg trick ⇒ 코트에서 당신의 기량을 크게 강화시킬 수 있는 강타 ¶

in vogue ⇒ 유행이다 ¶

tactic ⇒ inside out forehand ¶

tactic ⇒ 전략, 작전, 수단 ¶

coach ⇒ 운동 경기 기술을 지도하고 훈련시키다 ¶

trick ⇒ 요령, 재주, 속이다 ¶

vogue ⇒ 유행, 인기 ¶

[05]

Word&Phrase

shaky player 기량을 발휘 못하는 선수
the most devastating shot 가장 파괴적인 강타

Lead Sentence

The inside-out forehand, once seen as a sign of a shaky player, has become "the most devastating shot in the game."

한때 불안정한 선수의 표시로 보였던 인사이드 아웃 포핸드(the inside-out forehand) 전략은 이제 경기에서 가장 강력한 공격법이 되었다.

Bilingual Reading

The inside-out forehand, 인사이드-아웃 포핸드 전략은 **once seen as a sign of a shaky player,** 한때 불안정한 선수의 표시로 보였던 **has become "the most devastating shot in the game."** 경기에서 가장 파괴적인 강타가 되었다

Allianz takes Pimco's fall from grace in stride

With assets under management and profit falling, the German insurer's Pimco arm is still reeling from boss Bill Gross' acrimonious exit. But Allianz can ride it out. Its insurance division and a growing in-house asset manager mean it can stick to full-year targets.

Headline

Allianz takes Pimco's fall from grace in stride

알리안츠는 좋았던 영업실적 이후 핌코의 실적 부진에 대한 책임을 인정하고 있다.

일반 표현

Allianz takes responsibility for Pimco's poor result after its good performance.

Matrix Core

헤드라인 영어문장은 리드 문장에서 압축된 의미가 풀린다. ¶

Decoded Core

배경을 알고 있으면 헤드라인 문장에 대한 이해가 쉬워진다.
⇒ 영업실적은 좋지 않지만 핌코의 보험과 자산 관리 부서에서는 떨어진 영업실적을 다시 회복시키려고 노력하고 있다. 알리안츠는 핌코의 영업실적 부진에 대한 책임을 느끼고 있다. ¶

take one's fall ⇒ 책임을 인정하다 ¶

Pimco's fall ⇒ 핌코(채권 투자 펀드업체)의 영업실적 부진 ¶

grace in stride ⇒ 큰 행보의 영광, 좋았던 발전 ¶

Allianz ⇒ 알리안츠. 독일 생명보험사이자 핌코의 모기업 ¶

Pimco ⇒ Pacific Investment Management Company, 태평양 투자 관리 회사 ¶

[06]

Word&Phrase

asset 재산, 이점
reel 비틀거리다, 휘청대다, 릴
acrimonious 호된, 매서운

Lead Sentence

With assets under management and profit falling, the German insurer's Pimco arm is still reeling from boss Bill Gross' acrimonious exit. But Allianz can ride it out. Its insurance division and a growing in-house asset manager mean it can stick to full-year targets.

운용자산과 이익의 하락 추세 속에 독일 보험사의 자회사인 핌코는 사장 빌 그로스가 험악한 분위기 속에 회사를 떠난 뒤에도 여전히 휘청거리고 있다. 그러나 알리안츠는 이 상황을 잘 헤쳐 나갈 수 있다. 기업의 보험과와 규모가 커져가는 사내 자산 관리를 바탕으로 금년 목표 이익을 달성할 수 있다고 추측할 수 있다.

Bilingual Reading

With assets under management and profit falling, 운용자산과 이익이 떨어지고 있으므로 **the German insurer's Pimco arm** 독일 보험사의 Pimco 부문은 **is still reeling** 여전히 휘청거리고 있다 **from boss Bill Gross' acrimonious exit.** 사장 빌 그로스가 험악하게 회사를 떠나자 **But Allianz** 그러나 알리안츠는 **can ride it out.** 이 상황을 잘 헤쳐 나갈 수 있다 **Its insurance division** 이 회사의 보험과와 **and a growing in-house asset manager** 규모가 커져가는 사내 자산 관리 **mean it can stick to full-year targets.** 금년 목표치를 달성할 수 있다는 생각이다.

A new incarnation in London, with centuries of history

The Old War Office, whose interior resembles a grand country house more closely than it does government offices, is to become a hotel and residential development.

Headline

A new incarnation in London, with centuries of history

수 세기의 역사를 지닌 런던에 새로운 출현

수 세기의 역사를 지닌 한 웅장한 모습의 빌딩이 런던에 나타났다.

일반 표현

A newly imposing heritage building with centuries of history was built in London.

Matrix Core

헤드라인 영어문장은 동사 없이 몇 개의 단어로 나타낸다. ¶

Decoded Core

incarnation ⇒ 새로운 현신, 새로운 모습으로 탄생 ¶

with centuries of history ⇒ a new incarnation in London'을 수식하는 형용사구 ¶

[07]

Word&Phrase

resembles ~more closely than something 무엇이라기보다 ~을 더 닮다
government office 정부 사무실, 정부 청사
residential 주거지, 주택의

Lead Sentence

The Old War Office, whose interior resembles a grand country house more closely than it does government offices, is to become a hotel and residential development.

내부가 정부 청사라기보다 거대한 시골 저택을 더 닮은 옛 전쟁 사무처는 호텔 또는 주거단지가 될 예정이다.

Bilingual Reading

The Old War Office, 옛 전쟁 사무처는 **whose interior resembles a grand country house more closely** 그 내부가 거대한 시골 저택을 더 닮은 **than it does government offices,** 정부 사무실을 닮았다기보다 **is to become a hotel and residential development.** 호텔 또는 주거단지가 될 예정이다.

Indian automaker Tata aims to restore Jaguar's cachet in U.S.

Sales of Jaguar, the British brand acquired in 2008 from Ford by Tata, along with Land Rover, have been lagging this year.

Headline

Indian automaker Tata aims to restore Jaguar's cachet in U.S.

인도의 자동차업체 '타타'는 미국 내의 재규어 판매가 완전히 회복될 것을 목표로 한다.

일반 표현

Tata motors of India wants a full-fledged recovery in demand of Jaguar in the U.S.

Matrix Core

헤드라인 영어문장은 기본구조로 나타낸다. ¶

Decoded Core

aim to ⇒ 주로 의도하다, 또는 어떤 목적을 위해 나아가다
※ to direct for a particular purpose ¶

cachet ⇒ 카셰. 높은 신분의 인정, 특징, 보증의 인장, 관인 ¶

Tata ⇒ 타타. 인도 자동차 생산업체, 2008년에 재규어와 랜드로버를 인수했다. ¶

[08]

Word&Phrase

restore 회복시키다 : recover
acquire 인수, 구입
lag 지연, 더딘, 느린, 처지다

Lead Sentence

Sales of Jaguar, the British brand acquired in 2008 from Ford by Tata, along with Land Rover, have been lagging this year.

타타가 2008년 포드로부터 매입한 영국 브랜드 '재규어'의 판매는 랜드로버와 더불어 올해 실적이 부실한 상태다.

Bilingual Reading

Sales of Jaguar, 재규어 판매는 **the British brand** 영국 브랜드인 **acquired in 2008 from Ford by Tata,** 타타가 2008년 포드로부터 매입한 **along with Land Rover,** 랜드로버와 더불어 **have been lagging this year.** 올해 판매가 계속 부실했다.

Google's driverless cars run into problem: cars with drivers

The cars have been involved in a smattering of minor accidents because they observe traffic laws to the letter–and people don't.

Headline

Google's driverless cars run into problem: cars with drivers

구글의 운전자 없는
셀프 드라이빙 자동차가
장애물을 만났다:
운전자 있는 차들이다

일반 표현

Google's self-driving car has an odd safety problem, because it just follow the letter of the law.

Matrix Core

헤드라인 영어문장은 기본구조로 나타낸다. ¶

Decoded Core

run into ⇒ 우연히 만나다, 마주하다, 나타나다 ¶

driverless car ⇒ 운전자가 필요 없는 자동차 ¶

problem ⇒ 즉 문제점은 '운전자 있는 차'라는 의미 ⁂ 구글의 셀프 드라이빙 차는 교통법에 쓰인 문자만 따르기 때문에 가끔 안전문제를 야기한다는 뜻으로 운전자 없는 차가 운전자 있는 차를 만날 때 발생하는 문제점이라는 흥미 있는 표현 ¶

[09]

Word&Phrase

smattering 극소수의, 적은 양의 : a small amount of something
smattering of minor accident 아주 적은 양의 교통사고
observe traffic law to the letter 글자대로만 법규를 지키다
odd 가끔 : occasional

Lead Sentence

The cars have been involved in a smattering of minor accidents because they observe traffic laws to the letter- and people don't.

자동차들은 사람을 살피지 않고 교통법규의 글자만 보고 움직이므로 가벼운 교통사고를 내곤 했다.

Bilingual Reading

The cars 자동차들은 **have been involved** 관련이 있다 **in a smattering of minor accidents** 가벼운 일부 교통사고와 **because** 왜냐하면 **they** 그들은 **observe traffic laws to the letter** 교통법규 글자만 살피므로 **-and people don't.** 사람은 살피지 않고

As Americans figure out the roundabout, it spreads across the U.S.

Navigating roundabouts can be confusing, but they tend to reduce congestion and accidents at intersections. One is coming to the Bronx.

Headline

As Americans figure out the roundabout, it spreads across the U.S.

미국인들이 로터리를
이해하게 되면서
미국 전역으로 퍼지고 있다.

일반 표현

'Stop sign has been replaced with' drive roundabout,'
it is reducing congestion on the clogged road in U.S.
Americans have adopted a new traffic system to go roundabout,
the new law spreeds across the U.S.

Matrix Core

헤드라인 영어문장은
기본구조로 나타낸다. ¶

Decoded Core

figure out ⇒ 알다, 이해하다, 생각하다 ¶

roundabout ⇒ 우회하는 ¶

spread across ⇒ 펼치다, 퍼지다 ¶

[10]

Word&Phrase

navigate 길을 찾다, 돌아다니다, 안내하다
tend to 경향이 있다
congestion 혼잡, 정체, 밀집
intersection 교차로, 사거리

Lead Sentence

Navigating roundabouts can be confusing, but they tend to reduce congestion and accidents at intersections. One is coming to the Bronx.

우회도로를 찾는 것은 혼란스러울 수도 있다. 그러나 이는 교차로에서 체증을 줄이고 사고를 줄일 수 있다. 이 제도가 브롱스 구에도 곧 시행된다.

Bilingual Reading

Navigating roundabouts 우회도로를 찾는 것은 **can be confusing,** 혼란스러울 수도 있지만 **but they** 이는 **tend to reduce** 줄일 수 있다 **congestion and accidents** 체증과 사고를 **at intersections.** 교차로에서 **One** 이 제도가 **is coming** 곧 시행된다 **to the Bronx.** 브롱스 구에도

Part.4 LIFE

Villa on an old Roman road, with ties to film

A 20-room estate located within the park of the Old Appian Way and once owned by the film producer Carlo Ponti is on the market for $44.9 million.

Headline

Villa on an old Roman road, with ties to film

영화와 관계가 있는
'old Roman road'에 있는 빌라

일반 표현

Villa of an old Roman road with ties to film is on sale.

Matrix Core

헤드라인 영어문장은 동사를 생략한다. ¶

Decoded Core

with ties to film ⇒ 'Roman road'를 수식하는 형용사구 ¶

ties to film ⇒ 영화와 관계가 있는 ¶

on an old Roman road ⇒ 옛 로마 거리에 있는 ¶

[11]

Word&Phrase

on the market 시중에 나오다, 매물로 나오다
with ties to film 영화와 관계 있다

Lead Sentence

A 20-room estate located within the park of the Old Appian Way and once owned by the film producer Carlo Ponti is on the market for $44.9 million.

한때 영화 제작자 카를로 폰티가 소유했던 아피아 가도 공원에 위치한 침실 20개짜리 빌라가 4,490만 달러에 매물로 나왔다.

Bilingual Reading

A 20-room estate 방 20개 짜리 저택이 **located** 위치한 **within the park of the Old Appian Way** 아피아 가도 공원 내에 **and once** 한때 **owned by the film producer Carlo Ponti** 영화 제작자 카를로 폰티가 소유했던 **is on the market for $44.9 million.** 4,490만 달러 가격에 시장에 나와 있다.

For one apparel brand, staying fit is just part of the job

The Outdoor Voices crew has adopted certain endorphin-pumping office practices, which they share with T.

Headline

For one apparel brand, staying fit is just part of the job

특정 의류 브랜드의 경우 몸매를 유지하는 것은 업무의 중요한 부분이다.

일반 표현

The job of one apparel brand clothes is to stay fit.

Matrix Core

헤드라인 영어문장은 리드 문장에서 압축된 의미가 풀린다. ¶

Decoded Core

배경을 알기 위해 리드 문장을 검토하면 도움이 된다.
stay fit ⇒ 몸매를 유지하다 ¶

just part of the job ⇒ 바로 그 일, 옷의 중요한 부분이다 ¶

[12]

Word&Phrase

apparel brand 의류 브랜드
stay fit 몸매를 유지하다
share with 필요로 하는 사람과 나누어 쓰다, 나누어 갖다 : share with those in need

Lead Sentence

The Outdoor Voices crew has adopted certain endorphin-pumping office practices, which they share with T.

아웃도어 보이스의 직원들은 티셔츠를 함께 입으면서 활기찬 분위기 속에 업무를 해내고 있다.

Bilingual Reading

The Outdoor Voices crew 아웃도어 보이스 직원들은 **has adopted** 도입했다 **certain endorphin-pumping office practices,** 활기찬 작업들 **which they share with T.** T라는 공통분모를 공유하는

Why you should consider bilingual education

Across the country, more and more schools are implementing dual-language programs, in which students attend an equal number of classes in English and in another language, such as Spanish, Portuguese or Mandarin. Half of the school districts in Utah-by far the most progressive state when it comes to bilingual education-offer dual-language immersion, to great success.

Headline

Why you should consider bilingual education

왜 이중 언어 교육을 고려해야 하는가?

일반 표현

Why do we need to think carefully about bilingual education?

Matrix Core

헤드라인 영어문장은 의문부호를 생략한다. ¶

Decoded Core

should consider ⇒ need to consider, 충분히 생각해야 한다 ¶
consider ⇒ 신중히 생각하다 ¶
review ⇒ 검토하다 ¶

[13]

Word&Phrase

implement 도입하다 : introduce
bilingual education 이중 언어 교육
by far 지금까지
the most progressive state 가장 진보적인 주

dual-language immersion program
이중 언어 몰입 교육, 제2 언어를 이용하여 일반 과목(수학, 과학 등) 수업을 진행하는 프로그램
immersion 몰입, 집중

Lead Sentence

Across the country, more and more schools are implementing dual-language programs, in which students attend an equal number of classes in English and in another language, such as Spanish, Portuguese or Mandarin. Half of the school districts in Utah–by far the most progressive state when it comes to bilingual education–offer dual-language immersion, to great success.

미국 전역에서 점점 더 많은 학교들이 영어와 다른 언어, 즉 스페인어, 포르투갈어, 중국어를 똑같이 배워야 하는 2개 국어 프로그램을 도입하고 있다. 이중 언어 교육 분야에서 가장 진보적인 유타 주의 경우 학구의 절반에 달하는 학교가 이중 언어 몰입 교육 프로그램을 제공하고 큰 성공을 얻고 있다.

Bilingual Reading

Across the country, 미국 전역에서 **more and more schools** 점점 더 많은 학교들이 **are implementing dual-language programs,** 이중 언어 프로그램을 도입하고 있다 **in which** 그 제도에서 **students** 학생들은 **attend** 출석한다 **an equal number of classes** 같은 시간으로 **in English and in another language,** 영어와 다른 언어 **such as Spanish, Portuguese or Mandarin.** 즉 스페인어, 포르투갈어, 중국어 같은 **Half of the school districts in Utah** 유타 주 학구 학교 절반이 **–by far the most progressive state** 현재 가장 진보적이라 할 수 있는 **when it comes to bilingual education** 이중 언어 교육에 있어서 **–offer dual-language immersion,** 이중 언어 몰입 프로그램을 제시하고 **to great success.** 큰 성공을 얻고 있다.

A culture of nagging helps California save water

The rise of domestic and neighborhood self-enforcement is having an effect on the wasting of water amid the drought.

Headline

A culture of nagging helps California save water

물을 절약하자는 주 정부의 다그침은 캘리포니아의 물 부족을 해소하는 데 도움이 되었다.

일반 표현

A culture of asking people to conserve water has helped California save water.

Matrix Core

헤드라인 영어문장은 몇 개의 단어나 기본구조로 나타낸다. ¶

Decoded Core

nagging ⇒ 심하게 잔소리하다, 계속하다, 누그러지지 않다, 귀찮게 하다 ⋮ constantly harass to do something ¶

a culture of nagging ⇒ 지속적으로 다그치다 ¶

save water ⇒ 물을 아끼다 ¶

[14]

Word&Phrase

self-enforcement 자체시행령
domestic and neighborhood 주의 내외에
drought 가뭄, 한발, 고갈

Lead Sentence

The rise of domestic and neighborhood self-enforcement is having an effect on the wasting of water amid the drought.

캘리포니아 주와 이웃 지역의 물 아끼기 운동은 가뭄이 계속되는 가운데 물 소비에 대해 긍정적인 효과를 주고 있다.

Bilingual Reading

The rise 운동은 **of domestic** 캘리포니아 주와 **and neighborhood** 이웃 지역 **self-enforcement** 자체의 물 아끼기 **is having an effect** 좋은 효과를 주고 있다 **on the wasting of water** 물 소비에 대해 **amid the drought.** 가뭄 중에

Why tipping is wrong

THE announcement on Wednesday by the New York restaurateur Danny Meyer that he was eliminating tipping at his restaurants shows that he understands the impact tipping really has: It has created a two-tiered wage system with deep social and economic consequences for millions.

Headline

Why tipping is wrong

왜 팁을 주는 것이
잘못된 것인가?

일반 표현

Why overpayment as tipping is wrong?
Why paying of tip is not fair?

Matrix Core

헤드라인 영어문장은 리드 문장에서 압축의 의미가 풀린다. ¶

헤드라인 영어문장은 의문부호를 생략한다. ¶

Decoded Core

tipping ⇒ 식당 등에서 손님이 만족하는 서비스를 제공받았을 때 계산된 금액 이외에 추가로 고맙다는 의미로 지불하는 돈. 대체로 계산금액의 15% 내외의 금액을 주는 것이 관례다. ¶

Why tipping is wrong ⇒ 의문부호를 생략하면서 'Why is tipping wrong?' 문형의 모습을 바꾸었다. ¶

[15]

Word&Phrase

eliminate 제거하다, 없애다
impact 영향, 충격, 효과
two-tiered wage system 2단계 임금제도

Lead Sentence

THE announcement on Wednesday by the New York restaurateur Danny Meyer that he was eliminating tipping at his restaurants shows that he understands the impact tipping really has: It has created a two-tiered wage system with deep social and economic consequences for millions.

뉴욕 주 한 식당주인 데니 메이어가 수요일 자기 식당에 팁 지불 관례를 없애겠다고 발표한 것은 팁이 가져오는 영향을 잘 알고 있다는 것을 말해준다. 즉 이 식당은 사회 구석구석에 경제적 영향을 미칠 2단계 임금제도를 시행했다.

Bilingual Reading

THE announcement on Wednesday 수요일에 발표에서 **by the New York restaurateur Danny Meyer** 뉴욕 주 어느 식당주인 데니 메이어는 **that he was eliminating tipping at his restaurants** 자기식당에 팁 지불 관례를 없애겠다는 그의 발표는 **shows** 나타낸다 **that he understands** 그가 알고 있다는 것을 **the impact tipping really has:** 팁이 가져오는 실제적인 영향을 **It has created a two-tiered wage system** 즉, 이 식당은 이 단계 임금제도를 시행했다 **with deep social and economic consequences for millions.** 사회 구석구석에 경제적 영향을 미칠

Art forgers beware: DNA could thwart fakes

The artist Eric Fischl remembers the time a friend waved a catalog at him to alert him that one of his paintings was up for auction for six figures in London. In reality, the work was a fake, but so convincing, Mr. Fischl said, "I thought I was losing my mind."

Headline

**Art forgers beware:
DNA could thwart fakes**

예술품 위조범 주의:
DNA 검사를 통해
예술품 위조를 막을 수 있다.

일반 표현

Beware of art forgers:
DNA check can prevent art from being fakes.

Matrix Core

헤드라인 영어문장은 주어와 동사의 위치를 바꾼다. ¶

Decoded Core

Art forger beware ⇒ Beware of art forgers, "미술 위조범을 조심하세요", 주로 경고문을 만들 때 사용하는 패턴 ¶

thwart ⇒ 어떤 사람이 무엇을 못하게 저지하다 ≒ prevent (someone) from doing something ¶

could ⇒ if가 없는 문장에 could, would, might와 같은 조동사가 오면 그 문장 안에 if 의 의미가 들어있다. ¶

DNA could thwart fakes ⇒
DNA 검사를 하면 (if) 그 예술품이 모조품인지 알 수 있다.
즉, DNA 검사는 모조품을 막을 수 있다 는 의미 ¶

[16]

Word&Phrase

convincing 어떤 사람으로 하여금 어떤 것이 사실이라고 믿게 만드는
The art was convincing 그 예술품은 진품이라고 믿을 수밖에 없었다
Something up for auction for six figures 어떤 물건이 6자리 숫자 액수로 경매에 나왔다

Lead Sentence

The artist Eric Fischl remembers the time a friend waved a catalog at him to alert him that one of his paintings was up for auction for six figures in London. In reality, the work was a fake, but so convincing, Mr. Fischl said, "I thought I was losing my mind."

화가 에릭 피슬은 한 친구가 자신을 향해 카탈로그를 흔들면서 자신의 작품 중 하나가 런던 옥션에 6자리 가격으로 나왔다고 알려 주었던 때를 떠올렸다. 사실 그 작품은 위조품이었다. 그러나 너무나도 진품과 같아서 "나도 내 정신이 어떻게 된 것 같았다"라고 그 예술가는 이야기했다.

Bilingual Reading

The artist Eric Fischl 예술가 에릭 피슬은 **remembers the time** 그 당시를 기억한다 **a friend** 친구 한 사람이 **waved a catalog at him** 그에게 카탈로그를 흔들면서 **to alert him** 알려 주었다 **that one of his paintings** 자기의 그림 중 하나가 **was up for auction** 경매에 나왔다는 것을 **for six figures in London.** 런던에서 6자리 숫자 가격으로 **In reality, the work was a fake,** 사실 그 작품은 위조품이었다 **but so convincing,** 그러나 너무나도 진품과 같아서 **Mr. Fischl said,** 피슬이 말했다 **"I thought I was losing my mind."** "나도 내 정신이 어떻게 된 것이 아닌가 하고 생각했다."

Silence your smartphone – without missing any notifications

Had it with the ringtones on your iPhone or Android phone? Let these cute notification gadgets alert you in muted, amusing ways.

Headline

**Silence your smartphone
– without missing
any notifications**

스마트폰의 벨소리를 꺼놓아도
알람을 놓치지 않고 받을 수 있다.

일반 표현

Even if you silence your smartphone, you never miss any notifications.

Matrix Core

헤드라인 영어문장은 몇 개의 단어로 나타낸다. ¶

Decoded Core

Silence your smartphone ⇒
Even if you silence your smartphone,
당신의 스마트폰 벨소리를 꺼놓아도 ¶

without missing any notifications ⇒
you never miss any notifications,
당신은 알람을 놓치지 않는다 ¶

[17]

Word&Phrase

ringtones on your iphone or Android phone
당신의 스마트폰에 설정된 벨소리

Lead Sentence

Had it with the ringtones on your iPhone or Android phone? Let these cute notification gadgets alert you in muted, amusing ways.

당신의 아이폰이나 안드로이드폰의 알람을 벨소리로 설정해 놓으셨나요? 핸드폰이 묵음 상태에 있어도 이 작은 장치가 깜찍하게 당신에게 알람이 왔음을 알릴 수 있습니다.

Bilingual Reading

Had it with the ringtones 알람음이 벨소리로 설정되어 있는 **on your iPhone** 당신의 아이폰이나 **or Android phone?** 안드로이드폰 **Let these cute notification gadgets** 이 깜직한 알림 장치로 하여금 **alert you** 당신에게 알리다 **in muted,** 묵음 상태에서도 **amusing ways.** 즐거운 방법으로

Russia resisting Europe request for tough U.N. anti-smuggling step

Russia's United Nations ambassador, the current Security Council president, said in an interview that he opposed any measure allowing military action.

Headline

Russia resisting Europe request for tough U.N. anti-smuggling step

밀매에 대해 강력한 재제 조치를 취해줄 것을 유럽이 유엔에 요구했으나 러시아의 반대에 부딪히고 있다.

일반 표현

Europe request for tough U.N. anti-smuggling step is running into t opposition from Russia.

Matrix Core

헤드라인 영어문장은 과거를 현재분사로 나타낸다. ¶

Decoded Core

Russia resisting ⇒ Russia resisted, 러시아는 거부했다 ¶

Europe request ⇒ European request, 유럽의 요청 ¶

[18]

Word&Phrase

Russia's U.N. Ambassador 러시아 유엔 대사
current security council president 현 상임이사국(안전보장이사회) 의장
resist 저항하다, 참다, 반대하다
smuggle 밀수입하다, 밀매하다
military action 군사 행동

Lead Sentence

Russia's United Nations ambassador, the current Security Council president, said in an interview that he opposed any measure allowing military action.

러시아의 유엔 대사이자 현 상임이사회 의장은 한 인터뷰에서 군사적 행동을 허용하는 어떠한 조치도 반대한다고 말했다.

Bilingual Reading

Russia's United Nations ambassador, 러시아의 유엔 대사이자 **the current Security Council president,** 현 상임이사회 의장은 **said** 말했다 **in an interview** 한 인터뷰에서 **that he** 자기는 **opposed** 반대한다고 **any measure** 어떠한 조치도 **allowing military action.** 군사적 행동을 허용하는

Part 4 LIFE

Psychologists welcome analysis casting doubt on their work

To some, the news that most studies do not hold up when retested came as a relief, like the field had "come clean," one expert said.

Headline

Psychologists welcome analysis casting doubt on their work

심리학자들은 자신들의 이론에 의심을 던지는 것을 환영한다.

일반 표현

A new analysis found that some of previous analyses were different from original experiments.

Matrix Core

헤드라인에 사용된 단어의 정확한 이해가 필요하다. ¶

Decoded Core

analysis ⇒ 분석, 실험 결과를 의미 ¶

on their work ⇒ 그들이 지금까지 받아들이고 있는 이론 ¶

cast doubt ⇒ 의심을 던지다 ¶

Welcome analysis casting doubt on their work ⇒ welcome the analysis finding which is different from their previous finding, 그들의 이론을 의심하는 분석 ¶

psychologist ⇒ 정신과 의사, 심리학자 ¶

Word&Phrase

analysis 실험분석
cast doubt on their work 이론에 대해 의심을 던지다
psychologist 심리학자, 정신과 의사
relief 구조, 안도, 완화
hold up 받치다, 뒷받침하다

Lead Sentence

To some, the news that most studies do not hold up when retested came as a relief, like the field had "come clean," one expert said.

재실험을 실시했을 때 많은 경우 다른 결과가 나온다는 소식은 일부 사람들에게 안도감을 주었다. 업계가 "실토했다"고 한 전문가는 말했다.

Bilingual Reading

To some, 일부 사람들에게 **the news** 그 뉴스는 **that most studies** 대부분의 연구결과가 **do not hold up when retested** 재실험에서 처음과 다른 결과가 나왔다는 **came as a relief,** 안도감을 주었다 **like the field** 그 분야가 **had "come clean,"** "고백했다"고 **one expert said.** 한 전문가가 말했다

Motorist suspected in fatal hit-and-run arrested

A 20-year-old motorist suspected of hitting two pedestrians and killing one before fleeing the scene Saturday has been arrested, a Los Angelis policeman said.

Headline

Motorist suspected in fatal hit-and-run arrested

끔찍한 뺑소니 사고 혐의를 받고 있던 운전자가 체포되었다.

일반 표현

Motorist suspected in fatal hit and run has been arrested.

Matrix Core

헤드라인 영어문장은 관계사를 생략하고 과거분사로 나타낸다. ¶

헤드라인 영어문장은 수동형을 과거분사로 나타낸다. ¶

Decoded Core

motorist suspected ⇒ motorist (who was) suspected 뺑소니 혐의를 받고 있던 운전자 ¶

arrested ⇒ (has been) arrested 체포되었다 ¶

[20]

Word&Phrase

motorist 자동차 운전자
suspect 의심하다, 생각하다
fatal 치명적인, 죽음에 이르는, 불행한
hit and run 뺑소니

fatal hit and run driver 뺑소니 운전자
pedestrian 보행, 보도, 평범한

Lead Sentence

A 20-year-old motorist suspected of hitting two pedestrians and killing one before fleeing the scene Saturday has been arrested, a Los Angelis policeman said.

토요일에 두 사람의 행인을 치고 그중 한 사람이 사망한 현장에서 도망친 혐의로 한 20세 운전자가 체포되었다고 로스엔젤리스 경찰이 말했다.

Bilingual Reading

A 20-year-old motorist suspected 혐의를 받은 20세 자동차 운전자가 **of hitting two pedestrians** 두 사람의 행인을 치고 **and killing one** 한 사람이 사망한 **before fleeing the scene** 현장을 도망친 **Saturday** 토요일에 **has been arrested,** 체포되었다 **a Los Angelis policeman said.** 로스엔젤리스 경찰이 말했다

311

The best way to turn your old iPhone into cash

With carriers' subsidized phone deals going out the window, there's never been a better-or more confusing-time to sell your old smartphone.

Headline

**The best way
to turn your old iPhone
into cash**

사용하던 아이폰을
현금으로 바꿀 수 있는
가장 좋은 방법

일반 표현

Trade-in is best for getting hard cash for your iphone.

Matrix Core

헤드라인 영어문장은 몇 개의 단어로 나타낸다. ¶

Decoded Core

turn something into cash ⇒ 어떤 것을 현금으로 바꾸다 ¶
to turn your old iphone into cash ⇒ 오래된 아이폰을 현금으로 바꾸다 ¶

[21]

Word&Phrase

go out the window 더 이상 존재하지 않다 : it does not exists, no longer exists
carrier 통신업체
subsidize 후원하다, 원조하다, 보조금
confuse 혼란스럽다, 식별할 수 없다

Lead Sentence

With carriers' subsidized phone deals going out the window, there's never been a better-or more confusing-time to sell your old smartphone.

더 이상 보조금을 받고 휴대폰을 살 수 없기 때문에 당신의 낡은 휴대폰을 팔 수 있는 시기는 지금이 가장 좋을 때이다.

Bilingual Reading

With carriers' 휴대폰 통신업체 **subsidized** 보조금을 받는 **phone deals going out the window,** 휴대폰이 거래되지 않는다 **there's never been a better** 지금이 가장 좋을 때다 **-or more confusing** 또는 더 혼란스럽다 **-time to sell your old smartphone.** 당신의 오래된 휴대폰을 팔 수 있는 시기는

313

Recipes for getting the best return on a surplus of vegetables

It's that crazy time of year when there's almost more produce than we can handle. The pro move? These vegetable stew recipes that bridge the transition from summer to fall.

Headline

Recipes for getting the best return on a surplus of vegetables

남은 채소로 만들 수 있는 최고의 레시피

일반 표현

There are more recipes for getting the best dish from surplus of vegetables.

Matrix Core

헤드라인 영어문장은 문장이 아닌 단어로 의미를 나타낸다. ¶

Decoded Core

get the best return ⇒ 가장 큰 이윤을 얻다 ¶

getting the best return ⇒ 최고 보답을 얻다 ⁑ get more than you expect ¶

on a surplus of vegetable ⇒ 풍성한 채소들, 남은 채소 ¶

[22]

Word&Phrase

recipe 비결, 처방
crazy time 제철

Lead Sentence

It's that crazy time of year when there's almost more produce than we can handle. The pro move? These vegetable stew recipes that bridge the transition from summer to fall.

지금은 우리가 처리할 수 없을 정도로 많은 농산물이 생산되는 계절이다. 좋은 해결 방안은 무엇일까? 바로 여름에서 가을까지 활용할 수 있는 채소 스튜 레시피들이다.

Bilingual Reading

It's that crazy time of year 지금은 풍성한 계절이다 **when there's almost more produce** 더 많은 농산물이 나오는 **than we can handle.** 우리가 처리할 수 있는 것보다 **The pro move?** 좋은 방법은? **These vegetable stew recipes** 채소 스튜 레시피 **that bridge the transition** 연결시켜주는 **from summer to fall.** 여름에서 가을까지

Best chapter in Pearson breakup story yet to come

The media group can soon sell its 47 pct stake in publisher Penguin Random House to co-owner Bertelsmann. Including future synergies, the stake could fetch $2.7 billion, twice what Pearson got for the FT. Since the venture could get more valuable still, waiting looks better.

Headline

Best chapter in Pearson breakup story yet to come

피어슨 지분 매각의 클라이맥스 장은 아직 쓰여지지 않았다.

일반 표현

Best chapter in Pearson breakup story is not yet written.

Matrix Core

헤드라인 영어문장은 대체로 be 동사를 생략한다. ¶

Decoded Core

story yet to come ⇒ story (is) not come ¶

yet to come ⇒ 아직 오지 않았다는 의미,
피어슨 그룹의 출판사 펭귄 랜덤의 지분 47%를 매각할 예정인데 아직 계약이 성사되지 않았다는 이야기. ¶

Pearson ⇒ 미디어 그룹 ¶

[23]

Word&Phrase

co-owner 공동 소유주
breakup 분할 (지분 매각)
yet to come 아직 오지 않았다, 이루어지지 않았다
fetch 가져오다, 데려오다, 낙찰되다

Lead Sentence

The media group can soon sell its 47 pct stake in publisher Penguin Random House to co-owner Bertelsmann. Including future synergies, the stake could fetch $2.7 billion, twice what Pearson got for the FT. Since the venture could get more valuable still, waiting looks better.

미디어 그룹 피어슨은 자회사인 펭귄랜덤하우스 출판사의 지분 47%를 공동 소유주 베텔스만에게 곧 매각할 수 있다. 훗날의 시너지 효과를 포함해서 이 거래를 통해 피어슨이 〈파이낸셜 타임스〉 매각으로 받은 금액의 2배인 27억 달러를 받을 수 있다. 이 사업은 여전히 이익을 가져올 수 있으므로 기다리는 것도 좋다.

Bilingual Reading

The media group 미디어 그룹 피어슨은 **can soon sell** 곧 매각할 수 있다 **its 47 pct stake** 지분 47%를 **in publisher Penguin Random House** 펭귄랜덤하우스 출판사의 **to co-owner Bertelsmann.** 그의 소유주 베텔스만에게 **Including future synergies,** 미래 시너지 효과를 포함해서 **the stake** 이 지분은 **could fetch $2.7 billion,** 27억 달러를 받을 수 있다 **twice** 2배인 **what Pearson** 피어슨이 **got for the FT.** 〈파이낸셜 타임스〉 매각 금액의 **Since the venture could get more valuable** 이익을 가져올 수 있으므로 **still,** 이 사업은 여전히 **waiting looks better.** 기다리는 것도 좋다

Olympics committee gets it right with Beijing 2022

The Winter Games won't boost China's growth, end repression, or win the country much extra respect. It might help soft power, but then most countries already do whatever China asks. Freed from such false hopes, everyone can sit back, have fun and admire the fake snow.

Headline

Olympics committee gets it right with Beijing 2022

2022년 베이징 올림픽에 대해 올림픽위원회의 설명이 필요하다

일반 표현

Olympics committee has made a right decision with Beijing 2022.

Matrix Core

헤드라인 영어문장은 기본구조로 나타낸다. ¶

Decoded Core

get it right ⇒ make a right decision ¶

Olympics committeet ⇒ 올림픽 조직 위원회 ¶

[24]

Word&Phrase

soft power
정보과학이나 문화·예술 등이 행사하는 영향력, 국제 관계에 있어서 경제적 문화적 영향력을 이용하여 설득시키는 정책(국제적 영향력)

won't win the country much extra respect
그 나라에 추가적인 존경심은 가져다주지 못할 것이다

Lead Sentence

The Winter Games won't boost China's growth, end repression, or win the country much extra respect. It might help soft power, but then most countries already do whatever China asks. Freed from such false hopes, everyone can sit back, have fun and admire the fake snow.

동계올림픽은 중국의 성장을 끌어올리는 데 큰 도움이 되지 않을 것이고, 정치적 억압도 중단시키지 못할 것이며, 별도의 국제적 위신 향상도 가져다주지 못할 것이다. 다만 (문화적인) 영향력에는 도움을 줄지 모르지만, 이미 대부분의 국가는 중국이 원하는 것을 무엇이든 하고 있다. 이러한 그릇된 희망과 무관한 사람들은 뒤에 앉아서 즐기며 가짜 눈을 보고 찬양할 것이다.

Bilingual Reading

The Winter Games 동계올림픽은 **won't boost** 끌어올리지 못할 것이고 **China's growth,** 중국의 성장을 **end repression,** 정치적 억압도 중단시키지 못할 것이며 **or win the country much extra respect.** 국가적 명성도 얻지 못할 것이다 **It might help** 이것은 도움이 될 수 있다 **soft power,** 국제적 영향력에 **but** 하지만 **then most countries already** 대부분의 국가는 이미 **do whatever China asks.** 중국이 원하는 것을 무엇이든 한다 **Freed from such false hopes,** 그런 그릇된 희망과 무관한 **everyone** 모든 (중국) 사람들은 **can sit back, have fun** 뒤에 앉아서 즐기고 **and admire the fake snow.** 그리고 가짜 눈을 보고 찬양할 것이다

Art market bracing for an uncertain sales season

International auctions and fairs expect reverberations from China's economic woes.

Headline

Art market bracing for an uncertain sales season

미술품 시장은 불확실한 판매 시즌을 대비하고 있다.

일반 표현

Art market is preparing for an uncertain sales season.

Matrix Core

헤드라인 영어문장은 대체로 be 동사를 생략한다. ¶

Decoded Core

market bracing ⇒ market is bracing ¶

brace for ⇒ 대비하다, 준비하다 ‡ prepare for ¶

[25]

Word&Phrase

brace for 대비하다
auctions and fairs 경매 전시장
reverberation 반향, 영향, 여진
woe 우려, 어려움

Lead Sentence

International auctions and fairs expect reverberations from China's economic woes.

국제 미술품 경매시장은 중국의 경제적 어려움으로부터 발생되는 영향을 생각하고 있다.

Bilingual Reading

International auctions and fairs 국제 미술품 경매시장은 **expect reverberations from China's economic woes.** 중국의 경제적 어려움으로부터 오는 영향을 생각한다.

With a revamped Apple TV, company hopes to camp in your home

At Apple's product event on Wednesday, it is expected to introduce a TV device with more capabilities as the company seeks a bigger presence in homes.

Headline

With a revamped Apple TV, company hopes to camp in your home

애플 TV는 새로운 모습과 더 개선된 기능을 가지고 당신의 집을 찾아가려고 한다.

일반 표현

Apple device is expected to introduce a T.V. to your home with its new appearance and more capabilities.

Matrix Core

헤드라인 영어문장은 with 구문으로 나타낸다. ¶

Decoded Core

with ⇒ with 구문은 '~함으로, 했으므로, 했기 때문에'라는 의미 ¶

revamp ⇒ 어떤 것에 대해 새로운 모습 또는 새로운 형태를 부여하다 ː give new image or improved appearance to something ¶

with a revamped Apple TV ⇒ 애플 TV를 개선함으로 해서, 새로운 모습을 갖추고 ¶

[26]

Word&Phrase

revamp 개조하다, 새로운 모습으로 바꾸다

Lead Sentence

At Apple's product event on Wednesday, it is expected to introduce a TV device with more capabilities as the company seeks a bigger presence in homes.

수요일에 열린 애플 상품 행사에서 애플이 가정에 더 큰 존재감을 추구하고자 더 다양한 기능을 갖춘 TV를 소개하려고 한다.

Bilingual Reading

At Apple's product event on Wednesday, 수요일 애플 상품행사에서 **it is expected to introduce a TV device** TV를 소개하려고 한다 **with more capabilities** 더 다양한 기능을 갖춘 **as the company** 그 회사가 **seeks a bigger presence in homes.** 가정에 더 큰 존재감을 추구하고자

Part 4 LIFE

323

Competitors accuse Google of using search to diminish apps

In November, Google will start penalizing the search rankings of sites that show "please install our app" ads, a move that rivals say has less to do with providing users with a good experience and more to do with protecting Google's business.

Headline

Competitors accuse Google of using search to diminish apps

경쟁사들은 구글이 타사의 앱 사용을 방해한다고 주장했다.

일반 표현

Several websites (competitors) claimed that Google had been unfairly highlighting its search.

Matrix Core

헤드라인 영어문장은 완료형을 현재로 나타낸다. ¶

Decoded Core

accuse ⇒ have accused ~를 범죄로 기소하다, 고발하다 ⁑ to charge someone with crime ¶

accuse someone of something ⇒ ~를 ~의 혐의로 기소하다 ¶

diminish ⇒ 감소하다, ~이 줄다, 사라지다 ¶

[27]

Word&Phrase

penalize 벌점을 부과하다, 유죄로 하다
install 설치하다

Lead Sentence

In November, Google will start penalizing the search rankings of sites that show "please install our app" ads, a move that rivals say has less to do with providing users with a good experience and more to do with protecting Google's business.

11월 안으로 구글은 "우리 어플리케이션을 설치하세요"라는 광고 문구를 보여주는 검색결과 사이트에 패널티를 부과할 것이다. 경쟁사들은 이런 정책은 유능한 공급자(경쟁자)를 줄여 구글의 사업을 보다 더 보호할 것이라고 주장한다.

Bilingual Reading

In November, 11월 안에 Google 구글 **will start penalizing** 처벌할 것이다 **the search rankings of sites** 검색 사이트에 대해 **that show "please install our app" ads,** "우리 앱을 설치하세요"라는 광고를 보여준 **a move** 이런 정책 **that rivals say** 경쟁사들이 말한다 **has less to do with providing users with a good experience** 유능한 공급자(경쟁자)를 줄이다 **and more to do with protecting Google's business.** 구글의 사업을 보다 더 보호하게 되다